Creative Resources

of BIRDS, ANIMALS, SEASONS, and HOLIDAYS

Creative Resources

of BIRDS, ANIMALS, SEASONS, and HOLIDAYS

Judy Herr

Yvonne Libby

Delmar Publishers

I(T)P® International Thomson Publishing

Albany • Bonn • Boston • Cincinnati • Detroit • London • Madrid
Melbourne • Mexico City • New York • Pacific Grove • Paris • San Francisco
Singapore • Tokyo • Toronto • Washington

NOTICE TO THE READER

Cover Design by: Ron Sohn

Delmar Staff
Acquisitions Editor: Jay S. Whitney
Associate Editor: Erin O'Connor-Traylor
Developmental Editor: Ellen Smith
Project Editor: Karen Leet
Production Coordinator: Sandra Woods
Art & Design Coordinator: Carol Keohane

COPYRIGHT © 1998
By Delmar Publishers
a division of International Thomson Publishing Company

I(T)P® The ITP logo is a trademark under license.

Printed in the United States of America

For more information, contact:

Delmar Publishers
3 Columbia Circle Drive, Box 15015
Albany, New York 12212-5015

International Thomson Publishing
Berkshire House
168-173 High Holborn
London, WC1V7AA
England

Thomas Nelson Australia
102 Dodds Street
South Melbourne 3205
Victoria, Australia

Nelson Canada
1120 Birchmont Road
Scarborough, Ontario
M1K 5G4, Canada

International Thomson Editores
Campos Eliseos 385, Piso 7
Col Polanco
11560 Mexico, DF Mexico

International Thomson Publishing GmbH
Konigswinterer Str. 418
53227 Bonn
Germany

International Thomson Publishing Asia
221 Henderson Bldg. #05-10
Singapore 0315

International Thomson Publishing Japan
Hirakawacho Kyowa Building, 3F
2-2-1 Hirakawacho
Chiyoda-ku, Tokyo 102
Japan

1 2 3 4 5 6 7 8 9 10 XXX 03 02 01 00 99 98 97

Library of Congress Cataloging-in-Publication Data

Herr, Judy.
    Creative resources of birds, animals, seasons, and holidays / Judy
Herr, Yvonne Libby.
        p.   cm.
    ISBN 0-7668-0016-4
    1. Education, Preschool—Curricula. 2. Creative activities and
seat work. 3. Unit method of teaching. 4. Animals—Study and
teaching—Activity programs. 5. Seasons—Study and teaching—
Activity programs. 6. Holidays—Study and teaching—Activity
programs. I. Libby, Yvonne. II. Title.
LB1140.4.H48   1998
372.21—DC21
                                    97-11207
                                    CIP

CONTENTS

PREFACE

While reviewing early childhood curriculum resources, it becomes apparent that few books are available using a thematic or unit approach for teaching young children. As a result, our university students, colleagues, and alumni convinced us of the importance of such a book. Likewise, they convinced us of the contribution the book could make to early childhood teachers and, subsequently, the lives of young children.

Before preparing the manuscript, we surveyed hundreds of child care, preschool, and kindergarten teachers. Specifically, we wanted them to share their curriculum problems and concerns. Our response has been to design and write a reference book tailored to their teaching needs using a thematic approach. Each theme or unit contains a flowchart, theme goals, concepts for the children to learn, theme-related vocabulary words, music, fingerplays, science, dramatic play, creative art experiences, sensory, mathematics, cooking experiences, and resources. Additionally, creative ideas for designing child-involvement bulletin boards and parent letters have been included. These resources were identified, by the teachers included in our survey, as being critical components that have been lacking in other curriculum guides.

In addition to the themes included in this book, others can be found in *Creative Resources of Art, Brushes, Buildings . . .* and *Creative Resources of Colors, Food, Plants, and Occupations.* More can and should be developed for teaching young children. The authors, however, wish to caution the readers that it is the teacher's responsibility to select, plan, and introduce developmentally appropriate themes and learning experiences for his group of children. Specifically, the teacher must tailor the curriculum to meet the individual needs of the children. Consequently, we encourage all teachers to carefully select, adapt, or change any of the activities in this book to meet the needs, abilities, and interests of their group of children to ensure developmental appropriateness. A handy reference for checking developmental norms is included on pages xiii and xiv.

As you use this guide, you will note that some themes readily lend themselves to particular curriculum areas. As a result, the number of activities listed under each curriculum area will vary from theme to theme.

The detailed Introduction that follows is designed to help teachers use the book most effectively. It includes:

1. a discussion on how to develop the curriculum using a thematic approach;
2. a list of possible themes;
3. suggestions for writing parent letters;
4. methods for constructing and evaluating creative involvement bulletin boards; and
5. criteria for selecting children's books.

This book would not have been possible without the constant encouragement provided by our families, the laboratory teachers in the Child and Family Study Center, and the faculty, students, and alumni of the University of Wisconsin-Stout. Our thanks to all of these people and especially to Carla Ahmann, Susan Babler, Mary Babula, Terry Bloomberg, Margaret Braun, Renee Bruce, Anne Budde, Michelle Case, Jill Church, Bruce Cunningham, Jeanette Daines, Carol Davenport, Jill Davis, Mary DeJardin, Linda DeMoe, Rita Devery, Donna Dixon, Esther Fahm, Lisa Fuerst, Shirley Gebhart, Judy Gifford, Nancy Graese, Barbara Grundleger, Betty Herman, Patti Herman, John Herr, Mark Herr, Joan Herwig, Carol Hillmer, Priscilla Huffman, Margy Ingram, Paula Iverson, Angela Kaiser, Elizabeth (Betz) Kaster, Trudy King, Leslie Koepke, Beth Libby, Janet Maffet, Marian Marion, Janet Massa, Nancy McCarthy, Julie Meyers, Betty Misselt, Teresa Mitchell, Kathy Mueller, LaVonne Mueller, Robin Muza, Paula Noll, Sue Paulson, Mary Pugmire, Kelli Railton, Lori Register, Peg Saienga, Kathy Schaeffer, Mary Selkey, Cheryl Smith, Sue Smith, Amy Sprengler, Karen Stephens, Barbara Suihkonen, Judy Teske, Penny Warner, Connie Weber, Ed Wenzell, Mary Eileen Zenk, and Karen Zimmerman. We are also grateful to our reviewers: Gerri A. Carey, McLennan Community College, Waco, TX; Billie Coffman, PA College of Technology, Williamsport, PA; Ione Garcia, IL State University, Normal, IL; Ned Sauls, Wayne Community College, Goldsboro, NC; and Becky Wyatt, Murray State College, Tishomingo, OK. Finally, our special thanks to two individuals whose assistance made this book possible. Jay Whitney, our editor from Delmar, provided continous encouragement, support, and creative suggestions. Also, special thanks to Robin Muza, our typist and research assistant.

INTRODUCTION

The purpose of this introduction is to explain the process involved in curriculum planning for young children using the thematic, or unit approach. To support each theme, planning and construction ideas are included for bulletin boards, parent letters, and a wide variety of classroom learning experiences.

Curriculum Planning

As you use this guide, remember that children learn best when they can control and act upon their environment. Many opportunities should be available for seeing, touching, tasting, learning, and self-expression. Children need hands-on activities and choices. To construct knowledge, children need to actively manipulate their environment. To provide these opportunities, the teacher's primary role is to set the stage by offering many experiences that stimulate the children's senses and curiosity; children learn by doing and play is their work. As a result, it is the authors' intention that this book will be used as a resource. Specifically, the ideas in this book should help you to enrich, organize, and structure the children's environment, providing them an opportunity to make choices among a wide variety of activities that stimulate their natural curiosity. Knowledge of child development and curriculum must be interwoven. To illustrate, play in the classroom should be child-centered and self-initiated. To provide an environment that promotes these types of play, it is the teacher's role to provide unstructured time, space, and materials. Using a theme approach to plan curriculum is one way to ensure that a wide variety of classroom experiences are provided. Successful early childhood programs provide interesting, challenging, and engaging environments. Children need to learn to think, reason, and become decision makers.

It is important that all curricula be adapted to match the developmental needs of children at a particular age or stage of development. An activity that is appropriate for one group of children may be inappropriate for another. To develop an appropriate curriculum, knowledge of the typical development of children is needed. For this reason, the section following this Introduction contains such information. Review these developmental norms before selecting a theme or specific activities.

Theme Planning

A developmentally appropriate curriculum for young children integrates the children's needs, interests, and abilities and focuses on the whole child. Cognitive, social, emotional, and physical development are all included. Before planning curriculum, observe the children's development. Record notes of what you see. At the same time, note the children's interests and listen carefully. Children's conversations provide clues; this information is vital in theme selection. After this, review your observations by discussing them with other staff members. An appropriate curriculum for young children cannot be planned without understanding their development and interests.

There are many methods for planning a curriculum other than using themes. In fact, you may prefer not to use a theme during parts of the year. If this is your choice, you may wish to use the book as a source of ideas, integrating activities and experiences from a variety of the themes outlined in the book.

Planning a curriculum using a theme approach involves several steps. The first step involves selecting a theme that is appropriate for the developmental level and interests of your group of children. Themes based on the children's interests provide intrinsic motivation for exploration and learning. Meaningful experiences are more easily comprehended and remembered. Moreover, curiosity, enjoyment of participation, and self-direction are heightened. After selecting a theme, the next step is developing a flowchart. From the flowchart, goals, conceptual understandings, and vocabulary words can easily be extracted. The final step in curriculum planning is selecting activities based upon the children's stages of development and available resources. While doing this, refer to pages xiii and xiv, Developmental Benchmarks, to review development characteristics for children of different ages.

To help you understand the theme approach to curriculum development, each step of the process will be discussed. Included are assessing the children's needs, and developing flowcharts, theme goals, concepts, vocabulary, and activities. In addition, suggestions are given for writing parent letters, designing bulletin boards, and selecting children's books.

Assessment

Assessment is important for planning curriculum, identifying children with special needs, and communicating a child's progress to parents. Assessment needs to be a continuous process. It involves a process of observing children during activities throughout the day, recording their behaviors, and documenting their work. Assessment involves records and descriptions of what you observe while the behavior is occurring. Logs and journals can be developed. The developmental norms that follow this Introduction can be used as a checklist of behavior. You can create a profile of the children's individualized progress in developing skills. Your observations should tell what the children like, don't like, have discovered, know, and want to learn.

Samples of the children's work in an individual portfolio collection should be maintained. A portfolio documents the children's progress, achievements, and efforts. Included should be samples of the children's paintings, drawings, storytelling experiences, oral and written language. Thus, the portfolio will include products and evidence of the children's accomplishments.

By reviewing the assessment materials you can deduce the children's developmental needs and interests. This information will be important in selecting a theme that interests the children and in selecting developmentally appropriate learning experiences.

Flowcharts/Webbings. The flowchart is a simple way to record all possible subconcepts that relate to the major concept or theme. To illustrate, plan a theme on apples. In the center of a piece of paper, write the word "apple." Then using an encyclopedia as a resource, record the subconcepts that are related. Include origin, parts, colors, tastes, sizes, textures, food preparation, and nutrition. The flowchart on page ix includes these concepts. In addition, under each subconcept, list content that could be included. For example, apples may be colored green, yellow, or red. By using a thematic approach, we teach children the way environments and humans interconnect. This process helps children make sense out of the human experience.

Theme Goals. Once you have prepared a flowchart webbing, abstracting the theme goals is a simple process. Begin by reviewing the chart. Notice the subheadings listed. For the unit on apples, the subheadings include: foods, parts, forms, and colors. Writing each of these subheadings as a goal is the next step of the process.

Since there were four subheadings, each of these can be included as a goal. In some cases, subheadings may be combined. For example, note the fourth goal listed. It combines several subheadings.

Through participation in the experiences provided by using apples as a curriculum theme, the children may learn:

1. Parts of an apple.
2. Preparation of apples for eating.
3. Apple tastes.
4. Textures, sizes, and colors of apples.
5. The origin of an apple.

Concepts. The concepts must be related to the goal; however, they are more specific. To write the concepts, study the goals. Then prepare sentences that are written in a simple form that children can understand. Examples of concepts for a unit on apples may include:

1. An apple is a fruit.
2. An apple has five parts: seed, core, meat, skin, and stem.
3. Apples grow on trees.
4. A group of apple trees is called an orchard.
5. Bread, pies, puddings, applesauce, dumplings, butter, and jellies can be prepared from apples.
6. Some apples are sweet; others are sour.
7. Apples can be colored green, yellow, or red.
8. Apples can be large or small.
9. Apples can be hard or soft.
10. Apples can be eaten raw.
11. Seeds from an apple can grow into a tree.

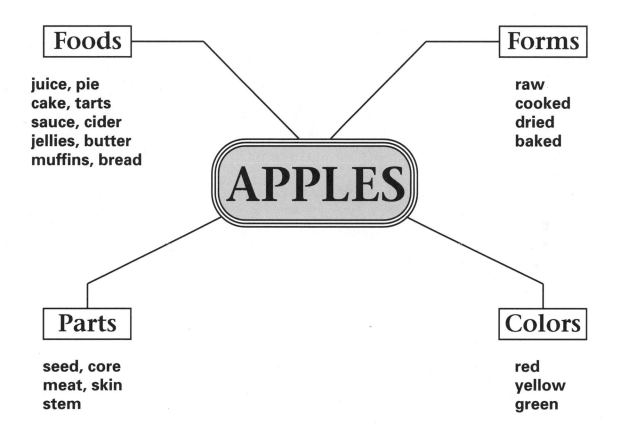

Foods

juice, pie
cake, tarts
sauce, cider
jellies, butter
muffins, bread

Forms

raw
cooked
dried
baked

APPLES

Parts

seed, core
meat, skin
stem

Colors

red
yellow
green

Vocabulary. The vocabulary should include new words that you want to informally introduce to the children. Vocabulary words need to be tailored to meet the specific needs of your group of children. The number of vocabulary words will vary, depending upon the theme and the developmental level of the children. For example, it might be assumed that the children know the word sweet, but not tart. So, the definition of the word tart is included. Collectively, the following words could be introduced in this unit: apple, texture, core, blossom, and apple butter. Definitions for these words could include:

1. apple—a fruit that is grown on a tree.
2. texture—how something feels.
3. core—the part of the apple that contains the seeds.
4. apple blossom—a flower on the apple tree.
5. apple butter—a spread for bread made from apples.

Activities. Now that you have learned how to develop goals related to a theme using a flowchart, you will need to learn how to select developmentally appropriate activities. You will find that many theme goals can be accomplished by additions to the environment, bulletin boards, field trips, and stories or resource people at group time. Your major role as an adult, or teacher, is that of a facilitator, planning and preparing the environment to stimulate the child's natural curiosity.

To begin this process, review each goal and determine how it can be introduced in the classroom. For example, if you were going to develop a theme on apples, review the goals. A bulletin board or game could introduce the three colors of apples. The children could also learn these colors through cooking experiences. The third vehicle for teaching the colors of apples would be placing the three colors of apples on a science table.

The five parts of an apple could also be introduced through participation in a tasting or cooking experience, bulletin board, or even discussion on a field trip or at the snack table. Always remember that children need to observe and manipulate the concrete object while engaged in child-initiated or child-directed play that is teacher supported. For that reason, fresh apples could be cut horizontally and placed on the science table with a magnifying glass. Likewise, simultaneously, apple seeds and paper could be available on the art table to construct a collage. Always remember that the best activities for young children are hands-on and open-ended. That is: focus on the process, rather than the product. Children need to learn to think, reason, and become problem solvers. As a teacher, you should take the ideas in this book and use and adapt them for planning and preparing the environment. Always remember that successful early childhood programs provide interesting, challenging, and engaging environments.

Parent Letters

Communication between the child's home and school is important. It builds mutual understanding and cooperation. With the efficiency of modern technology, parent letters are a form of written communication that can be shared on a weekly basis. The most interesting parent letters are written in the active voice. They state that the subject did something. To illustrate, "Mark played with blocks and read books today."

When writing the parent letter, consider the parent's educational level. Then write the letter in a clear, friendly, concise style. To do this, eliminate all words that are not needed. Limit the length of the letter to a page or two. To assist you with the process, an example of a parent letter is included for each theme.

Parent letters can be divided into three sections. Included should be a general introduction, school activities, and home activities. One way to begin the letter is by introducing new children or staff, or sharing something that happened the previous week. After this, introduce the theme for the coming week by explaining why it was chosen.

The second section of the parent letter could include some of the goals and special activities for the theme. Share with the parents all of the interesting things you will be doing at school throughout the week. By having this information, parents can initiate verbal interaction with their child.

The third section of the parent letter should be related to home activities. Suggest developmentally appropriate activities that the parents can provide in the home. These activities may or may not relate to the theme. Include the words of new songs and fingerplays. This section can also be used to provide parenting information such as the developmental value of specific activities for young children.

Bulletin Boards

Bulletin boards add color, decoration, and interest to the classroom. They also communicate what is happening in the classroom to parents and other visitors. The most effective bulletin boards involve the child. That is, the child will manipulate some pieces of the board. As a result, they are called involvement bulletin boards. Through the concrete experience of interacting with the bulletin board materials, children learn a variety of concepts and skills. Included may be size, shape, color, visual discrimination, eye-hand coordination, etc.

Carefully study the bulletin boards included for each theme in this book. They are simple, containing a replica of objects from the child's immediate environment. Each bulletin board has a purpose. It teaches a skill or concept.

As you prepare the bulletin boards provided in this book, you will become more creative. Gradually, you will combine ideas from several bulletin boards as you develop new themes for curriculum.

An opaque projector is a useful tool for individuals who feel uncomfortable with their drawing skills. Using the opaque projector, you can enlarge images from storybooks, coloring books, greeting cards, wrapping paper, etc. To do this, simply place the image to be copied in the projector. Then tape paper or tagboard on the wall. Turn on the projector. Using a pencil, color marker or crayon, trace the outline of the image onto the paper or tagboard.

Another useful tool for preparing bulletin boards is the overhead projector. Place a clear sheet of acetate on the picture desired for enlargement. This may include figures from a coloring book or storybook. Trace around the image using a washable marker designed for tranparencies. Project the image onto a wall and follow the same procedures as with the opaque projector.

To make your bulletin board pieces more durable, laminate them. If your center does not have a laminating machine, use clear contact paper. This process works just as well, but it can be more expensive.

Finally, the materials you choose to use on a bulletin board should be safe and durable. Careful attention should be given when selecting attachments. For two-, three- and four-year-old children, adhesive velcro and staples are preferred attachments. Push pins may be used with older children under careful supervision.

Selecting Books

Books for young children need to be selected with care. Before selecting books, once again, refer to the section following this Introduction and review the typical development for your group of young children. This information can provide a framework for selecting appropriate books.

There are some general guidelines for selecting books. First, children enjoy books that relate to their experiences. They also enjoy action. The words written in the book should be simple, descriptive, and within the child's understanding. The pictures should be large, colorful, and closely represent the actions.

A book that is good for one group of children may be inappropriate for another. You must know the child or group of children for whom the story is being selected. Consider their interests, attention span, and developmental level.

Developmental considerations are important. Two-year-olds enjoy stories about the things they do, know, and enjoy. Commonplace adventure is a preference for three-year-olds. They like to listen to things that could happen to them, including stories about community helpers. Four-year-old children are not as self-centered. These children do not have to be part of every situation that they hear about. Many are ready for short and simple fantasy stories. Five-year-olds like stories that add to their knowledge, that is, books that contain new information.

Curriculum Planning Guide

We hope you find this book to be a valuable guide in planning curriculum. The ideas should help you build curriculum based upon the children's natural interests. The book should also give you ideas so that your program will provide a wide variety of choices for children.

In planning a developmentally valid curriculum, consult the Index by Subject. It has been prepared to allow you easy selection from all the themes. So pick and choose and make it your own! The Index is arranged by subject as follows:

—Art
—Cooking
—Dramatic Play
—Features (by Theme)
—Field Trips/Resource People
—Fingerplays
—Group Time
—Large Muscle
—Math
—Rain Day
—Science
—Sensory
—Songs

Other Sources

Early childhood educators should refer to other Delmar publications when developing appropriate curriculum, including:

1. Oppenheim, Carol. *Science is Fun!*
2. Green, Moira. *474 Science Activities for Young Children.*

3. Herr, Judy and Libby, Yvonne. *Creative Resources of Art, Brushes, Buildings . . .*
4. Herr, Judy and Libby, Yvonne. *Creative Resources of Colors, Food, Plants, and Occupations.*
5. Green, Moira. *Themes With a Difference: 228 New Activities for Young Children.*
6. Green, Moira. Not! *The Same Old Activities for Early Childhood.*
7. Mayesky, Mary. *Creative Activities for Young Children* (5th ed.).
8. Pica, Rae. *Experiences in Movement with Music, Activities, and Theory.*
9. American Chemical Society and American Institute of Physics. *The Best of WonderScience.*
10. Wheeler, Ron. *Creative Resources for Elementary Classrooms and School-Age Programs.*
11. Bouza-Koster, Joan. *Growing Artists.*
12. Herr, Judy and Libby, Yvonne. *Creative Resources for the Early Childhood Classroom* (2nd ed.).

DEVELOPMENTAL BENCHMARKS

Ages	Fine Motor Skills	Gross Motor Skills
Two Year Olds	Turns pages in a book singly Imitates drawing a circle, vertical, and horizontal lines Fingers work together to scoop up small objects Constructs simple two- and three-piece puzzles Enjoys short, simple fingerplay games Strings large beads on shoelace Builds tower of up to eight blocks	Kicks large ball Jumps in place Runs without falling Throws ball without falling Walks up and down stairs alone Marches to music Tends to use legs and arms as pairs Uses whole arm usually to paint or color
Three Year Olds	Cuts paper Builds tower of nine small blocks Pastes using a finger Pours from a pitcher Copies a circle from a drawing Draws a straight line Uses fingers to pick up small objects Draws a person with three parts Strings beads and can arrange by color and shape Uses a knife to spread at meal or snack time	Catches ball with arms extended forward Throws ball underhand Completes forward somersault Walks up stairs with alternating feet Rides a tricycle skillfully Runs, walks, jumps, and gallops to music Throws ball without losing balance Hops on one foot
Four Year Olds	Buttons or unbuttons buttons Cuts on a line with scissors Completes a six- to eight-piece puzzle Copies a "t" Buckles a belt Zips separated fasteners Adds five parts to an incomplete man	Walks up and down stairs one foot per step Skips on one foot Rides a bicycle with training wheels
Five Year Olds	Uses a knife Copies most letters Traces objects Draws crude objects Colors within lines Copies square, triangle, and diamond shape Models objects from clay Laces shoes	Tries roller and ice skating Catches ball with hands Jumps from heights Jumps rope Walks on stilts Skips Climbs fences
Six Year Olds	Ties bows Hand preference established Reverses letters while printing Paints houses, trees, flowers, and clouds	Plays hopscotch Enjoys ball play Plays simple, organized games such as "hide-and-seek"

DEVELOPMENTAL BENCHMARKS

Ages	Emotional and Social Skills	Intellectual Skills
Two Year Olds	Takes toys away from others Plays near other children, but not cooperatively Unable to share toys Acts negatively at times Seeks teacher's attention Expresses fear of the dark Observes others to see how they do things	Talks mostly to himself Uses "me" instead of proper name Enjoys showing and naming objects Uses a two- to three-hundred word vocabulary Speaks in phrases or three-word sentences Answers yes/no questions Follows two-step commands Constructs negative sentences (no truck, no truck) Uses modifiers such as some, all, one Understands concepts big and little Uses such adjectives as red, old, and pretty
Three Year Olds	Plays in groups of two or three children Begins to take turns Sharing becomes evident with friends Enjoys independence by doing things for themselves, i.e., "Let me do it" or "I can do it." Yells "stop it" at times, as opposed to striking another child	Asks "how," "what," "when," and "why" questions Uses verb such as "could," "needs," "might," and "help" Uses adverbs such as "how about" and "maybe" Understands the pronouns you and they Understands "smaller" and "larger" Answers "how" questions appropriately Loves words such as "secret," "surprise," and "different" Uses words to define space such as "back," "up," "outside," "in front of," "in back of," "over," "next to"
Four Year Olds	Loves other children and having a "friend" Bases friendships on shared activities Seeks approval of friends Plays with small groups of children Delights in humorous stories Shows more interest in other children than adults Excludes children he does not like Loves to whisper and tell secrets	Experiences trouble telling the difference between reality and fantasy Exaggerates in practicing new words Loves silly language and to repeat new silly words Vocabulary of 1200 to 1500 words Begins to identify letters in his name Begins to appreciate bugs, trees, flowers, and birds Learns simple card games and dominoes Develops an awareness of "bad" and "good"
Five Year Olds	Prefers playing in small groups Prefers friends of same sex and age Protects younger children Plays well with older siblings Washes hands before meals Respects other people's property Becomes competitive Develops sense of fairness Verbally expresses anger	Names the days of the week Writes numbers from one to ten Retells main details of stories Recognizes the cause and effect of actions Uses a vocabulary of 2000 or more words Tells original stories Follows three-step command Recognizes square and rectangle shape Recognizes numerals 1-5
Six Year Olds	Prefers friends of the same sex Engages in cooperative play involving role assignments Enjoys being praised and complimented Enjoys "show and tell" time May be argumentative Competitive and wants to win	Identifies penny, nickel, and dime Counts ten objects Completes a 15-piece puzzle Acts out stories Plays Chinese checkers and dominoes Recognizes letters and words in books Identifies right from left hand Prints numbers from 1-20 Repeats an 8-10 word sentence Counts numbers to 30

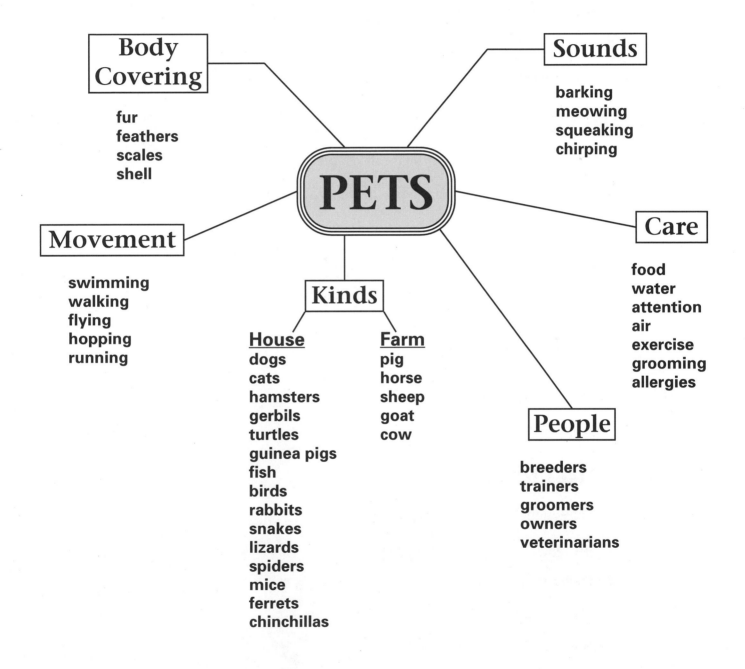

Body Covering
fur
feathers
scales
shell

Sounds
barking
meowing
squeaking
chirping

PETS

Movement
swimming
walking
flying
hopping
running

Care
food
water
attention
air
exercise
grooming
allergies

Kinds

House
dogs
cats
hamsters
gerbils
turtles
guinea pigs
fish
birds
rabbits
snakes
lizards
spiders
mice
ferrets
chinchillas

Farm
pig
horse
sheep
goat
cow

People
breeders
trainers
groomers
owners
veterinarians

Theme Goals:

Through participating in the experiences provided by this theme, the children may learn:

1. Some animals are kept as pets.

2. Pet care.

3. Places pets live.

4. Body coverings of pets.

5. Sounds of pets.

6. Movements of pets.

Concepts for the Children to Learn:

1. An animal kept for enjoyment is called a pet.

2. Dogs, cats, fish, hamsters, gerbils, and birds can all be house pets.

3. Pigs, ponies, horses, sheep, goats, and cows can be pets on a farm.

4. Pets need food, water, shelter, and loving care.

5. Barking, meowing, squeaking, and chirping are pet sounds.

6. To move, pets may swim, walk, fly, hop, or run.

7. The care of a pet depends on the type of animal.

8. Skin coverings on pets differ.

9. A veterinarian is an animal doctor.

Vocabulary:

1. **pet**—animal that is kept for pleasure.

2. **fur**—hairy coating of some animals.

3. **feathers**—skin covering of birds.

4. **scales**—skin covering of fish and other reptiles.

5. **veterinarian**—an animal doctor.

6. **collar**—a band worn around an animal's neck.

7. **leash**—a cord that attaches to a collar.

8. **whiskers**—stiff hair growing around the animal's nose, mouth, and eyes.

Bulletin Board

The purpose of this bulletin board is to encourage the development of mathematical skills. The children can count the fish in each water piece and match it to the corresponding numbered fishbowl. To prepare the bulletin board, construct fishbowls out of white tagboard or construction paper. Write a numeral beginning with one on each fishbowl and the corresponding number of dots. Hang the fishbowls on the bulletin board. Next, construct pieces as illustrated that will fit on top of the fishbowl to represent water in the bowl. Draw fish to match the numerals in each bowl. The pieces can be attached to each other to hang on the bulletin board by using magnet pieces, or push pins and a paper punch.

Parent Letter

Dear Parents,

Children are naturally curious about animals. Keeping that in mind, we will be starting a unit on pets, and I'm sure that we'll be busy! The children will discover the kinds of animals most people keep as pets. They will also learn the care that is involved in having a pet.

At School

The following are some of the learning experiences your child will participate in during our pet unit:

- making a special treat for Greta, our classroom gerbil.
- creating a large doghouse out of an appliance box for the dramatic play area.
- interacting with a variety of pets. Dani and Donny will bring their rabbit on Tuesday, and Cindy will bring her bird on Wednesday. If you are willing to bring your family pet to school to show the children, we welcome you. Contact me and we can arrange a time that would be convenient for you (and your pet).
- listening to the story, *Clifford, The Big Red Dog*, by Norman Bridwell.

At Home

Is your family considering adding a pet to your household? If so, there are many variables to be taken into consideration because not all households are meant to include pets. Allergies, fears, and life-styles are three things that need to be considered. Also, you will need to consider your child's readiness for a pet.

To develop fine motor skills, provide magazines and newspapers for your child to cut or tear out pictures of animals. These can be used to create an animal alphabet book or a collage to hang in your child's bedroom.

Enjoy your child!

Children enjoy feeding baby animals.

Music:

1. **"Rags"**
    (Sing this song to one of the children's favorite tunes)

    I have a dog and his name is Rags.
        (point to self)
    He eats so much that his tummy sags.
        (hold tummy)
    His ears flip-flop and his tail wig-wags.
        (flip hands by ears and wag hands at back)
    And when he walks he zigs and zags.
        (put hands together and zig-zag them)

    Flip-flop
    Wiggle-waggle
    Zig-zag   (Repeat the same actions)
    Flip-flop
    Wiggle-waggle
    Zig-zag

2. **"Six Little Pets"**
    (Sing to the tune of "Six Little Ducks," a traditional early childhood song)

    Six little gerbils I once knew, fat ones, skinny ones, fair ones too. But the one little gerbil was so much fun. He would play until the day was done.

    Six little dogs that I once knew, fat ones, skinny ones, fair ones too. But the one little dog with the brown curly fur, he led the others with a grr, grr, grr.

    Six little fish that I once knew, fat ones, skinny ones, fair ones too. But the one little fish who was the leader of the crowd, he led the others around and around.

    Six little birds that I once knew, fat ones, skinny ones, fair ones too. But the one little bird with the pretty little beak, he led the others with a tweet, tweet, tweet.

    Six little cats that I once knew, fat ones, skinny ones, fair ones too. But the one little cat who was as fluffy as a ball, he was the prettiest one of all.

3. **"Have You Ever Seen a Rabbit?"**
    (Sing to the tune of "Have You Ever Seen A Lassie?")

    Have you ever seen a rabbit, a rabbit, a rabbit?
    Have you ever seen a rabbit go hopping around?
    Go hopping, go hopping, go hopping, go hopping
    Have you ever seen a rabbit go hopping around?

Fingerplays:

MY PUPPY

I like to pet my puppy.
 (pet puppy)
He has such nice soft fur.
 (pet puppy)
And if I don't pull his tail
 (pull tail)
He won't say "Grr!"
 (make face)

IF I WERE

If I were a dog
I'd have four legs to run and play.
 (down on all four hands and feet)
If I were a fish
I'd have fins to swim all day.
 (hands at side fluttering like wings)
If I were a bird
I could spread my wings out wide.
And fly all over the countryside.
 (arms out from sides fluttering like wings)
But I'm just me.
I have two legs, don't you see?
And I'm just as happy as can be.

THE BUNNY

Once there was a bunny
 (fist with two fingers tall)
And a green, green cabbage head.
 (fist of other hand)
"I think I'll have some breakfast," this little
bunny said.
So he nibbled and he cocked his ears to say,
"I think it's time that I be on my way."

SAMMY

Sammy is a super snake.
 (wave finger on opposite palm)
He sleeps on the shore of a silver lake.
 (curl finger to indicate sleep)
He squirms and squiggles to snatch a snack
 (wave finger and pounce)
And snoozes and snores till his hunger is back.
 (curl finger on palm)

NOT SAY A SINGLE WORD

We'll hop, hop, hop like a bunny
 (make hopping motion with hand)
And run, run, run like a dog.
 (make running motion with fingers)
We'll walk, walk, walk like an elephant
 (make walking motion with arms)
And jump, jump, jump like a frog.
 (make jumping motions with arms)
We'll swim, swim, swim like a goldfish
 (make swimming motion with hand)
And fly, fly, fly like a bird.
 (make flying motion with arms)
We'll sit right down and fold our hands
 (fold hands in lap)
And not say a single word!

Science:

1. **Pet Foods**

   Cut pictures of pets and pet foods and place on the science table. Include different foods such as meat, fish, carrots, lettuce, nuts, and acorns. The children can match the food to a picture of the animal that would eat each type of food.

2. **Bird Feathers**

   Bird feathers with a magnifying glass can be placed on the science table for the children to examine.

3. **Hamster and Gerbil Pet Food**

   The children can assist in preparing the pet food for hamsters or gerbils. The recipe is as follows:

   1/2 cup cracked corn
   1/2 cup flour
   1/4 cup water
   1/2 teaspoon salt

   Mix the water with flour in a bowl. Add salt. Form into balls and roll into cracked corn. Cool to harden. Serve once a day.

   Source: Reynolds, Michelle. (1979). *Critter's Kitchen.* New York: Athenum Publishing Company.

Dramatic Play:

1. **Pet Store**

   The children can all bring in their stuffed animals to set up a pet store. A counter, a cash register, and several empty pet food containers should be provided to stimulate play.

2. **Veterinarian Prop Box**

   Collect materials for a veterinarian prop box. Include a stethoscope, empty pill bottles, fabric cut as bandages, splints, and stuffed animals.

Arts and Crafts:

1. **Pet Sponge Painting**

   Cut sponges into a variety of pet shapes. Place on the art table with paper and a shallow pan of tempera paint.

2. **Doghouse**

   Provide an old large cardboard box for the children to make a doghouse with adult supervision. They can cut holes, paint, and decorate it. When dry, the doghouse can be moved into the dramatic play area or to the outdoor play yard.

3. **Cookie Cutters and Playdough**

   Pet-shaped cookie cutters and playdough can be placed on the art table.

Sensory:

Minnows

Fill the sensory table with cold water. Place minnows purchased from a bait store into the water. The children will attempt to catch the minnows. Teachers should stress the importance of being gentle with the fish and follow through with limits set for the activity. After participating in this activity, the children should wash their hands.

Field Trips/Resource People:

1. **Pet Show**

   Plan a pet show. Each child who wants to show a pet should sign up for a time and day. If children can all bring in a pet the same day, have a big pet show. Award prizes for longest tail, longest ears, biggest, smallest, best groomed, loudest barker, most obedient, etc. Children who do not have a pet or cannot arrange to bring it to school can bring a stuffed toy.

2. **Veterinarian**

   Invite a veterinarian to talk to the children about how a veterinarian helps pets and animals. Pet care can also be addressed.

3. **Pet Store**

   Visit a pet store to observe types of pets, their toys, and other accessories. Pictures can be taken on the trip and later placed on the bulletin board of the classroom.

4. **Pet Groomer**

   Visit a pet groomer. Observe how the pet is bathed and groomed.

Social Studies:

1. **Animal Sounds**

   Tape several animal sounds and play them back for the children to identify.

2. **Feeding Chart**

   Design and prepare a feeding chart for the classroom pets.

3. **Weekend Visitor**

   Let children take turns bringing class pets home on weekends. Prepare a card for each animal's cage outlining feeding and behavioral expectations.

Cooking:

Animal Cookies

1 1/2 cups powdered sugar
1 cup butter or margarine
1 egg
1 teaspoon vanilla extract
1/2 teaspoon almond extract
2 1/2 cups flour

1 teaspoon baking soda
1 teaspoon cream of tartar

Mix powdered sugar, margarine, egg, and vanilla and almond extracts. Mix in flour, baking soda, and cream of tartar. Cover and refrigerate for 2 hours. Preheat oven to 375 degrees. Divide dough into halves. Roll out 1/2-inch thick on a lightly floured, cloth-covered board. Cut the dough into animal shapes with cookie cutters or let children cut. Place on lightly greased cookie sheet. Bake 7 to 10 minutes. Serve for snack.

Multimedia:

The following resources can be found in educational catalogs:

1. Palmer, Hap. *Walk Like the Animals* [record].

2. Palmer, Hap. *Walter the Waltzing Worm* [record].

Books:

The following books can be used to complement the theme:

1. Blacker, Terrance. (1990). *Herbie Hamster, Where Are You?* New York: Random House.

2. Robbins, Sandra. (1990). *How the Turtle Got Its Shell: An African Tale. New York: Berrent* Publications.

3. Yolen, Jane. (1990). *Sky Dog*. San Diego: Harcourt Brace Jovanovich.

4. Szekeres, Cyndy. (1990). *What Bunny Loves*. Racine, WI: Western Publishing Co.

5. Cohen, C. (1988). *The Mud Pony: A Traditional Skidi Pawnee Tale*. New York: Scholastic.

6. Brown, Marc. (1990). *Arthur's Pet Business*. Boston: Joy Street Books.

7. Rogers, Fred. (1988). *When a Pet Dies*. New York: G. P. Putnam.

8. Berry, Joy. (1987). *Teach Me About Pets*. Chicago: Children's Press.

9. Cousins, Lucy. (1991). *Pet Animals*. New York: William Morrow and Co.

10. Dupont, Marie. (1991). *Your First Kitten*. Neptune City, NJ: TFH Publications, Inc.

11. Pienkowski, Jan. (1992). *Pets*. New York: Simon and Schuster Trade.

12. Smith, Lane. (1991). *The Big Pets*. New York: Viking Children's Books.

13. Davies, Andrew, & Davies, Diana. (1990). *Poonam's Pets*. New York: Viking Children's Books.

14. Erickson, Gina C., & Foster, Kelli C. (1992). *The Best Pets Yet*. Hauppauge, NY: Barron's Educational Series, Inc.

15. Garland, Sarah. (1992). *Billy and Belle*. New York: Viking Children's Press.

16. Tusan, Stan. (1992). *Who Will Be My Pet?* Racine, WI: Western Publishing Co.

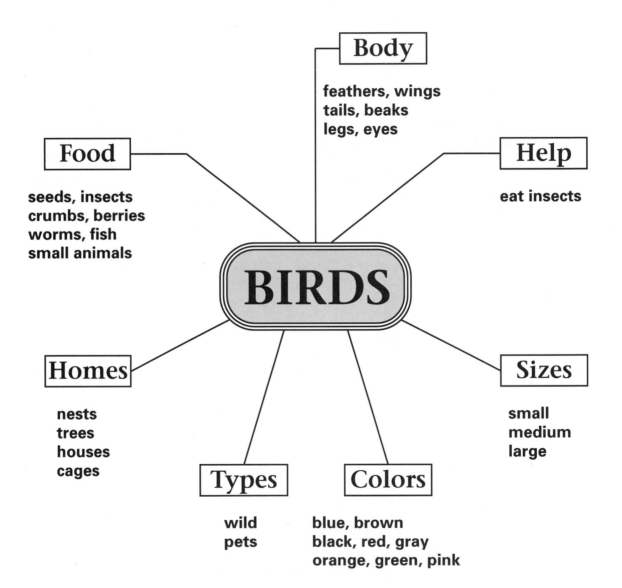

Body

feathers, wings
tails, beaks
legs, eyes

Food

seeds, insects
crumbs, berries
worms, fish
small animals

Help

eat insects

BIRDS

Homes

nests
trees
houses
cages

Sizes

small
medium
large

Types

wild
pets

Colors

blue, brown
black, red, gray
orange, green, pink

Theme Goals:

Through participating in the experiences provided by this theme, the children may learn:

1. The bird's body parts.
2. Types of birds.
3. Bird homes.
4. Foods that birds eat.
5. Ways birds help.
6. Sizes of birds.
7. Colors of birds.

Concepts for the Children to Learn:

1. There are many kinds of birds.
2. Birds hatch from eggs.
3. Birds have feathers, wings, and beaks.
4. Most birds fly.
5. Birds live in nests, trees, houses, and cages.
6. Some birds are pets.
7. Many birds make sounds.
8. Birds eat seeds, insects, crumbs, and worms.
9. Some birds eat fish and small animals.
10. Some birds help us by eating insects.

Vocabulary:

1. **beak**—the part around a bird's mouth.
2. **bird watching**—watching birds.
3. **bird feeder**—a container for bird food.
4. **feathers**—covers skin of a bird.
5. **hatch**—to come from an egg.
6. **nest**—bed or home prepared by a bird.
7. **perch**—a pole for a bird to stand on.
8. **wing**—movable body part that helps most birds fly.

Bulletin Board

The purpose of this bulletin board is to develop skills in matching a set to its corresponding numeral. To construct the board, cut ten bird nests out of brown-colored tagboard. Draw a set of dots, beginning with one on each bird nest. Tack the nest on the bulletin board. Next, construct the same number of birds out of tagboard. On each bird, write a numeral beginning with one. By matching the numeral on each bird to the number of dots on the nests, the children can help each bird find a home. The number of birds and nests on this bulletin board should match the children's developmental needs.

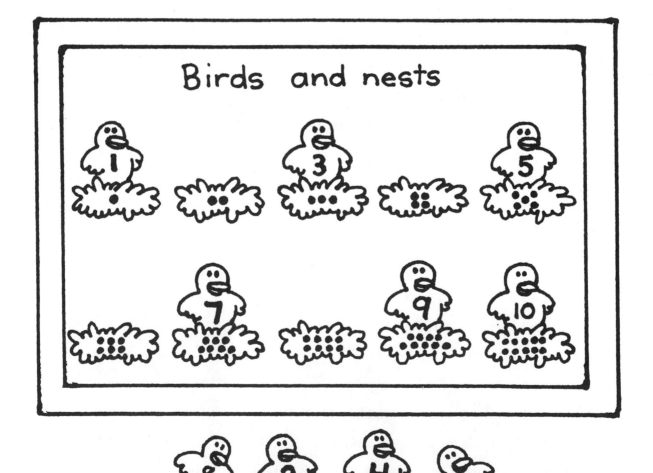

Parent Letter

Dear Parents,

Our class will be discussing our "feathered friends"—birds, which is the focus of our next unit. The children will be introduced to birds kept as pets and birds in the wild. In addition, they will discover the unique body parts of birds and the homes in which they live. The children will learn that birds are more similar than they are dissimilar.

At School

Some of the activities planned for the unit on birds include:

- observing different types of bird nests with a magnifying glass at the science table.
- visiting with Jodi's pet canary on Wednesday.
- creating collages using birdseed and glue in the art area.
- making bird feeders to hang outdoors in our play yard.

At Home

Whether you live in the city or country, chances are there are birds nearby. The following game may be fun to play with your child. Set an egg or kitchen timer for three to five minutes. Then look out the window and see how many birds you can see. For each bird, drop a button in a jar. When the timer goes off, count how many buttons are in the jar. This game will strengthen your child's observation skills and increase his understanding of number concepts. Variations of this game would be to observe for cars, squirrels, or any other object that can be counted.

Happy bird watching!

Children enjoy exploring bird habitats.

Music:

1. **"Birds"**
   (Sing to the tune of "Here We Go Round the Mulberry Bush")
   The first verse remains the same, with the children walking around in a circle holding hands.

   This is the way we scratch for worms.
   (children move foot in a scratching motion like a chicken)
   This is the way we peck our food.
   (children peck)
   This is the way we sit on our eggs.
   (children squat down)
   This is the way we flap our wings.
   (bend arms at elbows, and put thumbs under armpits, flap)
   This is the way we fly away.
   (children can "fly" anywhere they want, but return to the circle at the end of the verse)

2. **"Pretty Birds"**
   (Sing to the tune of "Ten Little Indians")

   One pretty, two pretty
   Three pretty birdies.
   Four pretty, five pretty,
   Six pretty birdies.
   Seven pretty, eight pretty,
   Nine pretty birdies,
   All sitting in a tree.

Fingerplays:

THE DUCK

I waddle when I walk.
(hold arms and elbows high and twist trunk side to side or squat down)
I quack when I walk
(place palms together and open and close)
And I have webbed toes on my feet.
(spread fingers wide)
Rain coming down, makes me smile, not frown
(smile)
And I dive for something to eat.
(put hands together and make diving motion)

Source: Hillert, Margaret. (1982). *Action Verse for Early Childhood*. Minneapolis: T.S. Denison and Co. Inc.

THE OWL

There's a wide-eyed owl
(encircle each eye with thumb and forefinger)
With a pointed nose.
(direct forefingers to a point downside of nose)
And two pointed ears
(extend forefingers up from top of head)
And claws for toes.
(curve fingers like claws)
He lives high in a tree.
(point overhead)
When he looks at you
(point to another child)
He flaps his wings
(bend elbows and flap arms like wings)
And says "whoo, whoo, whoo."

Source: Hillert, Margaret. (1982). *Action Verse for Early Childhood*. Minneapolis: T.S. Denison and Co. Inc.

HOUSES

Here is a nest for a robin.
    (cup both hands)
Here is a hive for a bee.
    (fists together)
Here is a hole for the bunny;
    (finger and thumb make circle)
And here is a house for me!
    (fingertips together to make roof)

TWO LITTLE BLACKBIRDS

Two little blackbirds sitting on a hill,
    (close fists, extend index fingers)
One named Jack. One named Jill.
    (talk to one finger; talk to other finger)
Fly away, Jack. Fly away, Jill.
    (toss index fingers over shoulder separately)
Come back, Jack. Come back, Jill.
    (bring back hands separately with index
    fingers extended)

BIRD FEEDER

Here is the bird feeder. Here are seeds and crumbs.
    (left hand out flat, right hand cupped)
Sprinkle them on and see what comes.
    (sprinkling motion with right hand over left
    hand)
One cardinal, one chickadee, one junco, one jay,
    (join fingers of right hand and peck at the
    bird feeder once for each bird)
Four of my bird friends are eating today.
    (hold up four fingers of left hand)

IF I WERE A BIRD

If I were a bird, I'd sing a song
And fly about the whole day long.
    (twine thumbs together and move hands
    like wings)
And when the night comes, go to rest,
    (tilt head and close eyes)
Up in my cozy little nest.
    (cup hands together to form nest)

TAP TAP TAP

Tap, tap, tap goes the woodpecker
    (tap with right pointer finger on inside of
    left wrist)
As he pecks a hole in a tree.
    (make hole with pointer finger and thumb)
He is making a house with a window
To peep at you and me.
    (hold circle made with finger and thumb in
    front of eye)

STRETCH, STRETCH

Stretch, stretch away up high:
On your tiptoes, reach the sky.
See the bluebirds flying high.
    (wave hands)
Now bend down and touch your toes.
Now sway as the North Wind blows.
Waddle as the gander goes!

Science:

1. **Bird Feeders**

   Make bird feeders. Suet can be purchased from a butcher shop or meat department of a supermarket. For each feeder, purchase 1/2 pound of suet, a 12" x 12" piece of netting, and birdseed. Begin by rolling the suet in birdseed. Place the seeded suet in the netting. Tie the four corners of the netting together and hang in tree or set outside on window ledge for children to observe.

2. **Grapefruit Cup Feeders**

   Place seeds in an empty grapefruit half. If possible, place the feeder in an observable location for the children. Some children may wish to take their feeders home.

3. **Science Table**

   On the science table, provide magnifying glasses and the following items:

   - feathers
   - eggs
   - nests

4. Observing a Bird

Arrange for a caged parakeet to visit the classroom. A parent may volunteer or a pet store may lend a bird for a week. Encourage the children to note the structure of the cage, the beauty of the bird, food eaten, and the behavior of the bird.

Dramatic Play:

1. Birdhouse

Construct a large birdhouse out of cardboard. Place in the dramatic play area, allowing the children to imitate birds. Unless adequate room is available, this may be more appropriate for an outdoor activity. Bird accessories such as teacher-made beaks and wings may be supplied to stimulate interest.

2. Bird Nest

Place several hay bales in the corner of a play yard, confining the materials to one area. Let the child rearrange the straw to simulate a bird nest.

3. Hatching

Here is a general idea of what you can say to create the hatching experience with young children. Say, "Close your eyes. Curl up very small; as small as you can. Lie on your side. Think of how dark it is inside your egg. Yes, you're in an egg! You're tiny and curled up and quiet. It's very dark. Very warm. But now, try to wiggle a little—just a little! Remember, your eggshell is all around you. You can wiggle your wingtips a little, and maybe your toes. You can shake your head just a little. Hey! Your beak is touching something. I think your beak is touching the eggshell. Tap the shell gently with your beak. Hear that? Yes, that's you making that noise. Keep tapping. A little harder. Something is happening. The shell has cracked—oh, close your eyes. It's bright out there. Now you can wiggle a little more. The shell is falling away. You can stretch out, stretch to be as long as you can make yourself.

Stretch your feet. Stretch your wings. Doesn't that feel good, after being in that little egg? Stretch! You're brand new—can you stand up, slowly? Can you see other new baby birds?"

Arts and Crafts:

1. Feather Painting

On the art table, place feathers, thin paper, and paint. Let the children experiment with different paint consistencies and types of feathers.

2. Birdseed Collages

Birdseed, paper, and white glue are needed for this activity. Apply glue to paper and sprinkle birdseed over the glue. For a variation, use additional types of seeds such as corn and sunflower seeds.

3. Eggshell Collage

Save eggshells and dye them. Crush the dyed shells into small pieces. Using glue, apply the eggshells to paper.

4. Robin Eggs

Cut easel paper into the shape of an egg. Provide light blue paint with sand for speckles.

5. Dying Eggs

Boil an egg for each child. Then let the children paint the eggs with easel brushes. The eggs can be eaten at snack time or taken home.

Sensory:

Additions to the Sensory Table

- feathers and sand
- eggshells
- sticks and twigs for nests
- worms and soil
- water, ducks, and other water toys
- birdseed and measuring tools

Field Trips/Resource People:

1. Pet Store

Take a field trip to a pet store. Arrange to have the manager show the children birds and bird cages. Ask the manager how to care for birds.

2. Bird Sanctuary

Take a field trip to a bird sanctuary, nature area, pond, or park. Observe where birds live.

3. Museum

Arrange to visit a nature museum or taxidermy studio to look at stuffed birds. Extend the activity by providing magnifying glasses.

4. Zoo

Visit the bird house. Observe the colors and sizes of birds.

5. Resource People

Invite resource people to visit the classroom. Suggestions include:

- wildlife management people
- ornithologists
- veterinarians
- bird owners
- bird watchers
- pet store owners

Math:

1. Feather Sorting

During the self-directed activity period, place a variety of feathers on a table. Encourage the children to sort them according to attributes such as color, size, and/or texture. This activity can be followed with other sorting activities including egg shapes and pictures of birds.

2. Cracked Eggs

Cut tagboard egg shapes. Using scissors, cut the eggs in half making a jagged line. Record a numeral on one side of the egg and corresponding dots on the other side. The number of eggs prepared should reflect the children's developmental level.

Social Studies:

1. Caring for Birds

Arrange for a pet canary to visit the classroom. The children can take turns feeding and caring for the bird. Responsibilities include cleaning the cage, providing water and birdseed. Also, a cuttlebone should be inserted in the bars of the cage within reach of the bird's bill. This bone will help keep the bird's bill sharp and clean, providing the bird uses it.

2. Bird Feeders

Purchase birdseed and small paper cups. The children can fill a cup with a small amount of seed. After this, the teacher can attach a small string to the cup for use as a handle. The bird feeders can then be hung in bushes outdoors. If bushes are not available, they can be placed on window sills.

Group Time (games, language):

1. Little Birds

This is a movement game that allows for activity. To add interest, the teacher may use a tambourine for rhythm. One child can be the mother bird and the remainder of the children can act out the story.

All the little birds are asleep in their nest.
All the little birds are taking a rest.
They do not even twitter, they do not even tweet.
Everything is quiet up and down the street.
Then came the mother bird and tapped them on the head.

© 1998, Delmar Publishers

They opened up one little eye and this is what was said,
"Come little birdies, it's time to learn to fly,
Come little birdies, fly way up in the sky."
Fly fly, oh fly away, fly, fly, fly
Fly fly, oh fly away, fly away so high.
Fly fly, oh, fly away, birds, can fly the best.
Fly fly, oh, fly away, now fly back to your nest.

2. Who Is Inside?

The purpose of this game is to encourage the child to develop listening skills. To prepare for the activity, find a piece of large muscle equipment such as a jungle gym to serve as the bird house. Cover it with a large blanket. To play the game one child looks away from the group or covers his eyes. A second child should go into the bird house. The first child says, "Who is inside?" The second child replies, "I am inside the bird house." Then the first child tries to guess who is in the bird house by recognizing the voice. Other clues may be asked for, if voice alone does not work.

3. Little Red Hen

Tell the story of the Little Red Hen. After listening to the story, let the children help make bread.

Cooking:

1. Egg Salad Sandwiches

eggs
bread
mayonnaise
dry mustard (just a pinch)
salt
pepper

Boil, shell, and mash the eggs, adding enough mayonnaise to provide a consistent texture. Add salt, pepper, and dry mustard to flavor. Spread on the bread.

2. French Bread Recipe

1/2 cup water
2 packages rapid rise yeast
1 tablespoon salt
2 cups lukewarm water
7 to 7 1/2 cups all-purpose flour

Soften the yeast in 1/2 cup lukewarm water. Be careful that the water isn't too warm or the activity of the yeast will be destroyed. Add salt to 2 cups of lukewarm warm water in a large bowl. Gradually, add 2 cups of flour and beat well. Add the softened yeast and gradually add the remaining flour, beating well after each addition. Turn the soft dough out on a lightly floured surface and knead until elastic. Lightly grease a bowl and place the dough into it, turning once to grease surface. Let rise until double. Divide into 2 portions. Bake in a 375-degree oven until light brown, about 35 minutes.

3. Bird's Nest Salad

1 grated carrot
1/2 cup canned Chinese noodles
mayonnaise to moisten
peas or grapes

Have the children grate a carrot. Next have them mix the carrot with 1/2 cup canned Chinese noodles and mayonnaise to moisten. Put a mound of this salad on a plate and push in the middle with a spoon to form a nest. Peas or grapes can be added to the nest to represent bird eggs. The nest could also be set on top of a lettuce leaf. Makes 2 salads.

Source: Warren, Jean. (1982). *Super Snacks.* Alderwood Manor, WA: Warren Publishing.

4. Egg Foo Young

12 eggs
1/2 cup finely chopped onion
1/3 cup chopped green pepper
3/4 teaspoon salt
dash of pepper
2 16-ounce cans bean sprouts, drained

Sauce:
2 tablespoons cornstarch
2 teaspoons sugar
2 cubes or 2 teaspoons chicken bouillon
dash of ginger
2 cups of water
3 tablespoons soy sauce

Heat oven to 300 degrees. Beat eggs in a large bowl. Add remaining ingredients, except sauce ingredients; mix well. Heat 2 tablespoons of oil in a large skillet. Drop egg mixture by table-spoons into skillet and fry until golden. Turn and brown other side. Drain on a paper towel. Continue to cook the remaining egg mixture, adding oil to skillet if necessary. Keep warm in 300-degree oven while preparing sauce. Combine the first four sauce ingredients in a saucepan. Add water and soy sauce. Cook until mixture boils and thickens, stirring constantly.

Multimedia:

The following resources can be found in educational catalogs:

1. *The Animal Fair* [record]. January Productions.

   - Six Little Ducks
   - Three Crows
   - Bird's Courting Song
   - I Bought Me a Rooster
   - Cluck Old Hen
   - The Old Grey Hen
   - Listen to the Mockingbird
   - Animal Fair

2. Palmer, Hap. *Folk Song Carnival* [record]. Activity Records.

   - Going to the Zoo
   - Blue Bird
   - Hush Little Baby

3. Mills, Alan. *Fourteen Numbers, Letters and Animal Songs* [record]. Folkways Records.

   - Animal Alphabet
   - Six Little Ducks

Books:

The following books may be used to complement this theme:

1. Oppenheim, Joanne. (1986). *Have You Seen Birds?* New York: Scholastic Books.

2. Van Laan, Nancy. (1989). *Rainbow Crow*. New York: Alfred A. Knopf.

3. Gibbons, Gail. (1991). *The Puffins Are Back*. New York: Harper Collins.

4. Carey, Valerie Scho. (1990). *Quail Song*. New York: Putnam.

5. Knutson, Barbara. (1990). *How the Guinea Fowl Got Her Spots*. Minneapolis: Carolrhoda Books.

6. Lester, Helen. (1988). *Tacky the Penguin*. Boston: Houghton Mifflin.

7. Maddox, Tony. (1989). *Spike: The Sparrow Who Couldn't Sing*. New York: Barron's.

8. Pomerantz, Charlotte. (1989). *Flap Your Wings and Try*. New York: Greenwillow.

9. Prelutsky, Jack. (1986). *Ride a Purple Pelican*. New York: Greenwillow.

10. Yolen, Jane. (1990). *Cardinal*. New York: Philomel.

11. Lawson, Amy. (1987). *The Talking Bird and the Story Pouch*. New York: Harper Collins.

12. Yolen, Jane. (1987). *Owl Moon*. New York: Philomel.

13. Busch, Laura C. (1990). *Canary Books*. Little Readers.

14. Rockwell, Anne. (1992). *Our Yard Is Full of Birds*. New York: Harper Collins Children's Books.

15. Packard, Mary. (1992). *I Wonder How Parrots Can Talk and Other Neat Facts About Birds*. Racine, WI: Western Publishing Co.

16. National Wildlife Federation. (1991). *Birds Birds Birds*. Vienna, VA: Author.

17. Hirschi, Ron. (1987). *What Is a Bird?* New York: Walker and Co.

18. Hirschi, Ron. (1987). *Where Do Birds Live?* New York: Walker and Co.

19. Ehlert, Lois. (1990). *Feathers for Lunch*. San Diego: Harcourt Brace Jovanovich.

20. Stewart, Frances T., & Stewart, Charles P. (1988). *Birds and Their Environments*. New York: Harper Collins Children's Books, Inc.

21. Livingston, P. (1992). *Gullible the Seagull*. Sound Publishers.

22. Lyon, David. (1987). *The Runaway Duck*. New York: Morrow.

23. McLerran, Alice. (1991). *The Mountain That Loved a Bird*. Saxonville, MA: Picture Book Studio.

24. Pirotta, Saviour. (1992). *Little Bird*. New York: Tambourine Books.

25. Ross, Michael E. (1992). *Become a Bird & Fly*. Brookfield, CT: Millbrook Press.

26. Wolff, Ashley. (1985). *A Year of Birds*. New York: Puffin Books.

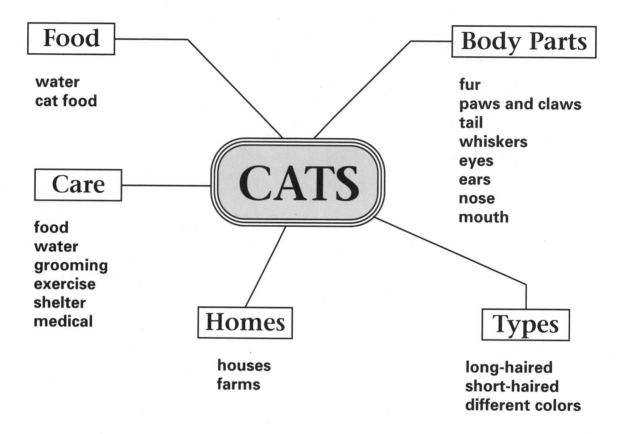

Food

water
cat food

Care

food
water
grooming
exercise
shelter
medical

CATS

Body Parts

fur
paws and claws
tail
whiskers
eyes
ears
nose
mouth

Homes

houses
farms

Types

long-haired
short-haired
different colors

Theme Goals:

Through participating in the experiences provided by this theme, the children may learn:

1. Types of cats.

2. Body parts of a cat.

3. Cats need special care.

4. What cats eat, drink, and where they live.

Concepts for the Children to Learn:

1. Cats can be black, brown, white, grey, yellow, or calico.

2. Cats use their claws for many things.

3. Cats meow and purr to communicate.

4. Cats have legs, eyes, ears, a mouth, nose, and a tail.

5. Cats have fur on their skin.

6. Cats should be handled carefully and gently.

7. There are many different sizes and types of cats.

8. Cats need food, water, and exercise every day.

9. Many different people help cats.

10. A kitten is a baby cat.

11. Cats like to play.

Vocabulary:

1. **kitten**—a baby cat.

2. **pet**—an animal kept for pleasure.

3. **paw**—the cat's foot.

4. **veterinarian**—an animal doctor.

5. **leash**—a rope, chain, or cord that attaches to a collar.

6. **collar**—a band worn around the cat's neck.

7. **whiskers**—stiff hair growing around the cat's nose, mouth, and eyes.

8. **coat**—hair covering the skin.

Bulletin Board

The purpose of this bulletin board is to promote visual discrimination and pattern matching skills. Construct cats' bodies and heads out of tagboard, coloring each a different color and fur pattern. Laminate all pieces. Attach cat bodies to the bulletin board. Children then match the heads to the corresponding body.

Parent Letter

Dear Parents,

We have many exciting activities planned at school as we begin our study on cats. We will be learning about a cat's body structure, how to care for and feed our cats, and the different types of cats.

At School

Some of the learning experiences planned include:

- taking a field trip to the veterinarian's office.
- making a chart of different types of cats.
- setting up a cat grooming area in dramatic play.

At Home

We will be learning the fingerplay "Two Little Kittens." You may want to try it with your child at home:

Two little kittens found a ball of yarn
    (hold up 2 fingers…cup hands together to form a ball)
As they were playing near a barn.
    (bring hands together pointed upward for barn)
One little kitten jumped in the hay,
    (hold up 1 finger…make jumping then wiggling motion)
The other little kitten ran away.
    (make running motion with other hand)

Fingerplays and rhymes help children develop language vocabulary and sequencing skills. The actions that often accompany fingerplays develop fine motor development.

Have fun with your child!

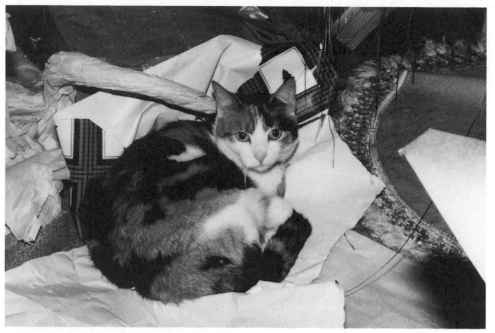

What is your favorite breed of cat?

Music:

1. **"Two Little Kittens"**
   (Sing to the tune of "Two Little Blackbirds")

   Two little kittens sitting on a hill
   One named Jack, one named Jill
   Run away Jack, run away Jill
   Come back Jack, come back Jill
   Two little kittens sitting on a hill
   One named Jack, one named Jill.

2. **"Kitty"**
   (Sing to the tune of "Bingo")

   I have a cat. She's very shy.
   But she comes when I call K-I-T-T-Y
   K-I-T-T-Y
   K-I-T-T-Y
   K-I-T-T-Y
   and Kitty is her name-o.

   Variation: Let children think of other names.

Fingerplays:

MRS. KITTY'S DINNER

Mrs. Kitty, sleek and fat,
   (put thumb up with fingers folded on right hand)

With her kittens four.
   (hold up four fingers on right hand)
Went to sleep upon the mat
   (make a fist)
By the kitchen door.

Mrs. Kitty heard a noise.
Up she jumped in glee.
   (thumb up on right hand)
"Kittens, maybe that's a mouse?
   (all 5 fingers on right hand up)
Let's go and see!"

Creeping, creeping, creeping on.
   (slowly sneaking with 5 fingers on floor)
Silently they stole.
But the little mouse had gone
   (mouse is thumb on left hand)
Back into his hole.

A KITTEN

A kitten is fast asleep under the chair.
   (thumb under hands)
And Donald can't find her.
He's looked everywhere.
   (fingers circling eyes to look)
Under the table
   (peek under one hand)
And under the bed
   (peek under other hand)

He looked in the corner, and then Donald said,
"Come Kitty, come Kitty, this milk is for you."
    (curve hands for dish)
And out came Kitty calling "mew, mew, mew."

THREE CATS

One little cat and two little cats
went out for a romp one day.
    (hold up 1 finger and then 2 fingers with
    other hand)
One little cat and two little cats
make how many cats at play?
    (ask how many that makes)
Three little cats had lots of fun
till growing tired away ran _____?
    (take 1 finger away and ask how many ran
    away)
I really think that he was most unkind
to the _____ little cats that were left behind.
    (ask how many are left)

KITTEN IS HIDING

A kitten is hiding under a chair,
    (hide one thumb in other hand)
I looked and looked for her everywhere.
    (peer about with hand on forehead)
Under the table and under the bed,
    (pretend to look)
I looked in the corner and then I said,
"Come Kitty, come Kitty, I have milk for you."
    (cup hands to make dish and extend)
Kitty came running and calling, "Mew, mew."
    (run fingers up arm)

TWO LITTLE KITTENS

Two little kittens found a ball of yarn
    (hold up 2 fingers…cup hands together to
    form a ball)
As they were playing near a barn.
    (bring hands together pointed upward for
    barn)
One little kitten jumped in the hay,
    (hold up one finger…make jumping, then
    wiggling motion)
The other little kitten ran away.
    (make running motion with other hand)

Science:

1. Provide a scale and different cat items (such as cat toys, collar, food dish, etc.) to weigh.

2. During the social studies activity, "Share Your Cat," arrange for a cat and a kitten to be in the classroom at the same time. With the help of parents, weigh the cats or kittens and discuss with the children the differences.

3. Set out a magnifying glass to observe different kinds of dry cat food.

4. Talk about a cat who has claws and one that is declawed. Ask various questions such as: Why do cats have claws? Why are cats declawed? Where do cats go to be declawed? etc.

5. Discuss the various parts of a cat's body and how they can protect the cat. (Examples: fur, whiskers, etc.)

6. Discuss what a cat's body does when it feels danger.

Dramatic Play:

1. **Cat Grooming**

   Provide the children with empty shampoo and conditioner bottles, brushes, combs, ribbons, collars, plastic bathtub, towels, and stuffed animal cats.

2. **Veterinarian's Office**

   Provide various medical supplies such as a stethoscope, bandages, and thermometers along with stuffed cats.

3. **Cats!**

   Let children pretend they are cats by using cat masks or costumes. Also, you may want to try using yarn balls, boxes to curl up in, and empty cat food boxes. Allow the children to act out the story, "The Three Little Kitttens" or other cat stories.

4. **Circus or Zoo**

   Lions, cheetas, panthers, leopards, and tigers are also cats. Use large boxes for cages.

Arts and Crafts:

1. **Kitty Collage**

   Let children find and cut or tear out pictures of cats from greeting cards and magazines. Children can then paste their cats on pieces of construction paper.

2. **Pom Pom Painting**

   Set out several different colors of tempera paint. Using pom-pom balls, let children create their own designs on construction paper.

3. **Cat Mask**

   Using paper plates or paper bags along with paper scraps, yarn, crayons, scissors, and paint, let the children design cat masks.

4. **Paw Prints**

   Let children pretend they are cats using their hands and paint to make prints.

Large Muscle:

1. **Bean Bag Toss**

   Make a cat shape on plywood with holes of different sizes cut out. The children can try from varying distances to throw bean bags through the holes.

2. **Yarn Balls**

   Set up baskets at varying distances from a masking tape line on the floor. Toss yarn balls into the baskets.

3. **Cat Pounce**

   Children pretend to be cats and pounce from one line to another.

4. **Climbing Cats**

   Bring into the classroom or play outside on a wooden climber. The children can pretend to be cats and climb on the climber.

5. **Cat Movements**

   Write down all the words that describe how cats move. Allow the children to demonstrate the movements. Also, use music in the background.

Field Trips/Resource People:

1. **Pet Store**

   Take a field trip to a pet store. Ask the manager how to care for cats. Observe the different types of cats, cages, collars, leashes, and food.

2. **Veterinarian's Office**

   Take a field trip to a veterinarian's office or animal hospital. Compare the similarities and differences to a doctor's office.

3. **Variety Store**

   Visit a variety store and observe pet accessories.

4. **Resource People**

   Invite resource people. Suggestions include:

   - cat groomer
   - humane society representative
   - pet store owner
   - veterinarian
   - parents to bring in pet cats

Math:

1. **Matching Game**

   Have the children match the number of cats on a card to the correct numeral. (Cat stickers work well.)

2. **How Many Paper Clips**

Make several different sizes of cats out of tagboard. Children measure each cat with the paper clips.

3. **Whisker Count**

Make several cat faces with one numeral on each face. Children attach the correct number of whiskers (pipe cleaners, felt, paper strips, etc.) according to the numeral on the cat.

Social Studies:

1. **Chart**

Make a chart with the children of different types of cats.

2. **Displays**

Display different pictures of cats around the room.

3. **Share Your Cat**

Invite the children and the parents to bring in a pet cat on specified days. (Have your camera ready! Take pictures and display them on a bulletin board.) Encourage the children to talk about their cat's colors, likes, body, etc.

4. **Cat Safety**

Discuss cat safety with the class. Items that may be discussed include why cats use their claws, what to do if you find a stray cat, the uses of collars and leashes.

Group Time (games, language):

1. **Copy Cats**

Have one child be the cat and clap a rhythm for the group. The other children listen and then be the copy cats. They clap the same rhythm as the cat did. Another child now becomes the cat and creates a rhythm for the copy cats to imitate.

2. **Nice Kitty**

One child is chosen to be the kitty. The rest of the children sit in a circle. As the kitty goes to each child in the circle he pets the kitty and says, "nice kitty," but the kitty makes no reply. Finally, the kitty meows in response to one child. That child must run around the outside of the circle as the kitty chases him. If the child returns to his original place before the kitty can catch him, the child becomes the new kitty. This activity is appropriate for four-, five-, and six-year-old children.

3. **Listen Carefully**

The children should sit in a circle. One child is selected to be the mother cat. After mother cat has left the room, choose several other children to be kittens. All of the children cover their mouths with both hands and the kittens start saying, "meow, meow, meow." When the mother cat returns she should listen carefully to find all of her kittens. When she has found them all, another child should be chosen mother cat and the game can continue.

4. **Farmer in the Dell**

The children can play "Farmer in the Dell."

Cooking:

1. **Cheese Cat**

English muffins
cheese slices

Allow the children to cut out a cat face on their own slice of cheese. Put the cheese on top of the English muffin and bake long enough to melt the cheese.

2. **Cat Face**

1/2 peach (head)
almonds (ears)
red hots (eyes)
raisin (nose)
stick pretzels (whiskers)

Create a cat face using the ideas above or a variety of other items.

28

Multimedia:

The following resources can be found in educational catalogs:

1. Crume, Marion. *I Like Cats* [record].

2. Carr, Rachel. "Stretch Like a Cat" on *Be a Frog, a Bird or a Tree* [record].

3. Sharon, Lois, & Bram. "The Cat Came Back" on *Singing, Swinging* [record].

4. Seeger, Pete. "My Little Kitty" on *Birds, Beasts, Bugs and Little Fishes* [record].

5. *Kittens, Kids and a Frog* [Apple/IBM software (Ages: 6–7)]. Hartley.

6. *Sugar and Snails and Kitty-Cat Tails* [Mac/Apple software, PK–2]. Entrex.

Books:

The following books can be used to complement the theme:

1. Brown, Ruth. (1986). *Our Cat Flossie*. New York: E. P. Dutton.

2. Kunhardt, Edith. (1987). *Kittens, Kittens, Kittens*. New York: Golden Books.

3. Matthias, Catherine. (1987). *I Love Cats*. Chicago: Children's Press.

4. Kanao, Keiko. (1987). *Kitten up a Tree*. New York: Alfred A. Knopf.

5. McCue, Lisa. (1990). *Kittens Love*. New York: Random House.

6. Mantegazza, Giovanna. (1992). *The Cat*. Honesdale, PA: Boyds Mills Press.

7. Martin, Bengt. (1992). *Olaf the Ship's Cat*. Checkerboard.

8. Parnell, Peter. (1989). *Cats from Away*. New York: Macmillan.

9. Pittman, Helena C. (1990). *Miss Hindy's Cats*. Minneapolis: Carolrhoda Books.

10. Polushkin, Maria. (1990). *Here's That Kitten!* New York: Macmillan.

11. Dupont, Marie. (1991). *Your First Kitten*. Neptune City, NJ: TFH Publications.

12. Nottridge, Rhoda. (1990). *Let's Look at Big Cats*. New York: Franklin Watts, Inc.

13. Petty, Kate. (1992). *Baby Animals: Kittens*. Hauppauge, NY: Barron's Educational Series, Inc.

14. Piers, Helen. (1992). *Taking Care of Your Cat*. Hauppauge, NY: Barron's Educational Series, Inc.

15. Carle, Eric. (1991). *Have You Seen My Cat?* Saxonville, MA: Picture Book Studio, Ltd.

16. Ehlert, Lois. (1990). *Feathers for Lunch*. San Diego: Harcourt Brace.

17. Hutchins, Hazel. (1992). *And You Can Be the Cat*. Buffalo, NY: Firefly Books, Ltd.

18. Moncure, Jane. (1990). *Caring for My Kitty*. Mankato, MN: Children's World, Inc.

19. Farjeon, Eleanor. (1990). *Cats Sleep Anywhere*. New York: Harper Collins Children's Books.

20. Kherdian, David, & Hogrogian, Nonny. (1990). *The Cat's Midsummer Jamboree*. New York: Philomel Books.

21. Bryan, Ashley. (1985). *The Cat's Purr*. New York: Atheneum.

22. Marzello, Jean. (1990). *Pretend You're a Cat*. New York: Dial Books for Young Readers.

23. Simon, Seymour. (1991). *Big Cats*. New York: Harper Collins.

24. Larrick, Nancy (Ed.). (1988). *Cats Are Cats*. New York: Philomel Books.

25. Kuklin, Susan. (1988). *Taking My Cat to the Vet*. New York: Bradbury Press.

26. Aylesworth, Jim. (1989). *Mother Halverson's New Cat*. New York: Macmillan.

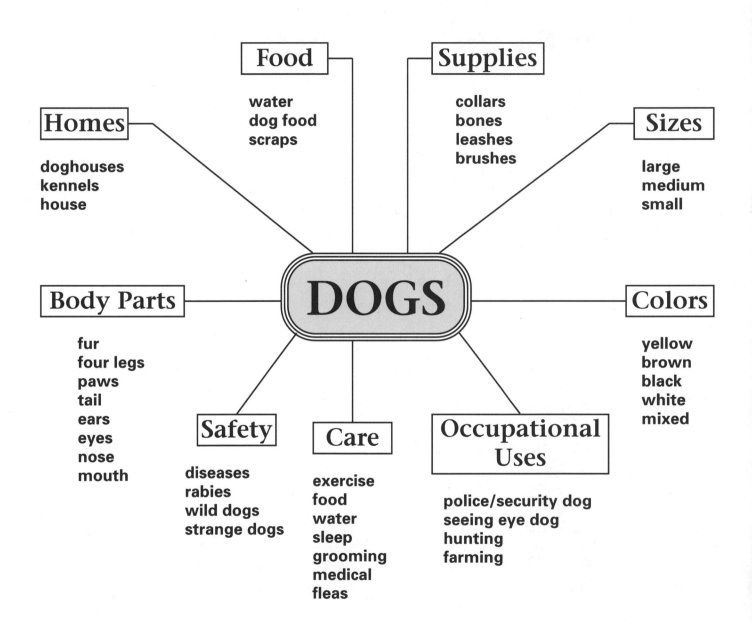

Food

water
dog food
scraps

Supplies

collars
bones
leashes
brushes

Homes

doghouses
kennels
house

Sizes

large
medium
small

DOGS

Body Parts

fur
four legs
paws
tail
ears
eyes
nose
mouth

Colors

yellow
brown
black
white
mixed

Safety

diseases
rabies
wild dogs
strange dogs

Care

exercise
food
water
sleep
grooming
medical
fleas

Occupational Uses

police/security dog
seeing eye dog
hunting
farming

Theme Goals:

Through participating in the experiences provided by this theme, the children may learn:

1. Dog's body parts.
2. Types of dogs.
3. Dogs need special care.
4. Dogs can be trained to do special tasks and tricks.

Concepts for the Children to Learn:

1. There are many different sizes of dogs.
2. Dogs have a keen sense of smell and hearing.
3. Dogs growl and bark to communicate.
4. Dogs may bark at strangers to protect their owners and their space.
5. Dogs have legs, eyes, ears, a mouth, nose, and tail.
6. Dogs have fur on their skin.
7. Dogs enjoy being handled carefully and gently.
8. Some dogs help people.
9. There are many different colors, sizes, and kinds of dogs.
10. Dogs need food, water, and exercise every day.
11. Dogs can be taught to do tricks.

Vocabulary:

1. **puppy**—a baby dog.
2. **pet**—an animal kept for pleasure.
3. **paw**—the dog's foot.
4. **veterinarian**—an animal doctor.
5. **guide dog**—a dog trained to help blind people.
6. **leash**—a rope, chain, or cord that attaches to a collar.
7. **collar**—a band worn around the dog's neck.
8. **obedience school**—a school where dogs are taught to obey.
9. **whiskers**—stiff hair growing around the dog's nose, mouth, and eyes.
10. **bone**—an object a dog uses to chew on.
11. **coat**—hair or fur covering the skin.
12. **doghouse**—a place for dogs to sleep and keep warm.

Bulletin Board

The purpose of this bulletin board is to develop color recognition and matching skills. Prepare the bulletin board by cutting dog shapes out of tagboard or construction paper. Use rubber cement to attach a different colored paper collar to each dog's neck. Also, cut out dog dishes from colored construction paper. Attach the pieces to the bulletin board as illustrated. Use lengths of yarn or string for children to match the color of each dog's collar to the corresponding dog dish.

Parent Letter

Dear Parents,

We will begin a unit on a favorite subject of children of all ages—dogs! We will be learning about their basic physical features such as coat and body. We will also learn about caring for a dog, the roles of dogs in people's lives, dog training, as well as things families need to consider when choosing a dog. This unit is designed so that the children will develop an awareness of and respect for dogs as pets.

At School

Some of the learning experiences planned include:

- creating paw prints at the art table (dipping paw-shaped sponges into paint and applying them to paper).
- sorting various-sized dog biscuits.
- listening to the children's stories about their own dogs.
- setting up a "pet store" in the dramatic play area, complete with stuffed animals and many dog accessories.
- baking dog biscuits!

At Home

To foster parent-child interaction and reinforce some of the concepts we are working on at school, try some of the following ideas:

- Look through magazines to find pictures of dogs and puppies. Help your child tear out pictures of dogs and puppies. This activity is good for the development of fine motor and visual discrimination skills. An interesting collage can be made by gluing these pictures onto a piece of paper.
- If you don't have access to a dog, visit a pet shop to observe the puppies. At the same time note all of the dog supplies available.

Enjoy your child!

What is your favorite breed of dog?

Music:

1. **"Bingo"**

   There was a farmer who had a dog
   And Bingo was his name-o.
   B-I-N-G-O
   B-I-N-G-O
   B-I-N-G-O
   And Bingo was his name-o.

2. **"Six Little Dogs"**
   (Sing to the tune of "Six Little Ducks")

   Six little dogs that I once knew,
   fat ones, skinny ones, fair ones too.
   But the one little dog with the brown curly fur,
   He led the others with a grr, grr, grr.
   Grr, grr, grr
   Grr, grr, grr
   He led the others with a grr, grr, GRR!

Fingerplays:

FRISKY'S DOGHOUSE

This is Frisky's doghouse;
   (pointer fingers touch to make a roof)
This is Frisky's bed;
   (motion of smoothing)
Here is Frisky's pan of milk;
   (cup hands)
So that he can be fed.

Frisky has a collar
   (point to neck with fingers)
With his name upon it, too;
Take a stick and throw it,
   (motion of throwing)
He'll bring it back to you.
   (clap once)

FIVE LITTLE PUPPIES

Five little puppies were playing in the sun.
   (hold up hands, fingers extended)
This one saw a rabbit, and he began to run.
   (bend down first finger)
This one saw a butterfly, and he began to race.
   (bend down second finger)
This one saw a cat, and he began to chase.
   (bend down third finger)
This one tried to catch his tail, and he went round and round.
   (bend down fourth finger)
This one was so quiet, he never made a sound.
   (bend down thumb)

FIVE LITTLE PUPPIES

Five little puppies jumping on the bed,
   (hold up five fingers)
One fell off and bumped his head,
   (hold up one finger—tap head)
Mama called the doctor and the doctor said,
"No more puppies jumping on the bed."
   (shake index finger)

Science:

1. Additions to the science table or area may include:

   • a magnifying glass with bones, dog hair, and dog food.

- dog tags of different sizes, including some with squeakers.
- a balance scale and dry dog food.

2. During a cooking activity, prepare dog biscuits. The recipe is listed under cooking.

Dramatic Play:

1. **Pet Store**

   Using stuffed animals simulate a pet store. Include a counter complete with cash register and money. Post a large sign that says, "Pet Store." Set out many stuffed dogs with collars and leashes. Children will enjoy pretending they have a new pet.

2. **Veterinarian's Office**

   Use some medical equipment and stuffed dogs to create a veterinarian's office.

3. **Pet Show**

   Encourage the children to bring a stuffed animal to school. Children can pretend that their stuffed animals can do tricks. Have ribbons available for them to look at and award to each other.

4. **Dog House**

   Construct a dog house from a large cardboard box. Provide dog ears and tails for the children to wear as they imitate the pet.

Arts and Crafts:

1. **Paw Prints**

   Make stamps out of erasers, sponges, or with the child's fist.

2. **Dog Puppets**

   Provide socks, paper bags, and/or paper plates to make dog puppets.

3. **Dog Masks**

   Use fake fur ears and pipe cleaners for whiskers.

4. **Bone Printing**

   Provide different meat bones, a tray of tempera paint, and paper to make prints.

5. **Bone Painting**

   Cut easel paper in bone shapes.

6. **Dog Collages**

   Provide dog pictures cut out of magazines to make a collage.

Large Muscle:

1. Encourage the children to dramatize the following movements:

   - a big dog
   - a tiny dog
   - a dog with heavy steps
   - a dog with light steps
   - a happy dog
   - a sad dog
   - a mad dog
   - a loud dog
   - a quiet dog
   - a hungry dog
   - a tired dog
   - a curious dog
   - a sick dog

2. **Dog Hoops**

   Provide hoops for the children to jump through as they imitate dogs.

3. **Scent Walk**

   Place prints of dog paws on the play yard leading to different activities. Encourage the child to crawl to each activity.

4. **Tracks**

   If snow is available, make tracks with boots that have different treads. Encourage children to follow one track.

5. **Bean Bag Bones**

Provide round bean bags or make special bone-shaped bean bags. Encourage the children to throw them into a large dog food bowl.

Field Trips/Resource People:

1. **Pet Store**

Take a field trip to a pet store. While there ask the manager how to care for dogs. Observe the different types of cages, collars, leashes, food, and toys.

2. **Veterinarian Office**

Take a field trip to a veterinarian's office or animal hospital. Compare its similarities and differences to a doctor's office.

3. **Kennel**

Visit a kennel and observe the different sizes of cages and dogs.

4. **Variety Store**

Visit a variety store and observe pet accessories.

5. **Grocery Store**

Take a field trip to the grocery store and purchase the ingredients needed to make dog biscuits.

6. **Dog Trainer**

Invite an obedience trainer to talk about teaching dogs.

7. **Additional Resource People**

- veterinarian
- pet store owner
- parents (bring in family dogs)
- humane society representative
- representative from a kennel
- dog groomer
- person with a seeing eye dog (guide dog)

Math:

1. **Dog Bones**

Cut dog bone shapes of four different sizes from tagboard. Encourage the children to sequence them.

2. **Classifying Dog Biscuits**

Purchase three sizes of dog biscuits. Using dog dishes, have the children sort them according to size and type.

3. **Weighing Biscuits**

Using the scale, encourage the children to weigh different sizes and amounts of dog biscuits.

Social Studies:

1. **Share Your Dog**

Individually invite the parents to bring their child's pet to school.

2. **Pictures of Dogs**

Display pictures of different types of dogs.

3. **Bulletin Board**

Prepare a bulletin board with pictures of the children's dogs.

4. **Slides**

Take slides of field trips and of resource people. Share them at group time. (This slide series may be shared with parents at meetings or coffees.)

5. **Dog Biscuits**

Prepare dog biscuits and donate to the local animal shelter. (See Cooking.)

6. **Chart**

Make a chart including each child's name, type of pet, size of pet, and the name of the pet. Count the number of dogs, cats, birds, etc. Discuss the most popular names.

7. Dogs

Using pictures or a real dog, talk about a dog's body. Some dogs have long noses so they can smell things very well; others have short hair to live in hot climates. Discuss why some dogs are good guard dogs. Discuss how dogs' tongues help them to cool off on hot days. Also talk about what else a dog's rough tongue is used for.

Group Time (games, language):

1. The Dog Catcher

Hide stuffed dogs or those cut from construction paper around the classroom and have children find them.

2. Child-created Stories

Bring in a picture of a dog or stuffed dog. Encourage the children to tell you a story about the picture or the stuffed dog. While the child speaks, record the words. Place the story in the book corner.

3. Dog Chart

Make a chart listing the color of each child's dog. A variation would be to have the children state their favorite color of dog. This activity can be repeated using size.

4. Doggie, Doggie, Where's Your Bone?

Bring in a clean bone or a bone cut from construction paper. Sit the children in a circle. Choose one child to be the dog. Have the child pretending to be the dog sit in the middle. The doggie closes his eyes. A child from the circle sneaks up and takes the bone. Children call, "Doggie, doggie, where's your bone? Someone stole it from your home!" The "dog" gets three guesses to find out who has the bone.

5. The Lost Dog

(This is a variation of the "Dog Catcher" game.) Using the children's stuffed animals from home, have the children trade dogs so that each is holding another's pet. One child begins by hiding the dog he is holding while the other children cover their eyes. He tells the owner, "Your dog is lost, but we can help you find it." As the dog owner looks, he can put the pet he is holding on his carpet square to free both hands. The group gives "hot" and "cold" clues to indicate whether the child is close to or far away from the pet. When the child finds his pet, he is the next one to hide a pet.

Cooking:

1. Hot "Dog" Kebabs on a Stick

paper plates and napkins
skewers
1 package hot dogs
2 green peppers, cut up
cherry tomatoes

Place 2 pieces of green pepper, 2 cherry tomatoes, and 2 hot dog pieces on each child's plate. Show the children how to thread the ingredients on skewers. Bake the kabobs in a preheated oven for 15 minutes at 350 degrees.

2. Dog Biscuits

2 1/2 cups whole wheat flour
1/2 cup powdered dry milk
1/2 teaspoon salt
1/2 teaspoon garlic powder
6 tablespoons margarine, shortening, or meat drippings
1 egg
1 teaspoon brown sugar
1/2 cup ice water

Combine flour, milk, salt, and flour. Cut in the shortening. Mix in egg. Add enough water until mixture forms a ball. Pat the dough to a half-inch thickness on a lightly oiled cookie sheet. Cut with cutters and remove scraps. Bake 25 to 30 minutes at 350 degrees. This recipe may be varied by adding pureed soup greens, liver powder, etc.

3. Dogs-in-a-Blanket

cheese crust
    1/2 teaspoon salt
    pinch baking powder
    1 cup white flour
    1/4 cup shortening

38

1/4 cup water
1/4 cup finely shredded cheddar cheese
hot dogs

Stir the dry ingredients in a large bowl. Cut in shortening and then add 1/4 cup water. Stir with a fork and add more water only if necessary to work in flour. Add cheese and knead together. Cut the cheese pie crust in strips and wrap each around a whole or half of a hot dog. Bake at 350 degrees until crust is light brown.

Source: Warren, Jean. (1982). *Super Snacks*. Alderwood Manor, WA: Warren Publishing House.

4. **Hush Puppies**

vegetable oil
2 1/4 cups yellow cornmeal
1 teaspoon salt
2 tablespoons finely chopped onion
3/4 teaspoon baking soda
1 1/2 cups buttermilk

Heat oil (about 1 inch deep) to 375 degrees. Mix cornmeal, salt, onion, and baking soda in a bowl. Add buttermilk. Drop by spoonfuls into hot oil. Fry until brown about 2 minutes.

Multimedia:

The following resources can be found in educational catalogs:

1. McCurdy, Ed. "I Had a Little Dog" on *Children's Stories and Songs* [record].

2. Barduhn, Art. "Animals" on *Children's Creative Play Songs* [record].

3. Mc Laughlin, Roberta & Wood, Lucille. "Kitty and Puppy" on *The Small Singer*. (Vol. 2.) [record].

4. Stewart, Georgiana Liccione. "Puppy Dog" on *Walk Like the Animals* [record].

Books:

The following books can be used to complement the theme:

1. Barrett, Norman. (1990). *Dogs*. New York: Franklin Watts, Inc.

2. Cole, Joanna. (1991). *My Puppy Is Born* (rev. ed.). New York: Morrow Junior Books.

3. Hanes, Harriet. (1992). *My New Puppy*. New York: Dorling Kindersley, Inc.

4. Perry, Kate. (1992). *Baby Animals: Puppies*. Hauppauge, NY: Barron's Educational Series, Inc.

5. Crozat, Francois. (1990). *I Am a Little Dog*. Hauppauge, NY: Barron's Educational Series, Inc.

6. Gottlieb, Dale. (1992). *Big Dog*. New York: Puffin Books.

7. Holland, Margaret. (1991). *Look Around Puppies and Dogs*. Pinellas Park, FL: Willowisp Press.

8. Johnson, Audean. (1993). *Fuzzy as a Puppy*. New York: Random House for Young Readers.

9. Pepin, Muriel. (1992). *Little Puppy Saves the Day*. New York: Readers Digest Association, Inc.

10. Robertus, Polly. (1992). *The Dog Who Had Kittens*. New York: Holiday House, Inc.

11. Weller, Frances Ward. (1990). *Riptide*. New York: Philomel Books.

12. Bridwell, Norman. (1988). *Clifford, the Big Red Dog*. New York: Scholastic.

13. Day, Alexandra. (1991). *Good Dog Carl*. New York: Simon & Schuster.

14. Dodd, Lynley. *Dogs & Puppies*. New York: Checkerboard Press.

15. McCue, Lisa. (1990). *Puppies Love*. New York: Simon & Schuster.

16. Taylor, Judy. (1989). *My Dog*. New York: Macmillan.

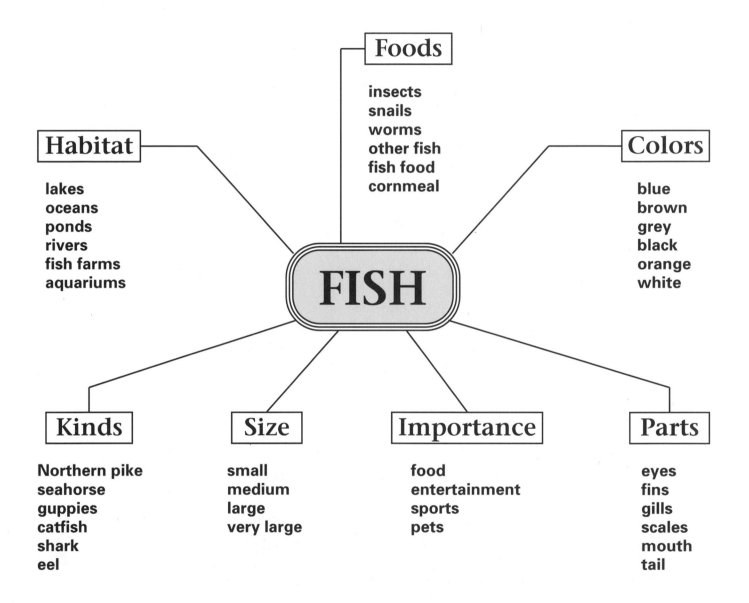

Foods

insects
snails
worms
other fish
fish food
cornmeal

Habitat

lakes
oceans
ponds
rivers
fish farms
aquariums

Colors

blue
brown
grey
black
orange
white

FISH

Kinds

Northern pike
seahorse
guppies
catfish
shark
eel

Size

small
medium
large
very large

Importance

food
entertainment
sports
pets

Parts

eyes
fins
gills
scales
mouth
tail

Theme Goals:

Through participating in the experiences provided by this theme, the children may learn:

1. Homes for fish.

2. The importance of fish.

3. Colors of fish.

4. Care of fish.

5. Kinds of fish.

6. Sizes of fish.

7. Parts of fish.

Concepts for the Children to Learn:

1. Most fish have eyes, fins, gills, scales, a mouth, and tail.

2. Fish vary in size. They may be small, medium, large, or very large.

3. Blue, brown, grey, white, black, and orange are colors of fish.

4. Fish may live in lakes, oceans, ponds, rivers, fish farms, and aquariums.

5. Fish need food and water to live.

6. Insects, snails, other fish, plants, worms, fish food, and cornmeal are foods fish eat.

7. There are many kinds of fish. Some kinds include Northern pike, seahorse, guppies, catfish, shark, and eel.

8. Fish are important to people. (They provide food, entertainment, pets, and sport.)

Vocabulary:

1. **scales**—skin covering of fish and other reptiles.

2. **gills**—the part of the fish body that helps it get air.

3. **fin**—the part that moves to help fish swim.

4. **tail**—the end body part that helps fish move.

5. **fish farm**—a place to raise fish for food.

6. **school**—a group of fish.

Bulletin Board

The purpose of this bulletin board is to promote identification of written numerals, as well as matching a set to a written numeral. To prepare the bulletin board begin by drawing and cutting fish shapes from construction paper. Decorate the fish as desired and print a numeral on each fish. Make another set of identical fish shapes from black construction paper to create fish "shadows." Cut small circles out of white construction paper to represent the fish air bubbles. Staple the fish shadows to the bulletin board. Above each fish shadow, staple a set of air bubbles. Children can then match the numerals on the fish to the corresponding set of air bubbles. The fish can be attached to the bulletin board with push pins or small adhesive magnet pieces.

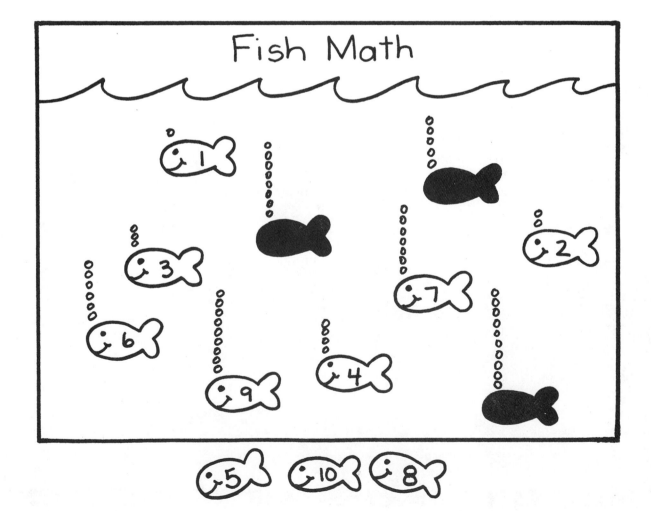

Parent Letter

Dear Parents,

Our next theme will focus on fish. Through participating in the experiences provided by this theme, the children will learn the color, size, kinds, and parts of a fish. They will also learn where fish live and the role fish play in our lives.

At School

Learning experiences that have been planned to complement this theme include:

- Visiting a pet store to observe different types and colors of fish. We will also purchase fish to bring back to our classroom.
- Listening to the story *Fish Eyes* by Lois Ehlert.
- Sorting, counting, and eating various fish-shaped crackers.
- Fishing in the dramatic play area.
- Observing minnows in the sensory table.

At Home

- Prepare a tuna salad using a favorite recipe with your child.
- Point out fishing gear in the sports section of a department store or in a catalog.
- Check out children's books about fish from the library. Look for:

  Fishes by Brian Wildsmith.
  Fish Is Fish and *Swimmy* by Leo Lionni.
  Gone Fishing by Earlene R. Long.
  A Million Fish…More or Less by Patricia C. McKissack.

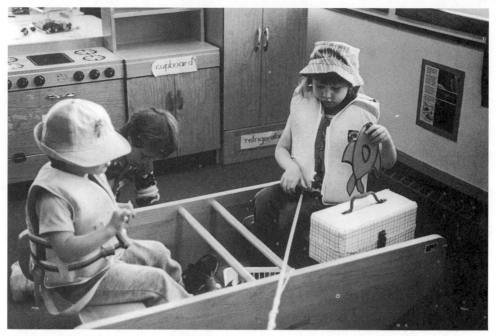

How many fish can you catch?

Music:

1. **"I'm a Little Fish"**
   (Sing to the tune of "I'm a Little Teapot")

   I'm a little fish in the lake so blue,
   There are so many things that I can do.
   I can swim around with my tail and fin.
   The water's fine—just jump right in.

2. **"Goldfish"**
   (Sing to the tune of "Have You Ever Seen a Lassie?")

   Have you ever seen a goldfish, a goldfish, a goldfish?
   Have you ever seen a goldfish, just swimming all around?
   He swims this way and that way,
   And this way and that way.
   Have you ever seen a goldfish, just swimming all around?

3. **"Six Little Fish"**
   (Sing to the tune of "Six Little Ducks")

   Six little fish that I once knew,
   Fat ones, skinny ones, fair ones, too.

But the one little fish who was the leader of the crowd.
He led the other fish around and around.

Fingerplays:

FISH STORY

One, two, three, four, five
   (hold up fingers while counting)
Once I caught a fish alive.
Six, seven, eight, nine, ten
   (hold up additional fingers)
Then I let it go again.
Why did I let it go?
Because it bit my finger so.
Which finger did it bite?
The little finger on the right.
   (hold up pinky on the right hand)

DIVE LITTLE GOLDFISH

Dive, little goldfish one.
   (hold up one finger)
Dive, little goldfish two.
   (hold up two fingers)
Dive, little goldfish three
   (hold up three fingers)

Here is food, you see!
    (sprinkling motion with fingers)
Dive, little gold fish four.
    (hold up four fingers)
Dive, little gold fish five.
    (hold up five fingers)
Dive, little goldfish six.
    (hold up six fingers)
I like your funny tricks.

Source: Scott, Louise Binder. *Rhymes for Learning Times.*

GOLD FISH PETS

One little goldfish lives in a bowl.
    (hold up one finger)
Two little goldfish eat their food whole.
    (hold up two fingers)
Three little goldfish swim all around.
    (hold up three fingers)
Although they move, they don't make a sound.
Four little goldfish have swishy tails.
    (hold up four fingers)
Five little goldfish have pretty scales.
    (hold up five fingers)

Source: Scott, Louise Binder. *Rhymes for Learning Times.*

Science:

1. **Aquarium**

    Set up an aquarium to place on the science table. Let the children take turns feeding the fish. Provide pictures and books about fish.

2. **Balance Scale**

    Place on the science table a balance scale and clean aquarium rocks. The children can use spoons and measuring cups to transfer the rocks into the scale containers. After this, they can experiment with the balance.

3. **Fish Tasting Party**

    Plan a tasting party. Prepare fish using different methods such as baked, broiled, fried, and prepared in a casserole. The results of the

children's favorite fish preparation can be discussed and charted.

Dramatic Play:

1. **Gone Fishing**

    Set up a fishing area in the dramatic play center. Provide props such as a wooden rocking boat, small wading pool, life vests, hats, tackle boxes, nets, and fishing poles. Fishing poles can be made by attaching string to a short dowel or paper towel tube. Tie a small magnet to the end of the string. Attach paper clips to the construction paper fish. Then, go fishing!

2. **Bait and Tackle Shop**

    Provide props to simulate a bait and tackle shop in the dramatic play area. Items can include a cash register, play money, plastic or paper fish of varying sizes, nets, fishing lures (remove hooks), tackle boxes, coolers, fishing poles, and life vests. Display pictures of fish and people fishing.

Arts and Crafts:

1. **Aquarium Crayon Resist**

    After observing fish or listening to stories about fish, encourage the children to use crayons to draw fish on a piece of white construction paper. Then, the children can paint over their crayon drawing with a thin wash of blue tempera or water color. The wax will repel the water paints leaving an interesting effect.

2. **Fish Sponge Painting**

    Cut sponges into fish shapes. Place the sponges on the art table with paper and several shallow trays of paint. Use thick tempera paint to color the fish. Also provide paper. The children can make prints by dipping the sponges into the paint and then pressing them onto paper.

3. **Fish Rubbings**

Cut fish shapes out of tagboard, adding details as desired. Place the fish shapes on the art table along with paper and crayons. The children can create designs by placing a tagboard fish beneath a piece of paper and rubbing over the top of the paper with a crayon. Repeat as discussed.

4. **Tackle Box Paint Container**

Use a discarded, clean tackle box as a container to hold paints at the art table. Paints can be placed in individual compartments, providing several choices for the children.

Sensory:

1. **Aquarium Rocks**

Place a bag of clean aquarium rocks in the sensory table. Provide cups, bowls, and pails for the children's use. Add water, if desired.

2. **Plastic Fish**

Purchase small plastic fish and place in the sensory table with water, strainers, and pails.

3. **Minnows**

Purchase minnows from a bait store. Place the minnows in a sensory table filled with cold water. Stress the importance of being gentle with the fish and follow through with limits set for the activity. After participating in this activity, the children need to wash their hands.

4. **Plastic Boats**

Place small plastic boats in a sensory table filled with water. Also provide small plastic people to ride and fish in the boats.

Field Trips/Resource People:

1. **Lake, Pond, or Stream**

If possible, visit a small body of water to observe fish habitat. Watch for people fishing.

(For safety purposes, the body of water will have to be carefully chosen. Likewise, additional supervision may be required.)

2. **Pet Store**

Visit a pet store to see many types of fish, as well as aquariums and fish supplies. Purchase one or more goldfish to take back to your classroom.

3. **Bait and Tackle Shop**

Make arrangements to visit a bait and tackle shop. Observe the many types of fishing poles and lures, as well as boat safety items.

4. **State or National Fish Hatchery**

These make a wonderful field trip. They also have coloring books, etc., for the children.

5. **Fish Sportsman or Sportswoman**

Invite a parent or another person who enjoys fishing to come talk with the children. Ask the person to bring fishing gear and pictures of fishing trips as well as fish caught.

Math:

1. **Sort the Fish**

Purchase a variety of small plastic fish or construct some out of tagboard. Put them in a large pail. The children can sort the fish by size, color, and type.

2. **Fish Seriation/Measurement**

Trace and cut shapes out of construction paper. Encourage the children to place them in order from smallest to largest. If developmentally appropriate, provide rulers and yardsticks for the children to measure the fish.

3. **Fishbowl Math**

Print numerals or sets of dots on small plastic fish. Place the fish in a clean bowl or container. The children can use small nets to take turns scooping out a fish and stating the numeral or counting the dots.

4. Fish Cracker Sort

Purchase a variety of flavors of small fish-shaped crackers. For each child, place a few of each kind of cracker in a paper cup. Before eating the crackers, encourage the children to sort the crackers. If appropriate, the children can count the number of each cracker flavor.

Group Time (games, language):

1. Fish Memory Game

Collect items associated with fish and place on a tray. At group time, show the tray containing the items and name them. To play the game, cover the tray with a towel. Then ask the children to recall the names of items on the tray. To vary the game, play again, this time removing an item from the tray while covered. The children then try to name the item missing from the tray. To ensure success, begin the activity with few objects. Additional objects can be added depending upon the developmental maturity of the children.

2. Go Fish!

Cut fish shapes out of various colors of construction paper. Attach a paper clip to each fish. Make a fishing pole by tying a string to a short dowel. Attach a small magnet to the end of the string. At group time, present the fishing pole and fish. Place the fish on the floor and allow the children to take turns fishing. As a fish is caught, the child removes it from the magnet and names the color. Repeat until all of the children have had a turn. The game can be varied by drawing a basic shape and printing a numeral or a letter on each fish for the children to identify.

Cooking:

1. Swimming Fish Snack

    8 ounces soft cream cheese
    blue food coloring

1 box rectangular-shaped crackers
2 cups small fish-shaped crackers (any flavor)

Add a few drops of blue food coloring to the cream cheese and stir. For each serving, spread cream cheese on a large, rectangular cracker. Place a few fish-shaped crackers on top of the cream cheese.

2. Fish Mix Snack

    2 cups toasted oat cereal
    2 cups pretzel sticks
    2 cups small fish-shaped crackers (any flavor)
    1/4 cup melted margarine
    2 teaspoons Worcestershire sauce

Combine oat cereal, pretzels, and fish-shaped crackers in a bowl. In a small bowl, stir together melted margarine and Worcestershire sauce. Drizzle over cereal mixture and toss to coat evenly. Transfer into 13 x 9 baking pan and bake in a 300-degree oven for 30 minutes, stirring occasionally. Remove from oven and cool. Makes approximately 6 cups.

3. Tuna Salad

    1 can of tuna (3 1/4-ounce), drained
    1/4 cup mayonnaise, salad dressing, or plain
        yogurt
    1/4 cup finely chopped apple
    3 tablespoons sunflower seeds
    4 slices of bread or 2 English muffins

Combine the tuna, mayonnaise, apple, and sunflower seeds in a bowl. Chill if desired. Toast the bread or English muffins. Spread tuna mixture on toasted muffins. (Makes four servings.)

4. Tartar Sauce for Fish Sticks

    1/2 cup mayonnaise or salad dressing
    1 tablespoon finely chopped pickle or pickle
        relish
    1 teaspoon dried parsley
    1/2 teaspoon grated onion or onion flakes

Combine all ingredients and chill. Bake frozen fish sticks as directed on the package and serve with tartar sauce.

Multimedia:

The following resources can be found in educational catalogs:

1. Poelker, Kathy. "A Pretty Little Fish" on *Amazing Musical Moments* [record].

2. Diamond, Charolette. "Octopus" on *Ten Carrot Diamond* [record].

3. *Undersea Adventure* [IBM software PK+]. Knowledge Adventure.

Books:

The following books can be used to complement the theme:

1. Adams, Georgie. (1993). *Fish Fish Fish*. New York: Dial Books for Young Readers.

2. Wildsmith, Brian. (1987). *Fishes*. New York: Oxford University Press.

3. Cazet, Denys. (1987). *A Fish in This Pocket*. New York: Orchard Books.

4. Seuss, Dr. (1987). *One Fish Two Fish Red Fish Blue Fish*. New York: Random House Books for Young Readers.

5. Ehlert, Lois. (1990). *Fish Eyes: A Book You Can Count On*. San Diego: Harcourt Brace Jovanovich.

6. Erickson, Gina C., & Foster, Kelli C. (1991). *Sometimes I Wish*. Hauppauge NY: Barron's Educational Series.

7. Luenn, Nancy. (1990). *Nessa's Fish*. New York: Macmillan Children's Book Group.

8. Wylie, Joanne, & Wylie, David. (1987). *A Big Fish Story Book*. Chicago: Children's Press.

9. Alexander, Sally H. (1992). *Maggie's Whopper*. New York: Macmillan Children's Book Group.

10. Long, Earlene R. (1987). *Gone Fishing*. Boston, MA: Houghton Mifflin Co.

11. McKissack, Patricia C. (1992). *A Million Fish...More or Less*. New York: Alfred A. Knopf Books for Young Readers.

12. Ward, Sally G. (1991). *Punky Goes Fishing*. New York: Dutton Children's Books.

13. George, William T., & George, Lindsay B. (1991). *Fishing at Long Pond*. New York: Greenwillow Books.

14. Bush, John, & Korky, Paul. (1991). *The Fish Who Could Wish*. Brooklyn, NY: Kane/Miller.

15. Edwards, Roberta. (1989). *Five Silly Fisherman: A Step One Book*. New York: Random House.

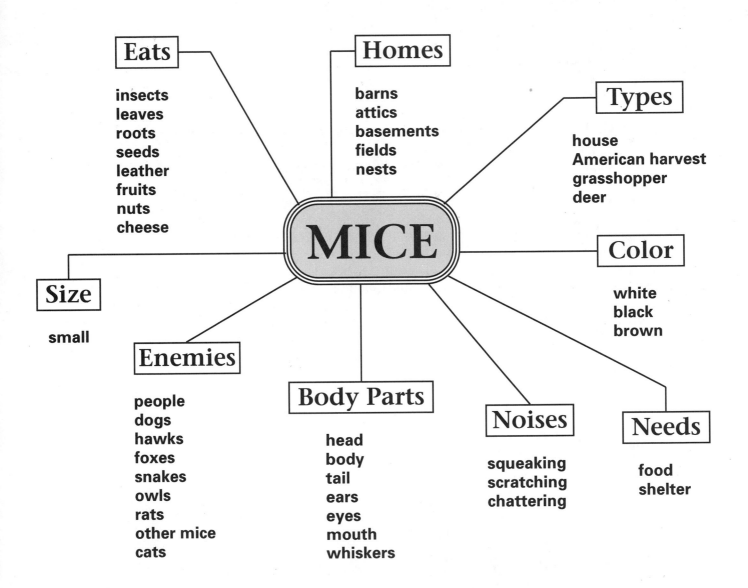

Eats

insects
leaves
roots
seeds
leather
fruits
nuts
cheese

Homes

barns
attics
basements
fields
nests

Types

house
American harvest
grasshopper
deer

MICE

Color

white
black
brown

Size

small

Enemies

people
dogs
hawks
foxes
snakes
owls
rats
other mice
cats

Body Parts

head
body
tail
ears
eyes
mouth
whiskers

Noises

squeaking
scratching
chattering

Needs

food
shelter

Theme Goals:

Through participating in the experiences provided by this theme, the children may learn:

1. Body parts of mice.
2. Size of mice.
3. Care of mice.
4. Color of mice.
5. Sounds made by mice.
6. Foods mice eat.
7. Homes mice make.
8. Enemies of mice.
9. Use of mice.

Concepts for the Children to Learn:

1. A mouse is a small animal.
2. Mice is the word to use when you refer to more than one mouse.
3. There are four main types of mice: house, American harvest, grasshopper, and deer.
4. The body of a mouse is 2 1/2 to 3 1/2 inches long. The tail is almost as long as the body.
5. The body of a mouse is covered with fur.
6. Mice may have white-, brown- or black-colored fur.
7. Mice need water, food, and shelter to live.
8. Mice eat plants, insects, leaves, roots, seeds, leather, fruits, and nuts.
9. Barns, attics, basements, fields, and nests are homes for mice.
10. Mice live where they can find food and shelter.
11. Mice have good hearing but poor sight.
12. Mice have strong, sharp front teeth that keep growing.
13. Mice have a head, body, tail, ears, eyes, mouth, and whiskers.
14. A house mouse has a brown back and white belly.
15. People can sometimes hear mice squeak, scratch, and chatter.
16. House mice are good climbers. People sometimes hear them running inside the walls of their homes.
17. Mice are sometimes used for pets and for health care discoveries.
18. People, cats, dogs, hawks, foxes, snakes, owls, rats, and other mice can be enemies of mice.

Vocabulary:

1. **mouse**—a small furry animal that has a head, ears, eyes, a mouth, whiskers, four legs, body, and tail.
2. **squeaking**—a clear, sharp sound made by a mouse.
3. **scratching**—a noise a mouse makes by rubbing his nails against a surface.

Bulletin Board

The purpose of this bulletin board is to promote the identification of written numerals as well as matching a set to a written numeral. Construct cheese and mice shapes out of construction paper or tagboard. Draw a set of dots on each piece of cheese. The number of dots used should correspond to the developmental level of the children. Print a corresponding numeral on each mouse. Staple the cheese pieces to the bulletin board along the side edges and the bottom, creating a pocket. The children should be encouraged to match the written numeral of each mouse to the corresponding set of dots on the cheese pieces and place the mice in the pockets.

Parent Letter

Dear Parents:

Squeak! Squeak! Squeak! We will be enjoying a new theme that will provide us with discoveries about small animals called mice. The children will be learning about types and colors of mice, care of mice, and enemies of mice.

At School

Learning experiences planned for this unit include:

- Visiting the pet store to observe mice.
- Pretending to be mice in the dramatic play area.
- Listening to the stories *Mouse Paint* and *Mouse Count* by Lois Ehlert.

At Home

Go to the library and check out some children's books about mice. Some titles to look for include:

- *If You Give a Mouse a Cookie* by Laura Numeroff
- *Mouse Poems* by John Foster

Have a nice week!

Can you squeak like a mouse?

Music:

1. **"Ten Little Mice"**
   (Sing to the tune of "Ten Little Indians.")

   One little, two little, three little mice.
   Four little, five little, six little mice.
   Seven little, eight little, nine little mice.

2. **"Two Little Brown Mice"**
   (Sing to the tune of "Two Little Blackbirds" or
   "Baa Baa Black Sheep.")

   Two little brown mice,
   Scampering through the hall.
   One named Sarah.
   One named Paul.

   Run away, Sarah.
   Run away, Paul.
   Come back, Sarah.
   Come back, Paul.

   Two little brown mice,
   Scampering through the hall.
   One named Sarah.
   One named Paul.

3. **"Find the Mouse"**
   (Sing to the tune of "The Muffin Man.")

Oh, can you find the little mouse.
The little mouse, the little mouse.
Can you find the little mouse,
He's somewhere in the house.

4. **"One Little Mouse"**
   (Sing to the tune of "Six Little Ducks.")

   One little brown and whiskery mouse
   Lived in a hole in a cozy house.
   When the cat came along to
   Take a little peek,
   The mouse ran away with a "Squeak, squeak,
   squeak."
   "Squeak, squeak, squeak."
   "Squeak, squeak, squeak."
   "The mouse ran away with a "Squeak, squeak,
   squeak."

5. **"Three Little Brown Mice"**
   (Sing to the tune of "Three Blind Mice.")

   Three brown mice, three brown mice.
   See how they run. See how they run.
   They were chased through the house by the
   big black cat.
   Lucky for them, she was lazy and fat.
   Did you ever see such a sight as that?
   Three brown mice, three brown mice.

Fingerplays:

WHERE ARE THE BABY MICE?

Where are the baby mice?
  (hide fists behind back)
Squeak, squeak, squeak!
I cannot see them.
Peek, peek, peek.
  (show fist)
Here they come out of their hole in the wall.
One, two, three, four, five, and that is all!
  (show fingers one at a time)

FIVE LITTLE BABY MICE

Five little mice on the kitchen floor.
  (hold up five fingers)
This little mouse peeked behind the door.
  (point to thumb)
This little mouse nibbled at the cake.
  (point to index finger)
This little mouse not a sound did he make.
  (point to middle finger)
This little mouse took a bite of cheese.
  (point to ring finger)
This little mouse heard the kitten sneeze.
  (point to pinky)
"Ah-choo!" sneezed the kitten,
And "squeak" they cried.
As they found a hole and ran inside.
  (move hand behind back)

LITTLE MOUSE

See the little mousie.
  (place index and middle finger on thumb to
  represent a mouse)
Creeping up the stair,
  (creep mouse slowly up the forearm)
Looking for a warm rest.
There—Oh! There!
  (spring mouse into a elbow corner)

HICKORY DICKORY DOCK

Hickory, dickory, dock.
  (bend arm at elbow; hold up and open
  palm)
The mouse ran up the dock.
  (run fingers up the arm)
The clock struck one,
  (hold up index finger)
The mouse ran down,
  (run fingers down arm)
Hickory, dickory, dock.

MOUSE

Here is a mouse with ears so funny,
  (place index and middle finger on thumb to
  represent a mouse)
And here is a hole in the ground.
  (make a hole with the other fist)
When a noise he hears, he pricks up his ears.
And runs to his hole in the ground.
  (jump mouse into hole in other fist)

Science:

Mice

Purchase or borrow mice from a pet store to keep as classroom pets. Place the cage on the science table for the children to observe. Allow the children to assist in caring for the animals.

Dramatic Play:

1. **Mouse House**

   The children can pretend to be mice! Construct mouse ears out of fabric or construction paper and attach to headbands. Provide large cardboard boxes to represent houses for the mice.

2. **Pet Store**

   Arrange the dramatic play area as a pet store. Provide props such as a cash register, play money, stuffed animals, animal cages, animal toys, and empty pet food boxes. Display posters of pets, including mice.

Arts and Crafts:

1. **Mouse Sponge Painting**

   Cut sponges into mice shapes. Place on the art table with paper and a shallow pan of thick tempera paint. The children can make designs by pressing the sponge into the paint and then on a piece of paper.

2. **Seed Collage**

Place a variety of seeds, glue, and paper on a table in the art area. The children can create designs with the materials.

Sensory:

Add to the sensory table:

- grains with scoops, cups, and spoons.
- seeds with pails and shovels.
- clean cedar chips (animal bedding) with measuring cups, scoops, and pails.

Field Trips:

1. **Pet Store**

Visit a pet store to observe the colors of pet mice and animal accessories. Photographs can be taken during the trip and later displayed in the classroom.

2. **Mouse Walk**

Take a walk around your school and look for places mice might live.

Group Time (games, language):

1. **"Mouse, Mouse, Where's Your Cheese?"**

This game is played in a circle formation. Arrange the chairs and place one in the center of the circle. Place a block to represent the cheese under the chair. Select one child, the "mouse," to sit on the chair and close his eyes. Then point to another child. This child must try to remove the cheese without making a sound. After the child returns to his chair in the circle, instruct all of the children to place their hands behind their backs. Then in unison the children say, "Mouse, Mouse, where is your cheese?" The mouse then opens his eyes and tries to guess who is holding the cheese.

2. **Language Chart**

Across the top of a piece of tagboard, print the question, "Where would you like to live if you were a mouse?" During group time introduce the chart and record the children's responses. Display the chart in the classroom.

Cooking:

1. **Macaroni and Cheese**

Purchase prepackaged macaroni and cheese. Prepare following the directions provided on the container. Compare the flavor to the recipe that follows:

3–3 1/2 cups of cooked macaroni
1/4 cup of butter or margarine
1/4 cup chopped onion (optional)
1/2 teaspoon salt
1/4 cup flour
1 1/2 cups of milk
1/2 pound of Swiss or American cheese cut into small cubes

Combine butter, onion, salt, and pepper in a saucepan; cook over medium heat until onion is tender. Blend in the flour. Lower heat and stir constantly until the mixture is smooth and bubbly. Add milk and heat to boiling, stirring constantly. Stir and boil one minute. Remove from heat. Add cheese and stir until melted.

Place macaroni in ungreased 1 1/2 quart casserole. Stir cheese sauce into the macaroni. Bake in an oven heated to 375 degrees for 30 minutes. (Makes five servings.)

2. **Mouse Cookies**

With the children, prepare a batch of drop cookie dough according to the recipe. Demonstrate how to drop three spoonfuls of dough onto a cookie sheet so that it will resemble a mouse head with two ears when baked. The mouse cookies can be frosted or details can be added with raisins, chocolate chips, and string licorice.

Multimedia:

The following resources can be found in educational catalogs:

1. Palmer, Hap. "The Mice Go Marching," *Rhythms on Parade* [record].

2. Sharon, Lois, & Bram. "Three Blind Mice" and "Hickory, Dickory, Dock," *Mainly Mother Goose* [record].

Books:

The following books can be used to complement the theme:

1. Cartlidge, Michelle. (1991). *Mouse in the House*. New York: Dutton Children's Books, Inc.

2. Watts, Barrie. (1992). *Mouse*. New York: Dutton Children's Books, Inc.

3. Baker, Alan. (1991). *Two Tiny Mice*. New York: Dail Books for Young Readers.

4. Walsh, Ellen S. (1991). *Mouse Court*. San Diego: Harcourt Brace Jovanovich.

5. Cartlidge, Michelle. (1990). *Mouse House*. New York: Dutton Children's Books, Inc.

6. Duerrstein, Richard (Illus.). (1992). *Mickey Is Happy: A Disney Book of Feelings*. New York: Walt Disney Book Publishing Group.

7. Dunbar, Joyce. (1990). *Ten Little Mice*. San Diego: Harcourt Brace Jovanovich.

8. Geraghty, Paul. (1990). *Look Out Patrick!* New York: Macmillan Children's Book Group.

9. Holabird, Katharine. (1989). *Angelina Ballerina*. New York: Crown Books for Young Readers.

10. Holabird, Katharine. (1989). *Angelina on Stage*. New York: Crown Books for Young Readers.

11. Holabird, Katharine. (1989). *Angelina's Birthday Surprise*. New York: Crown Books for Young Readers.

12. Lionni, Leo. (1992). *A Busy Year*. New York: Alfred A. Knopf Books for Young Readers.

13. Lionni, Leo. (1987). *Frederick*. New York: Alfred A. Knopf Books for Young Readers.

14. Lionni, Leo. (1987). *Mr. McMouse*. New York: Alfred A. Knopf Books for Young Readers.

15. Majewski, Joe. (1991). *A Friend For Oscar Mouse*. New York: Puffin Books.

16. Shories, Pat. (1991). *Mouse Around*. New York: Farrar, Straus, and Giroux.

17. Foster, John. (1992). *Mouse Poems*. New York: Oxford University Press.

18. Beguinot, Brigitte. (1992). *Mouse Part: An Open-the-Door Book*. Honesdale, PA: Boyds Mills Press.

19. Brown, Marcia. (1989). *Once a Mouse*. New York: Macmillan.

20. *Cottage Mouse: Village Mouse Stories*. (1992). Los Angeles: Price Stern Sloan.

21. Lobel, Arnold. *Martha the Movie Mouse*. (1993). New York: Harper Collins.

22. Wohl, Lauren. (1993). *Matzoh Mouse*. New York: Harper Collins.

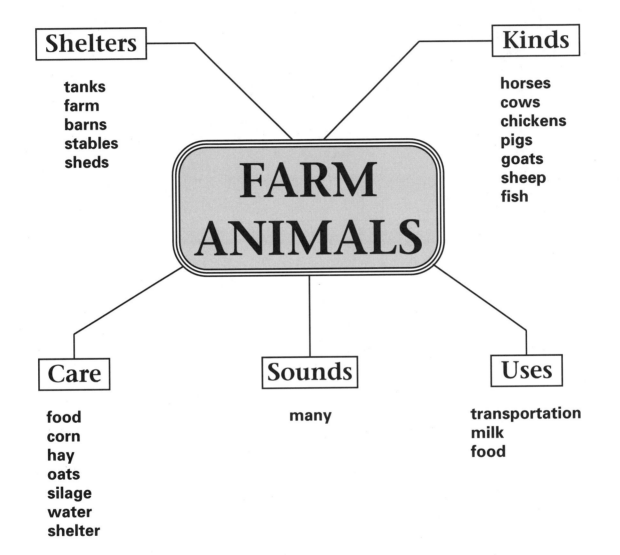

Shelters

tanks
farm
barns
stables
sheds

Kinds

horses
cows
chickens
pigs
goats
sheep
fish

FARM ANIMALS

Care

food
corn
hay
oats
silage
water
shelter

Sounds

many

Uses

transportation
milk
food

Theme Goals:

Through participating in the experiences provided by this theme, the children may learn:

1. Names of farm animals.

2. Uses for farm animals.

3. Farm animal shelters.

4. Food for farm animals.

5. Sounds of farm animals.

Concepts for the Children to Learn:

1. A farm animal lives on a farm.

2. Barns, stables, and sheds are homes for farm animals.

3. Horses are farm animals that can be used for transportation.

4. Cows, chickens, pigs, sheep, and goats are farm animals.

5. Some cows and goats give milk.

6. Farm animals eat corn, hay, oats, and silage.

7. A farmer cares for farm animals.

8. We can recognize some farm animals by their sounds.

9. Some farm animals supply us with food such as milk, meat, and eggs.

Vocabulary:

1. **herd**—a group of animals.

2. **stable**—building for horses and cattle.

3. **farmer**—person who cares for farm animals.

4. **barn**—building to house animals and store grain.

Bulletin Board

The purpose of this bulletin board is to foster one-to-one correspondence skills and matching sets to written numerals. Out of tagboard construct red barns as illustrated. The number of barns constructed will depend upon the maturity of your group of children. Place a numeral on each red barn. Construct the same number of black barns by tracing around the red barns onto black construction paper. After cutting out, place small white circles (dots from paper punch) onto the black barns. Laminate all barns. Staple black barns to the board. Punch a hole in each red barn window. During self-selected activity periods the children can hang red barns on push pins of corresponding black barns.

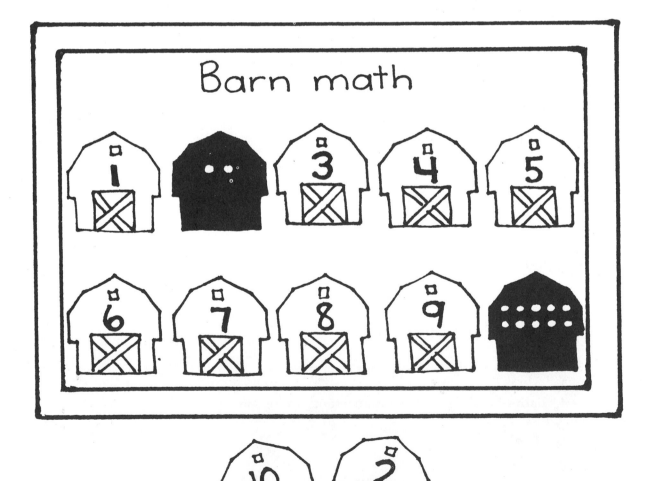

Parent Letter

Dear Parents,

Farm animals will be the focus of our next unit. The children will be learning the many different ways that farm animals help us. They will also become aware of the difference between pets and farm animals. The children will also discover that farm animals need homes and food.

At School

Some of the learning activities scheduled for this week include:

- making a barn out of a large cardboard box for the dramatic play area
- tasting different kinds of eggs, milk, and cheese for breakfast one day
- observing and comparing at the science table the many grains and seeds farm animals eat
- dressing up like farmers and farm animals
- making buttermilk chalk pictures

At Home

There are many ways you can integrate this unit into your family life. To stimulate imagination and movement skills ask your child to imitate different farm animals by walking and making that animal's noise. Also, your child will be learning this rhyme at school. You can also recite it at home to foster language skills.

If I Were a Horse

If I were a horse, I'd gallop all around.
  (slap thighs and gallop in a circle)
I'd shake my head and say "Neigh, neigh."
  (shake head)
I'd prance and gallop all over town.

Enjoy your child as you explore experiences related to farm animals.

Seesaws can be pretend horses.

Music:

1. **"Old Mac Donald Had a Farm"**
   (traditional)

2. **"The Animals on the Farm"**
   (Sing to the tune of "The Wheels on the Bus")

   The cows on the farm go moo, moo, moo.
   Moo, moo, moo, moo, moo, moo.
   The cows on the farm go moo, moo, moo
   all day long.

   The horses on the farm go neigh, neigh, neigh.
   Neigh, neigh, neigh, neigh, neigh, neigh.
   The horses on the farm go neigh, neigh, neigh
   all day long.

   (pigs—oink)
   (sheep—baa)
   (chicken—cluck)
   (turkeys—gobble)

3. **"The Farmer in the Dell"**
   (traditional)

   The farmer in the dell,
   The farmer in the dell,
   Hi-ho the dairy-o
   The farmer in the dell.

   The farmer takes a wife/husband.
   The farmer takes a wife/husband.
   Hi-ho the dairy-o
   The farmer in the dell.

   (The other verses are:)
   The wife/husband takes the child
   The child takes the nurse
   The nurse takes the dog
   The dog takes the cat
   The cat takes the rat
   The rat takes the cheese.

   (The final verse:)
   The cheese stands alone.
   The cheese stands alone.
   Hi-ho the dairy-o
   The cheese stands alone.

Fingerplays:

THIS LITTLE COW

   This little cow eats grass.
      (hold up one hand, fingers erect, bend down
      one finger)
   This little cow eats hay.
      (bend down another finger)

62

This little cow drinks water.
   (bend down another finger)
And this little cow does nothing.
   (bend down another finger)
But lie and sleep all day.

IF I WERE A HORSE

If I were a horse, I'd gallop all around.
   (slap thighs and gallop in a circle)
I'd shake my head and say "Neigh, neigh."
   (shake head)
I'd prance and gallop all over town.

THIS LITTLE PIG

This little pig went to market.
   (point to one finger at a time)
This little pig stayed home.
This little pig had roast beef.
This little pig had none.
This little pig cried, "Wee, wee, wee"
And ran all the way home.

EIGHT BABY PIGS

Two mother pigs lived in a pen.
   (thumbs)
Each had four babies and that made ten.
   (fingers of both hands)
These four babies were black and white.
   (fingers of one hand)
These four babies were black as night.
   (fingers of other hand)
All eight babies loved to play
   (wiggle fingers)
And they rolled in the mud all day!
   (roll hands)

THE FARM

The cows on the farm go, "Moo-oo, moo-oo";
The rooster cries, "Cock-a-doodle-doo";
The big brown horse goes, "Neigh, neigh";
The little lamb says, "Baa," when he wants to play.
The little chick goes, "Peep, peep, peep";
The cat says, "Meow," when it's not asleep;
The pig says, "Oink," when it wants to eat.
And we all say, "Hello," when our friends we meet.

Source of fingerplays: Cromwell, Hibner & Faitel. (1983). *Finger Frolics: Fingerplays for Young Children.* Michigan: Partner Press.

Science:

1. **Sheep Wool**

   Place various types of wool on a table for the children to observe. Included may be wool clippings, lanolin, dyed yarn, yarn spun into thread, wool cloth, wool articles such as mittens and socks.

2. **Feathers**

   Examine various types of feathers. Use a magnifying glass. Discuss their purposes such as keeping animals warm and helping ducks to float on water. Add the feathers to the water table to see if they float. Discuss why they float.

3. **Tasting Dairy Products**

   Plan a milk-tasting party. To do this, taste and compare the following types of milk products: cow milk, goat milk, cream, skimmed milk, whole milk, cottage cheese, sour cream, butter, margarine, and buttermilk.

4. **Eggs**

   Taste different kinds of eggs. Let children choose from scrambled, poached, deviled, hard-boiled, and fried. This could also be integrated as part of the breakfast menu.

5. **Cheese Types**

   Observe, taste, and compare different kinds of cheese. Examples include swiss, cheddar, colby, cottage cheese, and cheese curds.

6. **Egg Hatching**

   If possible, contact a hatchery to borrow an incubator. Watch the eggs hatch in the classroom.

7. **Feels from the Farm**

   Construct a feely box containing farm items. Examples may include an ear of corn, hay, sheep wool, a turkey feather, hard-boiled egg, etc.

Dramatic Play:

1. **Farmer**

   Clothes and props for a farmer can be placed in the dramatic play area. Include items such as hats, scarves, overalls, boots, etc.

2. **Saddle**

   A horse saddle can be placed on a bench in the classroom. The children can take turns sitting on it, pretending they are riding a horse.

3. **Barn**

   A barn and plastic animals can be added to the classroom. The children can use blocks as accessories to make pens, cages, etc.

4. **Veterinarian**

   Collect materials to make a veterinarian prop box. Stuffed animals can be used as patients.

Arts and Crafts:

1. **Yarn Collage**

   Provide the children with several types and lengths of yarn. Include clipped yarn, yarn fluffs, frayed yarn in several different colors, along with paper.

2. **Texture Collage**

   On the art table provide several colors, shapes, and types of fabric for creating a texture collage during the self-selected activity period for the children.

3. **Grain and Seed Collage**

   Corn, wheat, hay, oats, barley, and grains that farm animals eat can be placed on the art table. Paper and glue or paste should also be provided.

4. **Buttermilk Chalk Picture**

   Brush a piece of cardboard with 2 to 3 table-spoons of buttermilk or dip chalk in buttermilk. Create designs using colored chalk as a tool.

5. **Farm Animal Mobiles**

   Cut pictures of farm animals from magazines and hang them from hangers or branches.

6. **Eggshell Collages**

   Collect eggshells and crush into pieces. Place the eggshells in the art area for the children to glue on paper. Let dry. If desired, the shells can be painted. If preparation time is available, eggshells can be dyed with food coloring by teacher prior to the activity.

7. **Sponge Prints**

   Cut farm animal shapes out of sponges. If a pattern is needed, cut out of a coloring book. Once cut, the sponge forms can be dipped into a pan of thick tempera paint and used as a tool to apply a design.

Sensory:

Add to the Sensory Table:

- different types of grain, such as oats, wheat, barley, and corn, and measuring devices
- wool and feathers
- sand and plastic farm animals
- materials to make a barnyard. Include soil, hay, farm animals, barns, farm equipment toys, etc.

Large Muscle:

1. **Trikes**

   During outdoor play, encourage children to use trikes and wagons for hauling.

2. **Barn**

   Construct a large barn out of a large cardboard box. Let all the children help paint it outdoors. When dry, the children can play in it.

Field Trips/Resource People:

1. **Farmer**

   Invite a farmer to talk to the children. If possible, have him bring a smaller farm animal for the children to touch and observe.

64

2. **The Farm**

   Visit a farm. Observe the animals and machinery.

3. **Milk Station**

   Visit a milk station if there is one in your area.

4. **Grocery Store**

   Visit the dairy section of a grocery store. Look for dairy products.

Math:

1. **Puzzles**

   Laminate several pictures of farm animals; coloring books are a good source. Cut the pictures into puzzles for the children.

2. **Grouping and Sorting**

   Collect plastic farm animals. Place in a basket and let the children sort them according to size, color, where they live, how they move, etc.

Social Studies:

Farm Animal of the Day

   Throughout the week let children take care of and watch baby farm animals. Suggestions include a piglet, chicks, small ducks, rabbit, or lamb.

Group Time (games, language):

1. **"Duck, Duck, Goose"**

   Sit the children in a circle. Then choose one child to be "it." This child goes around the circle and touches each of the other children on the shoulder and says "Duck, Duck, Goose." The child who is tapped as "goose" gets up and chases the other child around the circle. The first child who returns back to the empty

spot sits down and the other child proceeds with the game of tapping children on the shoulder until someone else is tapped as the goose.

2. **Thank You**

   Write a thank-you note as a follow-up activity after a field trip or a visit from a resource person.

Miscellaneous:

Transition

   During transition time encourage the children to imitate different farm animals. They may gallop like a horse, hop like a bunny, waddle like a duck, move like a snake, etc.

Cooking:

1. **Make Butter**

   Fill baby food jars half-full with whipping cream. Allow the children to take turns shaking the jars until the cream separates. First it will appear like whipping cream, then like overwhipped cream, and finally an obvious separation will occur. Then pour off liquid and taste. Wash the butter in cold water in a bowl several times. Drain off milky liquid each time. Taste and then wash again until nearly clear. Work the butter in the water with a wooden spoon as you wash. Add salt to taste. Let the children spread the butter on crackers or bread.

2. **Make Cottage Cheese**

   Heat one quart of milk until lukewarm. Dissolve one rennet tablet in a small amount of the milk. Stir the rennet mixture into remaining milk. Let the mixture stand in a warm place until set. Drain the mixture through a strainer lined with cheesecloth. Bring the corners of the cloth together and squeeze or drain the mixture. Rinse the mixture with cold water and drain again. Add a small amount of butter and salt.

3. **Purple Cow Drink Mix**

1/2 gallon milk
1/2 gallon grape juice
6 ice cubes
blender

Mix the ingredients in a blender for one minute. Drink. Enjoy! This recipe will serve approximately 20 children.

4. **Animal Crackers**

Serve animal crackers and peanut butter for snack.

5. **Hungry Cheese Spread**

1 8-ounce goat cheese or 8-ounce soft cream cheese
1/4 cup soft butter
1 teaspoon salt
1 tablespoon paprika
1 teaspoon dry mustard
1 1/2 tablespoons caraway seeds

Blend the cheese and butter in the mixing bowl. Add the remaining ingredients. Mix them well. Put the blended cheese into a small serving bowl. Chill in the refrigerator for at least 30 minutes before serving.

Source: Cooper, Terry Touff, & Ratner, Marilyn. (1974). *Many Hands Cooking*. New York: Thomas Y. Crowell Company.

6. **Corn Bread**

2 cups cornmeal
1 teaspoon salt
1/2 teaspoon baking soda
1 1/2 teaspoons baking powder
1 tablespoon sugar
2 eggs
1 1/2 cups buttermilk
1/4 cup cooking oil

Heat oven to 400 degrees. Sift cornmeal, salt, soda, baking powder, and sugar into a bowl. Stir in unbeaten eggs, buttermilk, and cooking oil until all ingredients are mixed. Pour the batter into a greased 9-inch x 9-inch pan or cob-formed pans. Bake for 30 minutes until lightly browned.

Multimedia:

The following resources can be found in educational catalogs:

1. Poelker, Kathy Lecinski. "My Pony Stop and Go" on *Look at My World* [record]. Look at Me Company.

2. *McDonald's Farm* [47-minute video]. Edu-vid.

3. *Doing Things* [27-minute video]. Bo Peep Productions.

4. *Good Morning, Good Night* [17-minute video]. Bo Peep Productions.

Books:

The following books can be used to complement the theme:

1. Gibbons, Gail. (1985). *The Milk Makers*. New York: Macmillan.

2. Brura, Dick. (1984). *Farmer Brown*. Los Angeles: Price, Stern, Sloan.

3. Ziegler, Sandra. (1987). *A Visit to the Dairy Farm*. Chicago: Children's Press.

4. *Baby Animals on the Farm*. (1989). Auburn, ME: Ladybird Books, Inc.

5. Brown, Craig. (1991). *My Barn*. New York: Greenwillow Books.

6. Cousins, Lucy. (1991). *Farm Animals*. New York: Morrow, Williams and Co.

7. Sweet, Melissa. (1992). *Fiddle - I - Fee: A Farm Yard Song for the Very Young*. New York: Little, Brown and Co.

8. Wells, Donna K. (1990). *What Animals Give Us: So Many Things*. Mankato, MN: Child's World, Inc.

9. Carroll, Kathaleen S. (1992). *One Red Rooster*. Boston: Houghton Mifflin Co.

10. Lewison, Wendy C. (1992). *Going to Sleep on the Farm*. New York: Dial Books for Young Readers.

11. Most, Bernard. (1990). *The Cow That Went Oink*. San Diego: Harcourt Brace Jovanovich.

12. Curran, Ellen. (1985). *Hello, Farm Animals*. Mahwah, NJ: Troll.

13. Galdone, Paul. (1985). *The Little Red Hen*. Boston: Houghton Mifflin.

14. Hammar, Asa. (1992). *Fit for Pigs*. New York: Checkerboard Press.

15. Hellen, Nancy. (1990). *Old MacDonald Had a Farm*. New York: Orchard Books.

16. Archambault, John. (1989). *Counting Sheep*. New York: Henry Holt.

17. Cross, Verda. (1992). *Great Grandma Tells of Threshing Day*. Morton Grove, IL: Albert Whitman.

18. McPhail, David. (1992). *Farm Boy's Year*. New York: Macmillan.

19. Mother Goof. (1992). *The Sheep Who Was Allergic to Wool*. Sunflower Hill.

20. Snow, Nancy. (1991). *Sheep In a Shop*. Boston: Houghton Mifflin.

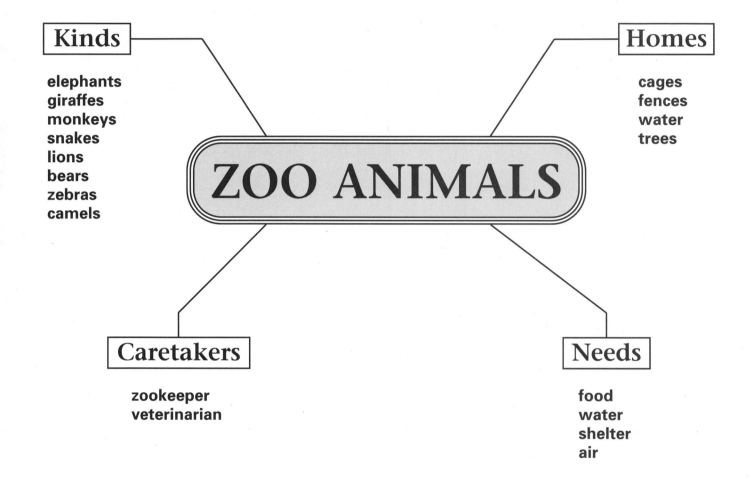

Kinds

elephants
giraffes
monkeys
snakes
lions
bears
zebras
camels

Homes

cages
fences
water
trees

ZOO ANIMALS

Caretakers

zookeeper
veterinarian

Needs

food
water
shelter
air

Theme Goals:

Through participating in the experiences provided by this theme, the children may learn:

1. Names of zoo animals.

2. Needs of zoo animals.

3. Types of animal homes.

4. The caretaker's role.

Concepts for the Children to Learn:

1. A zoo is a place for animals.

2. Zoo animals are kept in cages, fences, water, or in trees.

3. Elephants, giraffes, monkeys, snakes, lions, zebras, camels, and bears are zoo animals.

4. A zookeeper feeds and takes care of the animals.

5. Zoo animals need food, water, and shelter.

6. Veterinarians are animal doctors.

Vocabulary:

1. **zoo**—a place to look at animals.

2. **cage**—a home for animals.

3. **zookeeper**—a person who feeds the zoo animals.

4. **veterinarian**—an animal doctor.

Bulletin Board

The purpose of this bulletin board is to encourage the children to place the correct number of balls above each seal corresponding to the numeral on the drum. To prepare the bulletin board, construct seals sitting on a drum as illustrated. Place a numeral on each drum with the corresponding number of dots. Construct colored balls from tagboard. Laminate. Staple the seal figures and drums to the bulletin board. Place a magnetic strip above each seal. Also adhere a magnetic strip on the back of each ball.

Parent Letter

Dear Parents,

Our new theme is called zoo animals. This is an appropriate theme to introduce to the children because they are fascinated by the zoo and the animals that live there. Through our study of zoo animals, the children will become familiar with the names of many familiar zoo animals. They will also be introduced to new occupations: the zookeeper and the veterinarian.

At School

Some of the experiences planned for the zoo animal unit include:

- looking at peek-a-boo pictures of zoo animals.
- using zoo animal-shaped cookie cutters with playdough at the art table.
- pretending to be caged zoo animals using boxes as cages in the dramatic play area.

Field Trip

Our class will be taking a field trip to the Dunn County Reserve Park on Friday. There we can see some unusual animals. Please let me know by Wednesday if you are interested in accompanying the group. We will be leaving the center at 9:30 a.m. and be returning by 11:30 a.m.

At Home

To develop observation skills, you can show your child pictures of zoo animals from books or magazines. Plan a family trip to a zoo. Many opportunities for learning present themselves at the zoo. Children can actually see different kinds of animals and many times, such as at petting zoos, are able to touch and feed them. What a great way to develop an appreciation for and respect of animal life!

Enjoy your child!

Can you roar like a leopard?

Music:

1. **"Zoo Animals"**
   (Sing to the tune of "Muffin Man")

   Do you know the kangaroo
   The kangaroo, the kangaroo?
   Oh, do you know the kangaroo
   That lives in the zoo?

   (Adapt this song and use other zoo animals
   such as the monkey, elephant, giraffe, lion,
   turtle, bear, snake, etc.)

2. **"One Elephant"**

   One elephant went out to play
   On a spider web one day.
   He had such enormous fun
   That he called for another elephant to come.

   (Makes a nice flannel story or choose one child
   to be an "elephant." Add another "elephant"
   with each verse.)

3. **"Animals at the Zoo"**
   (Sing to the tune of "Frere Jacques")

   See the animals, see the animals
   At the zoo, at the zoo.
   Elephants and tigers, lions and seals
   Monkeys too, monkeys too.

Fingerplays:

LION

I knew a little lion who went roar, roar, roar.
   (make sounds)
Who walked around on all fours.
   (walk on both hands and feet)
He had a tail we could see behind the bars
   (point to tail)
And when we visit we should stand back far.
   (move backwards)

ALLIGATOR

The alligator likes to swim.
   (two hands flat on top of the other)
Sometimes his mouth opens wide.
   (hands open and shut)
But when he sees me on the shore,
Down under the water he'll hide.

THE MONKEY

The monkey claps, claps, claps his hands.
   (clap hands)
The monkey claps, claps, claps his hands.
   (clap hands)
Monkey see, monkey do.
The monkey does the same as you.
   (use pointer finger)
   (change actions)

ZOO ANIMALS

This is the way the elephant goes.
   (clasp hands together, extend arms, move
   back and forth)
With a curly trunk instead of a nose.
The buffalo, all shaggy and fat.
Has two sharp horns in place of a hat.
   (point to forehead)
The hippo with his mouth so wide—
Let's see what's inside.
   (hands together and open wide and close
   them)
The wiggly snake upon the ground
Crawls along without a sound.
   (weave hands back and forth)
But monkey see and monkey do is the funniest
animal in the zoo.
   (place thumbs in ears and wiggle fingers)

THE ZOO

The zoo holds many animals inside
   (make a circle with your hands and peer
   inside)
So unlatch the doors and open them wide.
   (open your hands wide)
Elephants, tigers, zebras, and bears
   (hold up one finger for each animal)
Are some of the animals you'll find there.

Science:

1. **Animal Skins**

   Place a piece of snakeskin, a patch of animal
   hide, and animal fur out on the science table.
   The children can look and feel the differences.
   These skins can usually be borrowed from the
   Department of Natural Resources.

2. **Habitat**

   On the science table, place a bowl of water, a
   tray of dirt, and a pile of hay or grass on the
   table. Also, include many small toy zoo
   animals. The children can place the animals in
   their correct habitat.

Dramatic Play:

1. **The Zoo**

   Collect large appliance boxes. Cut slits to
   resemble cages. Old fur coats or blankets can
   be added. The children may use the fur pieces
   pretending to be animals in the zoo.

2. **Pet Store**

   Cages and many small stuffed animals can be
   added to the dramatic play area.

3. **Block Play**

   Set out many blocks and rubber, plastic, or
   wooden models of zoo animals.

Arts and Crafts:

1. **Paper Plate Lions**

   Collect paper plates, sandwich bags, and
   yellow cotton. Color the cottonballs by
   pouring powdered tempera paint into the
   sandwich bag and shaking. The children can
   trim the cut side of the paper plate with the
   yellow cotton to represent a mane. Facial
   features can also be added. This activity is for
   older children.

2. **Cookie Cutters**

   Playdough and zoo animal-shaped cookie
   cutters can be placed on a table in the art area.

Sensory:

Additions to the sensory table include:

- sand and zoo animal models
- seeds and measuring scoops
- corn and scales
- hay
- water

Large Muscle:

1. Walk Like the Animals

"Walk Like the Animals" is played like "Simon Says." Say, "The zookeeper says to walk like a giraffe." The children can walk as they believe that particular zoo animal would walk. Repeat using different animals such as monkeys, elephants, lions, tigers, bears, etc. This activity can also be used for transition.

2. Zookeeper, May I?

Designate one child to be the zookeeper. This child should stand about six feet in front of the remainder of the children. The zookeeper provides directions for the other children. To illustrate, he may say take three elephant steps, one kangaroo hop, two alligator glides, etc. Once the children reach the zookeeper, the zookeeper chooses a child as his successor.

Field Trips:

1. Zoo

Visit a local zoo if available. Observe the animals that are of particular interest to the children such as the elephants, giraffes, bears, and monkeys.

2. Reserve Park

If your community has a reserve park, or an area where wild animals are caged in a natural environment, take the children to visit. Plan a picnic snack to take along.

Math:

1. Animal Sort

Collect pictures of elephants, lions, giraffes, monkeys, and other zoo animals from magazines, calendars, or coloring books. Encourage the children to sort the pictures into labeled baskets. For example, one basket may be for large animals and another for small animals.

2. Which Is Bigger?

Collect many toy models of zoo animals in various sizes. Encourage the children to order from smallest to biggest, etc.

3. Animal Sets

Cut and mount pictures of zoo animals. The children can classify the pictures by sorting. Examples might include birds, four-legged animals, furry animals, etc.

Social Studies:

Helpful Zoo Animals

Discuss how some animals can be useful during large group. Show the children pictures of various helping animals and discuss their uses. Examples include:

- camel (transportation in some countries).
- elephant (often used to pull things).
- dogs (seeing eye dogs, sled dogs).
- goats (used for milk).

Group Time (games, language):

What Am I?

Give the children verbal clues in which you describe an animal and the children guess which zoo animal you are talking about. An example is, "I am very large, gray-colored, and have a long nose that looks like a hose. What zoo animal am I?"

Cooking:

1. Animals on Grass

Take a graham cracker and spread either peanut butter or green-tinted cream cheese on the top. Stand an animal cracker on the top of the graham cracker.

2. Peanut Butter Log

1/2 cup peanut butter
1/2 cup raisins
2 1/2 tablespoons dry milk
2 tablespoons honey

Mix together, roll into log 1 inch x 10 inches long. Chill and slice.

Multimedia:

The following resources can be found in educational catalogs.

1. Palmer, Hap. *Animal Antics* [record].

2. *What's New at the Zoo?* [record]. Kimbo Records.

3. *Walk Like the Animals* [record]. Kimbo Records.

4. *Animal Walks* [record]. Kimbo Records.

5. *Ping & Kooky's Cuckoo Zoo* [IBM/Mac software, PK–1]. EA Kids.

6. *Kid's Zoo* [IBM/Mac software, PK+]. Knowledge Adventure.

7. *Alphabet Zoo* [Apple/IBM software, PK–2]. Queue.

Books:

The following books can be used to complement the theme:

1. Hoban, Tara. (1987). *A Children's Zoo*. New York: Morrow.

2. Ata, Te. (1989). *Baby Rattlesnake*. San Francisco: Children's Book Press.

3. Caduto, Michael, & Bruchac, Joseph. (1991). *Keepers of the Animals: Native American Stories & Wildlife Activities for Children*. Golden, CO: Fulcrum Publishing.

4. Arnold, Caroline. (1992). *Cheetah*. New York: Morrow.

5. Arnold, Caroline. (1992). *Hippo*. New York: Morrow.

6. Davis, Kerry. (1993). *The Swetsville Zoo*. Kerry Tales.

7. Douglas-Hamilton, Oria. (1991). *The Elephant Family Book*. Saxonville, MA: Picture Book Studios.

8. Hefer, Angelika. (1991). *The Lion Family Book*. Saxonville, MA: Picture Book Studios.

9. Moerbeek, Kees. (1989). *New at the Zoo*. New York: Random House.

10. Brown, Margaret W. (1993). *Don't Frighten the Lion!* New York: Harper Collins.

11. Baker, Keith. (1991). *Hide & Snake*. San Diego: Harcourt Brace.

12. Ruschak, Lynette. (1992). *Counting Zoo: A Pop-up Number Book*. New York: Macmillan Children's Group.

13. Brennan, John, & Keney, Leonie. (1989). *Zoo Day*. Minneapolis: Carolrhoda Books.

14. Carle, Eric. (1989). *One, Two, Three to the Zoo*. New York: Putnam Publishing Group.

15. Oremerod, Jan. (1991). *When We Went to the Zoo*. New York: Lothrop, Lee, & Shepard Books.

16. Parramon, J. M. (1990). *My First Visit to the Zoo*. Hauppauge, NY: Barron's Educational Series, Inc.

17. Unwin, Pippa. (1990). *Great Zoo Hunt!* New York: Doubleday and Co., Inc.

18. Lunn, Carolyn. (1991). *Bobby's Zoo Big Book*. Chicago: Children's Press.

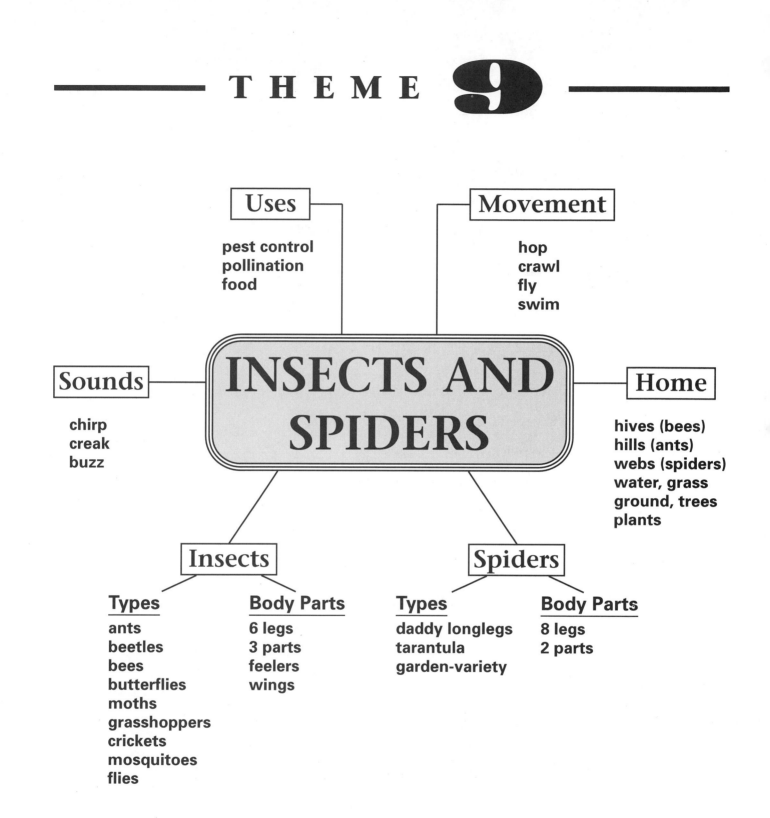

Uses

pest control
pollination
food

Movement

hop
crawl
fly
swim

Sounds

chirp
creak
buzz

INSECTS AND SPIDERS

Home

hives (bees)
hills (ants)
webs (spiders)
water, grass
ground, trees
plants

Insects

Types
ants
beetles
bees
butterflies
moths
grasshoppers
crickets
mosquitoes
flies

Body Parts
6 legs
3 parts
feelers
wings

Spiders

Types
daddy longlegs
tarantula
garden-variety

Body Parts
8 legs
2 parts

Theme Goals:

Through participating in the experiences provided by this theme, the children may learn:

1. Ways to identify different insects and spiders.

2. Ways insects help us.

3. Ways spiders help us.

4. Places where spiders and insects live.

5. Ways that spiders and insects move from place to place.

Concepts for the Children to Learn:

1. There are many kinds of insects.

2. Insects are different in many ways: size, shape, color, eyes, mouths, and number of wings.

3. Insects have six legs (three pairs) and, if winged, four wings.

4. Spiders have eight legs (four pairs) and no wings.

5. Insects and spiders come from eggs.

6. Insects can help us by making honey and pollinating fruits and flowers.

7. Spiders can help us by eating insect pests.

8. Most spiders spin a web.

9. Some insects fly, others walk.

10. Spiders spin a web to catch other insects to eat.

Vocabulary:

1. **insect**—small animal with three pairs of jointed legs.

2. **spider**—small animal with four pairs of legs.

3. **caterpillar**—the wormlike larvae of a butterfly or moth.

4. **pollinate**—the way insects help flowers to grow.

5. **spiderling**—a baby spider.

6. **antennae**—feelers on an insect that stick out from the head.

7. **pupa**—intermediate stage of an insect; chrysalis.

8. **moth**—night-flying insect with four wings related to the butterfly.

9. **wasp**—winged insect with a poisonous sting.

10. **cricket**—small leaping insect known for its chirping.

Bulletin Board

The purpose of this bulletin board is to develop visual discrimination skills. Construct several butterflies, each of a different shape, out of tagboard. Trace on black construction paper for shadows. Laminate. Staple shadow butterflies to bulletin board. Punch holes in colored butterflies for children to hang on the push pin of the corresponding shadow butterfly.

Parent Letter

Dear Parents,

We are continuing our study of animals. We are moving to a new category—insects and spiders. The children will become aware of the difference between insects and spiders and the ways that those creatures are helpful. Do you know the difference between insects and spiders? Most insects have three body parts and six legs. Spiders have two body parts and eight legs.

At School

Some of the learning experiences planned include:

- singing and acting out the song, "One Elephant Went Out to Play." It's about an elephant that plays on a spider web!
- listening to a flannel board version of the story, *The Very Hungry Caterpillar* by Eric Carle.
- watching and observing an ant farm set up in the science area.
- creating spiders and insects out of a variety of materials in the art area.

At Home

There are many ways to bring this unit into your home. Take a walk with your child and see how many spiders and insects you can find. Avoid touching unknown types of insects or spiders with your fingers. Instead, use a clear jar with a lid to observe the creature close up. Release the insect or spider after the observation.

We will be having a snack this week called ants on a log. Let your child make some for you! Spread peanut butter on pieces of celery. Top with raisins. Enjoy!

Enjoy your child!

Children enjoy observing bugs.

Music:

1. **"The Eensie Weensie Spider"**
   (traditional)

   The eensie weensie spider crawled up the water spout.
   (walk fingers of one hand up other hand)
   Down came the rain and washed the spider out.
   (lower hands to make rain, wash out spider by placing hands together in front and extending out to either side)
   Out came the sun and dried up all the rain
   (form sun with arms in circle over head)
   And the eensie weensie spider went up the spout again.
   (walk fingers up other arm)

2. **"The Elephant Song"**

One elephant went out to play
On a spider's web one day.
He had such enormous fun,
That he called for another elephant to come.

Elephant! Elephant! Come out to play!
Elephant! Elephant! Come out to play!

Two elephants…

3. **"The Insects and Spiders"**
   (Sing to the tune of "The Wheels on the Bus")

   The bugs in the air fly up and down,
   up and down, up and down.
   The bugs in the air fly up and down all through the day.

   The spiders on the bush spin a web.
   The crickets in the field hop up and down.
   The bees in their hive go buzz, buzz, buzz.

Fingerplays:

ANTS

Once I saw an ant hill, with no ants about.
So I said "Little ants, won't you please come out?"
Then as if they heard my call, one, two, three, four, five came out.
And that was all!

BUMBLEBEE

Brightly colored bumblebee
Looking for some honey.
Flap your wings and fly away
While it still is sunny.

THE CATERPILLAR

A caterpillar crawled to the top of a tree.
(index finger of left hand moves up right arm)
"I think I'll take a nap," said he.
So under a leaf, he began to creep
(wrap right hand over left fist)
To spin his chrysalis and he fell asleep.
All winter long he slept in his chrysalis bed,
(keep right hand over left fist)

Till spring came along one day, and said,
"Wake up, wake up little sleepy head."
    (shake left fist with right hand).
"Wake up, it's time to get out of bed!"
So, he opened his eyes that sun shiny day
    (shake fingers and look into hand)
Lo—he was a butterfly and flew away!
    (move hand into flying motion)

LITTLE MISS MUFFET

Little Miss Muffet
Sat on a tuffet
Eating her curds and whey.
Along came a spider
And sat down beside her
And frightened Miss Muffet away!

Spiders can be prepared in the art area.

Science:

1. Observe an ant farm.
   The children can watch the ants dig tunnels, build roads and tunnels, build roads and rooms, eat and store food, etc. (Ant farms are available in some commercial play catalogs.)

2. Go outside and observe anthills in the playground area.

3. Observe deceased flies and ants under a microscope.

4. Observe insects and spiders in a caged bug keeper or plastic jars with holes in the lids.

5. Listen to a cricket during quiet time.

6. Capture a caterpillar and watch it spin a chrysalis and turn into a butterfly.

Dramatic Play:

1. **Scientist**

   The children can dress up in white lab coats and observe spiders and insects with magnifying glasses.

2. **Spider Web**

Tie together a big piece of rope to resemble a spider web. Have children pretend they are spiders playing on their web.

3. **Spider Sac**

   Tape together a 10-foot by 25-foot piece of plastic on the sides. Blow it up with a fan to make a big bubble. Make a slit in the plastic for the entrance. The children can pretend to be baby spiders coming out of the spider sac when they are hatching.

4. The children can act out "Little Miss Muffet."

Arts and Crafts:

1. Cut easel paper in the shape of a butterfly.

2. Fingerpaint creepy crawly pictures.

3. Make insects and spiders out of clay. Use toothpicks, straws, and pipe cleaner segments for the appendages.

4. Make insects and spiders with thumbprints. Children can draw crayon legs to make prints look like insects and spiders.

5. Egg carton caterpillars. Cut egg cartons in half, lengthwise. Each child paints a carton half. When dry, children can make a face on the end of the carton and insert pipe cleaners or straws for feelers.

6. Have children make spiders from black construction paper—one large black circle for a body and eight strips for legs. Children can paste on two yellow circles for eyes. Hang by a string around the room.

7. Make ladybug shapes out of red and orange construction paper. Have children sponge paint dots and legs on the bugs.

8. Make butterfly templates.

9. Use butterfly templates and place crayon shavings between two pieces of waxed paper and iron. Put a butterfly template over the waxed paper and glue it on. A pretty butterfly will be the final product!

10. Tissue paper butterflies. Have children lightly paint white tissue paper or use colored tissue paper. Fasten a pipe cleaner around the middle. Add circles on the ends for antennaes.

11. Balloon bugs. Blow up several long balloons. Cover them with strips of paper dipped in wallpaper paste. Put on three to four layers of this sticky paper. Let dry for two to three days. Then paint your own giant bug!

12. Have insect and spider stencils set out for the children to draw and trace.

Sensory:

Add soil and plastic insects to the sensory table.

Large Muscle:

Have children pretend to walk as different insects when in transition from one activity to another.

Field Trips/Resource People:

1. Go on a walk to a nearby park to find bugs. Look under rocks, in cracks, in sidewalks, in bushes, etc.

2. Have someone who has a butterfly collection come in.

3. Visit a pet store. Ask them to show you what kind of insects they feed to the animals in the store. Do they sell any insects?

4. Invite a zoologist to come in and talk about insects and how important they are.

5. Invite an individual who raises bees to talk to the children. Ask him to bring in a honeycomb for the children to taste.

Math:

1. **Butterfly Match**

   Make several triangles of different colors. On one triangle put the numbers 1 to 10; on the other make dots to correspond to the numbers 1 to 10. Have the children match the dots to the numbers and clip them together with a clothespin to form a butterfly.

2. **Ladybug Houses**

   Paint several 1/2-pint milk cartons red. Write the numerals 1 to 10 on each. Make 50 small ladybugs dotting 5 sets of 1 to 10. Have children put ladybugs in their correct houses by matching dots to numerals.

3. **Numeral Caterpillar**

   Make a caterpillar with 10 body segments and a head. Have the children put the numbers in order to complete the caterpillar's body.

4. Sing the song, "The Ants Go Marching One by One," and have the children act out the song using their fingers as numbers.

5. Make an insect and spider lotto or concentration game with stickers for children to play.

Social Studies:

1. Take the children on an insect hunt near your school. When children are finished, have everyone show the rest of the class what they found. Talk about where they found the insects (on a tree, under a log, etc.).

2. Have children make homes for all the insects they found. They can put dirt, grass, twigs, and small rocks in plastic jars and cans.

3. Discuss what it is like to be a member of a family. Ask the children if each member of their family has a certain job. Then focus on ant colonies or families. Ants live together much like people do, except that ants live in a larger community. Each ant has a certain task within the community. Some of the jobs are:

- nurse: to look after the young
- soldier: defend colony and attack the enemies
- others: search for food; enlarge and clean the nest (house)

Group Time (games, language):

1. **Matching Insects**

   Divide children into two groups. Hand out pictures of different spiders and insects, one to each group that matches one in the other group. Point to a child from one group and have that child act out the insect she has in some way (movement or noises). The child that has the same insect from the other group must go and meet the child in the middle and act out the insect also.

2. Have many pictures of insects and spiders on display. Talk about a different insect or spider every day. Include where it lives, how it walks, what it might eat, etc.

Cooking:

1. **Honey Bees**

   1/2 cup peanut butter
   1 tablespoon honey
   1/3 cup nonfat dry milk
   2 tablespoons toasted wheat germ
   unsweetened cocoa powder
   sliced almonds

   In a mixing bowl, mix peanut butter and honey. Stir in dry milk and wheat germ until well mixed. Lay waxed paper on a baking sheet. Using 1 tablespoon at a time, shape peanut butter mixture into ovals to look like bees. Put on baking sheet. Dip a toothpick in cocoa powder and press lightly across the top of the bees to make stripes. Stick on almonds for wings. Chill for 30 minutes.

   Source: *Better Homes and Gardens Kids Snacks.* (1979). Iowa: Meredith Corporation.

2. **Ants on a Log** (traditional)

   Cut celery pieces into 3-inch strips. Fill the cavity of the celery stick with peanut butter. Garnish with raisins. (As with all recipes calling for celery, this might be more appropriate for older children.)

Multimedia:

The following resources can be found in educational catalogs:

1. Seeger, Pete. *Birds, Beasts, Bugs, and Little Fishies* [record].

2. Norfolk, Bobby. *Why Mosquitoes Buzz in People's Ears* [record].

3. *Bugs Don't Bug Us* [35-minute video]. Bo Peep Productions.

Books:

The following books can be used to complement the theme:

1. Carle, Eric. (1985). *The Very Busy Spider*. New York: Philomel Books.

2. Heller, Ruth. (1992). *How to Hide a Butterfly and Other Insects*. New York: Putnam.

3. Arvetis, Chris. (1987). *What Is a Butterfly?* Chicago: Children's Press.

4. de Bourgoing, Pascale. (1991). *Ladybug and Other Insects*. New York: Scholastic, Inc.

5. Fowler, Allen. (1990). *It's a Good Thing There Are Insects*. Chicago: Children's Press.

6. Kindersley, Dorling. (1992). *Insects and Crawly Creatures*. New York: Macmillan Children's Book Group.

7. Morris, Dean. (1990). *Insects That Live in Families*. Madison, NJ: Raintree Steck—Vaughn Publishers.

8. National Wildlife Federation Staff. (1991). *Incredible Insects*. Vienna, VA: Author.

9. Aylesworth, Jim. (1992). *Old Black Fly*. New York: Henry Holt and Co.

10. Carle, Eric. (1990). *The Very Quiet Cricket*. New York: Putnam Publishing Group.

11. Inkpen, Mick. (1992). *Billy's Beetle*. San Diego: Harcourt Brace Jovanovich.

12. Pienkowski, Jan. (1990). *Oh My a Fly*. Los Angeles: Price Stern Sloan, Inc.

13. Ross, Katharine. (1991). *Twinkle, Twinkle, Little Bug: A Sesame Street Book*. New York: Random House for Young Readers.

14. McDonald, Suse. (1991). *Space Spinners*. New York: Dial Books for Young Readers.

15. Patent, Dorothy H. (1989). *Looking at Ants*. New York: Holiday House, Inc.

16. Moses, Amy. (1992). *If I Were an Ant*. Chicago: Children's Press.

17. Butterfield, Moira. (1992). *Butterfly*. New York: Simon and Schuster Trade.

18. Gibbons, Gail. (1989). *Monarch Butterfly*. New York: Holiday House, Inc.

19. Van Allsburg, Chris. (1988). *Two Bad Ants*. Hoston: Houghton Mifflin.

20. Lunn, Carolyn. (1989). *Spiders & Webs*. Chicago: Children's Press.

21. Kimmel, Eric. (1992). *Anansi Goes Fishing*. New York: Doubleday.

22. Rodanas, Kristina. (1992). *Dragonfly's Tale*. New York: Clarion.

23. Hopkins, Lee Bennett (Ed.). (1992). *Flit, Flutter, Fly: Poems About Bugs and Other Crawly Creatures*. New York: Doubleday.

24. Henwood, Chris. (1988). *Earthworms*. New York: Watts.

25. Giganti, Paul, Jr. (1988). *How Many Snails?* New York: Greenwillow.

26. Parker, Nancy Winslow, & Wright, Joan Richards. (1987). *Bugs*. New York: Mulberry Books.

27. Ryder, Joanne. (1989). *Where Butterflies Grow*. New York: Lodestar.

28. Rounds, Glen. (1990). *I Know an Old Woman Who Swallowed a Fly*. New York: Holiday House.

29. Selsam, Millicent E. (1988). *Backyard Insects*. New York: Scholastic.

30. Thomson, Ruth. (1991). *Creepy Crawlies*. New York: Macmillan.

31. Fleming, Denise. (1993). *In the Tall, Tall Grass*. New York: Holt.

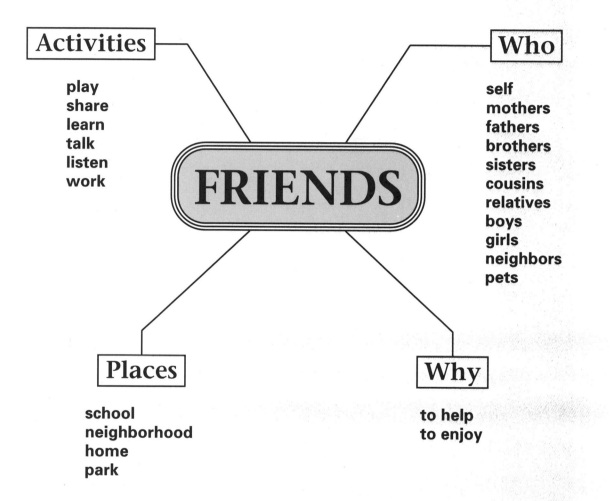

Activities

play
share
learn
talk
listen
work

Who

self
mothers
fathers
brothers
sisters
cousins
relatives
boys
girls
neighbors
pets

FRIENDS

Places

school
neighborhood
home
park

Why

to help
to enjoy

Theme Goals:

Through participating in the experiences provided by this theme, the children may learn:

1. Who friends are.

2. Why we have friends.

3. Activities we can do with our friends.

4. Places we can make friends.

Concepts for the Children to Learn:

1. A friend is someone who I like and who likes me.

2. My friends are special to me.

3. We have friends at school.

4. Our brothers and sisters can be our friends.

5. Friends can help us with our work.

6. We play with our friends.

7. We share and learn with friends.

8. Friends talk and listen to us.

9. A pet can be a friend.

10. Friends can be boys or girls.

Vocabulary:

1. **friend**—a person we enjoy.

2. **sharing**—giving and taking turns.

3. **like**—feeling good about someone or something.

4. **giving**—sharing something of your own with others.

5. **cooperating**—working together to help someone.

6. **togetherness**—being with one another and sharing a good feeling.

7. **pal or buddy**—other words for friend.

Bulletin Board

The purpose of this bulletin board is to help the children with recognition of their own and their friends' names. The bulletin board can also be used by the teacher as an attendance check. Prepare the board by constructing name cards for each child as illustrated. Then laminate and punch holes in each card. When the children arrive at school, they can attach their name card to the bulletin board with a push pin.

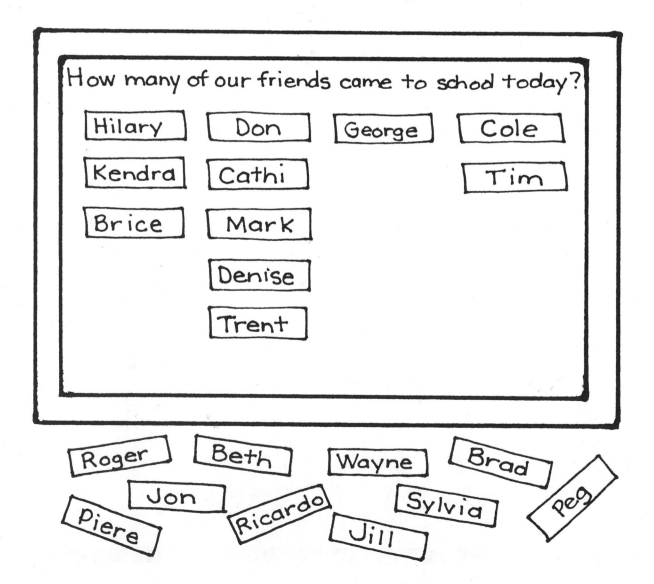

Parent Letter

Dear Parents,

We will be starting a unit on friends, which will include discovering people of all ages and even animal friends. The children have made many new friends at school with whom they are learning to take turns, cooperate, work, and play. Through this unit, the children will become more aware of what a friend is and activities friends can do together.

At School

Highlights of the learning experiences in this unit include:

- making friendship fortune cookies.
- sending notes to pen pals.
- creating a friendship chain with strips of paper.
- looking at pictures of our friends at school in our classroom photo album.

At Home

Your child may enjoy looking at photo albums of family and friends. Perhaps a friend could be invited to come and play with your child. Here is a poem about friends we will be learning to promote an enjoyment of language and poetry.

Friends

I like my friends.
So when we are at play,
I try to be very kind,
and nice in every way.

Be your child's best friend!

Tina is my best friend!

Music:

1. **"Do You Know This Friend of Mine"?**
   (Sing to the tune of "The Muffin Man")

   Do you know this friend of mine,
   This friend of mine,
   This friend of mine?
   Do you know this friend of mine?
   His name is _____.

   Yes, we know this friend of yours,
   This friend of yours,
   This friend of yours.
   Yes, we know this friend of yours.
   His name is _____.

2. **"The More We Are Together"**
   (Sing to the tune of "Have You Ever Seen a Lassie?")

   The more we are together, together, together,
   The more we are together, the happier we'll be.
   For your friends are my friends, and my
   friends are your friends.
   The more we are together the happier we'll be.

   We're all in school together, together, together,
   We're all in school together, and happy we'll be.
   There's Mary and Peter and Janet and Joshua

There's _____ and _____ and _____ and _____.
We're all in school together and happy we'll be.

Insert names of children in your classroom.

3. **"Beth Met a Friend"**
   (Sing to the tune of "The Farmer in the Dell")

   Beth met a friend,
   Beth met a friend,
   When she came to school today,
   Beth met a friend.

   Insert names of children in your classroom for
   each verse.

Fingerplays:

FRIENDS

I like my friends.
So when we are at play,
I try to be very kind
and nice in every way.

FIVE LITTLE FRIENDS
(hold up five fingers; subtract one with each
action)

Five little friends playing on the floor,
One got tired and then there were four.

Four little friends climbing in a tree,
One jumped down and then there were three.
Three little friends skipping to the zoo,
One went for lunch and then there were two.
Two little friends swimming in the sun,
One went home and then there was one.
One little friend going for a run,
Decided to take a nap and then there were
none.

Science:

1. **Comparing Heartbeats**

   Provide stethoscopes for the children to listen
   to their friends' heartbeats.

2. **Fingerprints**

   Ink pads and white paper can be provided for
   the children to make fingerprints. Also, a
   microscope can be provided to encourage the
   children to compare their fingerprints.

3. **Friends' Voices**

   Tape the children's voices throughout the
   course of the day. The following day, leave the
   tape recorder at the science table. The children
   can listen to the tape and try to guess which
   classmate is talking.

4. **Animal Friends**

   Prepare signs for the animal cages listing the
   animal's daily food intake and care.

Dramatic Play:

1. **Puppet Show**

   Set up a puppet stage with various types of
   puppets. The children can share puppets and
   act out friendships using the puppets in
   various situations.

2. **A Tea Party**

   Provide dress-up clothes, play dishes, and
   water in the dramatic play area.

Arts and Crafts:

1. **Friendship Chain**

   Provide strips of paper for the older children to
   print their names on. For those children who
   are not interested or unable, print their names
   for them. When all the names are on the strips
   of paper, the children can connect them to
   make a chain. The chain should symbolize that
   everyone in the class is a friend.

2. **Friendship Collage**

   Encourage the children to find magazine
   pictures of friends. These pictures can be
   pasted on a large sheet of paper for a collage.
   Later the paper can be used for decoration and
   discussion in the lobby or hallway.

3. **Friendship Exchange Art**

   Provide each child with a piece of construction
   paper with "To: _____" printed in the upper
   left corner and "From: _____" printed on the
   bottom. The teacher assists the children in
   printing their names on the bottom and the
   name of the person to their right on the top of
   the paper. Using paper scraps, tissue paper
   squares, fabric scraps, and glue, each child will
   construct a picture for a friend. When finished,
   have each child pass the paper to the friend it
   was made for.

Sensory:

The sensory table is an area where two to four
children can make new friends and share.
Materials that can be added to the sensory
table include:

- shaving cream
- playdough
- sand with toys
- water with boats
- wood shavings
- silly putty
  Mix equal parts of white glue and liquid
  starch. Food coloring can be added for color.
  Store in an airtight container.

- dry pasta with scoops and a balance scale
- goop
  Mix water and cornstarch. Add cornstarch to the water until you get the consistency that you want.

Large Muscle:

1. **Double Balance Beam**

   Place two balance beams side by side and encourage two children to hold hands and cross together.

2. **Bowling Game**

   Set up pins or plastic bottles. With a ball, have the children take turns knocking down the pins.

3. **Outdoor Obstacle Course**

   Design an obstacle course outdoors for two children to go through at one time. Use balance beams, climbers, slides, etc. Short and simple obstacle courses seem to work the best.

Field Trips/Resource People:

1. **The Zoo**

   Take a trip to the zoo to observe animals.

2. **The Nursing Home**

   Visit a nursing home allowing the children to interact with elderly friends.

3. **Resource People**

   Invite the following community helpers into the classroom:

   - police officer
   - trash collector
   - janitor/custodian
   - fire fighter
   - doctor, nurse, dentist
   - principal or director

Math:

1. **Group Pictures**

   Take pictures of the children in groups of 2, 3, 4, etc. Make separate corresponding number cards. The children then can match the correct numeral to the picture card.

2. **Friend Charts**

   Take individual pictures of the children and chart them according to hair color, eye color, etc. Encourage the children to compare their looks to the characteristics of their friends.

Social Studies:

Friends Bulletin Board

Ask the children to bring pictures of their friends into the classroom. Set up a bulletin board in the classroom where these pictures can be hung for all to see. Remind the children that friends can be family members and animals too.

Cooking:

1. **Pound Cake Brownies**

   3/4 cup butter or margarine, softened
   1 cup sugar
   3 eggs
   2 1-ounce squares unsweetened chocolate, melted and cooled
   1 teaspoon vanilla
   1 1/4 cups all-purpose flour
   1/2 teaspoon baking powder
   1/4 teaspoon salt
   1/2 cup chopped nuts

   Cream butter and sugar; beat in eggs. Blend in chocolate and vanilla. Stir flour with baking powder and salt. Add to creamed mixture. Mix well. Stir in nuts. Spread in a greased 9- x 9- x 2-inch baking pan. Bake at 350 degrees for 25 to 30 minutes. Cool. If desired, sift powdered sugar over the top. Cut into bars. Yields 24 bars.

TRANSITION ACTIVITIES

Clean-Up

"Do You Know What Time It is?"
(Sing to the tune of "The Muffin Man")

Oh, do you know what
    time it is,
What time it is, what time
    it is?
Oh, do you know what
    time it is?
It's almost clean-up time.
    (Or, it's time to clean
    up.)

"Clean-up Time"
(Sing to the tune of
    "London Bridge")

Clean-up time is already
    here,
Already here, already here.
Clean-up time is already
    here,
Already here.

"This Is the Way"
(Sing to the tune of
    "Mulberry Bush")

This is the way we pick up
    our toys,
Pick up our toys, pick up
    our toys.
This is the way we pick up
    our toys,
At clean-up time each day.

"Oh, It's Clean-up Time"
(Sing to the tune of "Oh,
    My Darling
    Clementine")

Oh, its clean-up time,
Oh, it's clean-up time,
Oh, it's clean-up time right
    now.
It's time to put the toys
    away,

It is clean-up time right
    now.

"A Helper I Will Be"
(Sing to the tune of "The
    Farmer in the Dell")

A helper I will be.
A helper I will be.
I'll pick up the toys and put
    them away.
A helper I will be.

**"We're Cleaning Up Our
    Room"**
(Sing to the tune of "The
    Farmer in the Dell")

We're cleaning up our
    room.
We're cleaning up our
    room.
We're putting all the toys
    away.
We're cleaning up our
    room.

"It's Clean-up Time"
(Sing to the chorus of
    "Looby Loo")

It's clean-up time at school.
It's time for boys and girls
To stop what they are
    doing
And put away their toys.

"Time to Clean-up"
(Sing to the tune of "Are
    You Sleeping?")

Time to clean-up.
Time to clean-up.
Everybody help.
Everybody help.
Put the toys away, put the
    toys away.
Then sit down. (Or, then
    come here.)

Specific toys can be men-
    tioned in place of "toys."

"Clean-up Time"
(Sing to the tune of "Hot
    Cross Buns")

Clean-up time.
Clean-up time.
Put all of the toys away.
It's clean-up time.

ROUTINES

"Passing Around"
(Sing to the tune of "Skip to
    My Loo")

Brad, take a napkin and
    pass them to Sara.
Sara, take a napkin and
    pass them to Tina.
Tina, take a napkin and
    pass them to Eric,
Passing around the
    napkins.

Fill in appropriate child's
    name and substitute
    napkin for any object
    that needs to be passed
    at meal time.

"Put Your Coat On"
(Sing to the tune of "Oh,
    My Darling
    Clementine")

Put your coat on.
Put your coat on.
Put your winter coat on
    now.
We are going to play
    outside.
Put your coat on right now.

Change coat to any article
    of clothing.

"Time to Go Outside"
(Sing to the tune of "When Johnny Comes Marching Home")

When it's time for us to go outside
To play, to play,
We find a place to put our toys
Away, away.
We'll march so quietly to the door.
We know exactly what's in store
When we go outside to play for a little while.

"We're Going on a Walk"
(Sing to the tune of "The Farmer in the Dell")

We're going for a walk.
We're going for a walk.
Hi-ho, the dairy-o,
We're going for a walk.

Additional verses:
What will we wear?

What will we see?
How will we go?
Who knows the way?

"Find a Partner"
(Sing to the tune of "Oh, My Darling Clementine")

Find a partner, find a partner,
Find a partner right now.
We are going for a walk.
Find a partner right now.

"Walk Along"
(Sing to the tune of "Clap Your Hands")

Walk, walk, walk along,
Walk along to the bathroom.
____ and ____ walk along,
Walk along to the bathroom.

Change "walk" to any other types of movement— jump, hop, skip, crawl.

"We're Going…."
(Sing to the tune of "Go in and out the Window")

We're going to the bathroom,
We're going to the bathroom,
We're going to the bathroom,
And then we'll wash our hands.

"It's Time to Change"
(Sing to the tune of "Hello, Everybody")

It's time to change, yes indeed,
Yes indeed, yes indeed.
It's time to change, yes indeed
Time to change groups.
    (Or, Time to go outside.)

Multimedia:

The following records can be found in educational catalogs:

1. Thomas, Marlo, & Friends. *Free to Be You and Me* [record]. Arista.

2. Palmer, Hap. *Getting to Know Myself* [record].

3. Palmer, Hap. *Ideas, Thoughts, and Feelings* [record].

4. Poelker, Kathy Lecinski. *Look at My World* [record]. Look at Me Company.

5. Rogers, Fred. *Let's Be Together Today* [record].

6. *Toddlers on Parade* [record]. Kimbo Records.

7. *Children's Songs Around the World* [record]. Alphabetical.

8. *Play-Along Games & Songs* [video]. Random House.

9. *Scruffy and Friends* [Mac/IBM/Apple Software]. Hartley. Age: 6.

Books:

The following books can be used to complement the theme:

1. Newman, Nanette. (1990). *Sharing*. New York: Doubleday and Co., Inc.

2. Daniel, Becky. (1991). *Count on Your Friends*. Carthage, IL: Good Apple.

3. Adams, Pam. (1991). *Playmates*. New York: Child's Play International.

4. Aliki. (1987). *We Are Best Friends*. New York: Morrow, William and Co., Inc.

5. dePaola, Tomie. (1992). *Bill and Pete*. New York: Putnam Publishing Group.

6. Isadora, Rachel. (1990). *Friends*. New York: Greenwillow Books.

7. Mason, Margo. (1990). *Two Good Friends*. New York: Bantam Books, Inc.

8. Rogers, Fred. (1987). *Making Friends*. New York: Putnam Publishing Group.

9. Kellogg, Steven. (1990). *Best Friends*. New York: Dial Books for Young Readers.

10. Wilheim, Hans. (1986). *Let's Be Friends Again*. New York: Crown.

11. Winthrop, Elizabeth. (1989). *The Best Friends Club*. New York: Lothrop, Lee, & Shepard.

12. Hutchins, Pat. (1989). *The Doorbell Rang*. New York: Morrow.

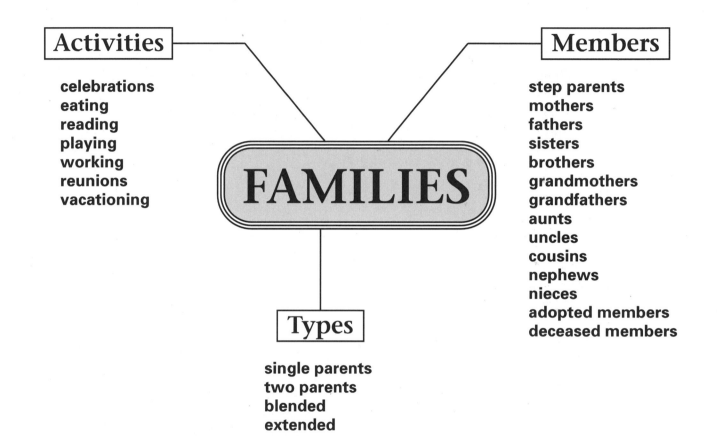

Activities

celebrations
eating
reading
playing
working
reunions
vacationing

FAMILIES

Members

step parents
mothers
fathers
sisters
brothers
grandmothers
grandfathers
aunts
uncles
cousins
nephews
nieces
adopted members
deceased members

Types

single parents
two parents
blended
extended

Theme Goals:

Through participating in the experiences provided by this theme, the children may learn:

1. The members in a family.
2. Roles of family members.
3. Family activities.

Concepts for the Children to Learn:

1. A family is a group of people who live together.
2. Mothers, fathers, sisters, and brothers are family members.
3. Grandmothers, grandfathers, aunts, uncles, cousins, nephews, and nieces are family members.
4. Camping, eating, working, reading, and watching television are all family activities.
5. Each family is a special group of people.
6. Families teach us about our world.
7. Family members care for us.
8. There are many types of families: one parent, two parent, blended, and extended.

Vocabulary:

1. **mother**—female parent.
2. **father**—male parent.
3. **children**—young people.
4. **sister**—a girl having the same parents as another person.
5. **brother**—a boy having the same parents as another person.
6. **grandmother**—mother of a parent.
7. **grandfather**—father of a parent.
8. **cousin**—son or daughter of an uncle or aunt.
9. **aunt**—sister of a parent.
10. **uncle**—brother of a parent.
11. **nephew**—son of a brother or sister.
12. **niece**—daughter of a brother or sister.
13. **love**—feeling of warmth toward another.
14. **family**—people living together.
15. **one-parent family**—a child or children who lives with only one parent, a father or mother.
16. **blended**—people from two or more families living together.
17. **extended**—includes aunts, uncles, grandparents, and cousins.

Bulletin Board

The purpose of this bulletin board is to foster awareness of various family sizes, as well as to identify family members. From tagboard construct a name card for each child. Print each child's name on one of the tagboard pieces. Then cut people figures as illustrated. Laminate the name cards and people. Staple the name cards to a bulletin board. Individually, the children can affix the people in their family after their name using tape, sticky putty, or a stapler.

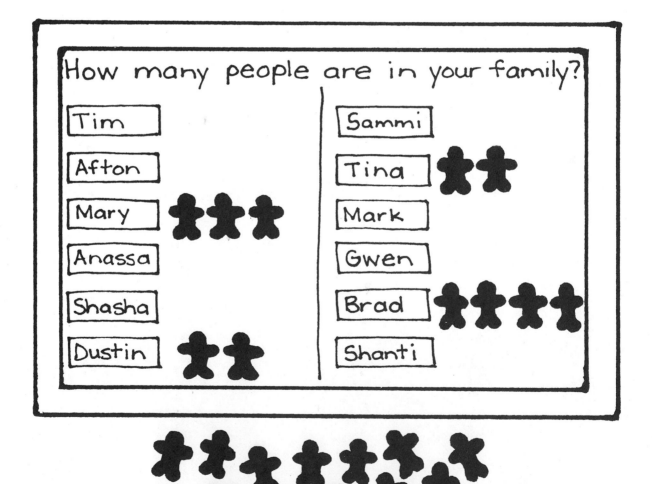

Parent Letter

Dear Parents,

Our next unit will focus on families. Through this unit, the children will develop an understanding of various family patterns. They will also discover what family members do for each other, as well as activities that families can participate in together.

At School

A few of this unit's highlights include:

- creating pictures of our families on a bulletin board.
- looking at photographs of classmates' families. To assist us with this unit, please send a picture of your family to school with your child. We will place the photograph in a special photo album to look at in the reading area.

At Home

There are several activities you can do at home to foster the concepts of this unit. Begin by looking through family photographs with your child. While doing this discuss family traditions or customs. You can also encourage your child to dictate a letter to you to write to a grandparent or other relative. Plan and participate in a family activity. This could be as simple as taking a walk together or going on a picnic.

We invite you and your family to visit us. This includes moms, dads, brothers, sisters, grandparents, and other relatives! If you are interested in coming, please let me know!

From all of us,

Families are an important part of life.

Music:

"Family Helper"
(Sing to the tune of "Here We Are Together")

It's fun to be a helper, a helper, a helper.
It's fun to be a helper, just any time.
Oh, I can set the table, the table, the table.
Oh, I can set the table at dinner time.
Oh, I can dry the dishes, the dishes, the dishes.
Oh, I can dry the dishes, and make them shine.

Fingerplays:

MY FAMILY

If you peek in my room at night,
(stand on toes as if peeking)
My family you will see,
(nod head)

They kiss my face and tuck me in tight,
(kiss into the air)
Why? Because they love me!
(hug yourself)

SEE MY FAMILY

See my family? See them all?
(hold up all five fingers)
Some are short
(hold up thumb)
Some are tall
(hold up middle finger)

Let's shake hands. "How do you do?"
(grasp hands and shake)
See them bow? "How are you?"
(bend fingers)

Father,
(hold up middle finger)
Mother,
(hold up pointer finger)
Sister,
(hold up ring finger)
Brother
(hold up thumb)
And me.
(hold up pinky finger)

THIS IS THE MOTHER

This is the mother, kind and dear.
(make a fist then point to the thumb)
This is the father sitting near.
(show each finger in turn)
This is the brother strong and tall.
This is the sister, who plays with her ball.
This is the baby, the littlest of all.
See my whole family large and small?
(wiggle all fingers)

I LOVE MY FAMILY

Some families are large.
(spread arms out wide)
Some families are small.
(bring arms close together)
But I love my family
(cross arms over chest)
Best of all!

A GOOD HOUSE

This is the roof of the house so good.
    (make roof with hands)
These are the walls that are made of wood.
    (hands straight, palms parallel)
These are the windows that let in the light.
    (thumbs and forefingers form window)
This is the door that shuts so tight.
    (hands straight by side)
This is the chimney so straight and tall.
    (arms up straight)
Oh! What a good house for one and all!

All fingerplays taken from Cromwell, Faitel & Hibner. (1983). *Finger Frolics: Fingerplays for Young Children*. Michigan: Partner Press.

Science:

1. **Sounds**

   Tape different sounds from around the house that families hear daily, such as a crying baby, brushing teeth, telephone ringing, toilet flushing, doorbell ringing, water running, electric shaver, alarm clock, etc. Play the tape for the children to identify the correct sound.

2. **Feely Box**

   Place objects pertaining to a family into a box. Include items such as a baby rattle, a toothbrush, a comb, baby bottle, etc. The children feel the objects and try to identify them.

3. **Animal Families**

   Gerbils or hamsters with young babies in a cage can be placed on the science table. Observe daily to see how they raise their babies. Compare the animal behavior to the children's own families.

Dramatic Play:

1. **Baby Clothing**

   Arrange the dramatic play area for washing baby dolls. Include a tub with soapy water,

washcloths, drying towels, play clothes, brush, and comb.

2. **Family Picnic**

   Collect items to make a picnic basket. Include paper napkins, cups, plates, plastic eating utensils, etc.

3. **Dollhouse**

   Set up a large dollhouse for children to play with. These can be constructed from cardboard. Include dolls to represent several members of a family.

Arts and Crafts:

1. **Family Collage**

   The children can cut out pictures of people from magazines. The pictures can be pasted on a sheet of paper to make a collage.

2. **My Body**

   Trace each child's body on a large piece of paper. The children can use crayons and felt-tip markers to color their own body picture. When finished, display the pictures around the room or in the center's entrance.

Sensory:

1. Washing baby dolls in lukewarm, soapy water
2. Washing dishes in warm water
3. Washing doll clothes and hanging them up to dry
4. Cars and houses placed on top of several inches of sand

Large Muscle:

Neighborhood Walk

Take a walk through a neighborhood and have children identify different homes. Observe the colors and sizes of the homes.

Resource People:

Family Day

Invite moms, dads, sisters, brothers, grand-fathers, grandmothers, and other family members to a tea at your center.

Math:

1. **Families—Biggest to Smallest**

   Cut out from magazines several members of a family. The children can place the members from largest to smallest, and then smallest to largest. They can also identify each family member as the biggest and the smallest.

2. **Family Member Chart**

   Graph the number of family members for each child's family in the classroom.

Social Studies:

Family Pictures

1. Display posters of all types of families. Discuss at group time ways that families help and care for each other.

2. Ask each child to bring in a family picture. Label each child's picture and place on a special bulletin board with the caption, "Our Families."

3. Discuss the Muslim celebration of Ramadan. Each year Muslims around the world observe the religious period of Ramadan by refraining from food, water, television, and other activities from sunrise to sunset. The fasting lasts for 28 days. Fasting teaches patience, discipline, and humility. Families and friends gather before sunrise (*Suhour*) and after sunset for meals. When it is time to break the fast (*Iftar*), the first thing one should eat is dates. Children learn that the Prophet Mohammed broke his fast on dates. Families then mostly have soup, because it is easy on the stomach and also helps rehydrate the thirsty.

Group Time (games, language):

A Hundred Ways to Get There

During outdoor play or large group, form a large circle. Begin the game by choosing a child to cross the circle by skipping, hopping, jumping, crawling, running, etc. Once the circle has been crossed the child takes the place of another person who then goes across the circle in another manner. Each child can try to think of something new.

Cooking:

1. **Peanut Butter and Jelly**

   Cut whole wheat bread into house shapes for snack one day. Put peanut butter, raisins, and jelly on the table with knives. Let children choose their own topping.

2. **Gingerbread Families**

   Use the following recipe to create gingerbread families.

   1 1/2 cups whole wheat pastry flour
   1 teaspoon baking soda
   1/2 teaspoon salt
   1/2 teaspoon ginger
   1 teaspoon cinnamon
   1/4 cup oil
   1/4 cup maple syrup
   1/4 cup honey
   1 large egg

   Preheat oven to 350 degrees. Measure all of the dry ingredients into a bowl and mix well. Measure all wet ingredients into a second bowl and mix well. Add the two mixtures together. Pour the combined mixture into an 8-inch square pan and bake for 30 to 35 minutes. When cool, roll the gingerbread dough into thin slices and provide cookie cutters for children to cut their family. Decorate the figures with raisins, peanut butter, wheat germ, etc. Enjoy for snack time.

3. Raisin Bran Muffins

4 cups raisin bran cereal
2 1/2 cups all-purpose flour
1 cup sugar
1/2 cup chopped walnuts
2 1/2 teaspoons baking soda
1 teaspoon salt
2 eggs, beaten
2 cups buttermilk
1/2 cup cooking oil

Stir the cereal, flour, sugar, nuts, baking soda, and salt together in a large mixing bowl. In a separate bowl beat the eggs, buttermilk, and oil together. Add this mixture to the dry ingredients and stir until moistened. The batter will be thick. Spoon the batter into greased or lined muffin cups, filling 3/4 full. Bake in a 375-degree oven for 20 to 25 minutes and remove from pans.

4. Kabbat hamudth (Meatball soup served during Ramadan, a Muslim celebration)

For the meatballs:

1 pound choice ground beef
14-oz. box cream of rice
1/2 teaspoon salt

Combine ingredients and mix well. Add a little water if necessary. Puree in small batches. Divide mixture into 30 balls. Cover and chill.

For the stuffing:

1 medium onion, chopped
1/2 pound choice ground beef
1 cup drained chickpeas, cut in half
1/4 cup chopped fresh parsley
1 scant teaspoon ground allspice

Brown onions and beef in a 10-inch skillet. Drain fat and add remaining stuffing ingredients. Set aside.

To form meatballs flatten each ball with your fingertips. Place 2–3 teaspoons of the stuffing in the center and reform beef into a ball around the stuffing. Cover and chill.

For the soup:

2–3 medium onions, quartered
1 pound turnips, chopped
2 tablespoons olive oil
16 cups beef broth
1 pound Swiss chard, coarsely chopped
1 cup drained canned chickpeas
1 teaspoon ground allspice (optional)
Salt and pepper to taste
3–4 tablespoons finely chopped fresh mint
    leaves or 2 teaspoons dried
1/2 cup lemon juice

Sauté onions and turnips in olive oil until onions are translucent. Bring broth to boil, lower heat, add onions, turnips, Swiss chard, and chickpeas. Season with allspice, salt, and pepper. Simmer until turnips are soft. Add mint and lemon juice. About 20 minutes before serving add meatballs.

Serve in bowls with 2–3 meatballs per serving. Caution must be taken regarding the temperature of the soup.

SNACK IDEAS

MILK

1. Dips (yogurt, cottage cheese, cream cheese)
2. Cheese (balls, wedges, cutouts, squares, faces, etc.)
3. Yogurt and fruit
4. Milk punches made with fruits and juices
5. Conventional cocoa
6. Cottage cheese (add pineapple, peaches, etc.)
7. Cheese fondues (pre-heated, no open flames in classroom)
8. Shakes (mix fruit and milk in a blender)

MEAT

1. Meat strips, chunks, cubes (beef, pork, chicken, turkey, ham, fish)

2. Meatballs, small kabobs
3. Meat roll-ups (cheese spread, mashed potatoes, spinach, lettuce leaves, or tortillas)
4. Meat salads (tuna, other fish, chicken, turkey, etc.) as spreads for crackers, stuffing for celery, rolled in spinach or lettuce
5. Sardines
6. Stuffing for potatoes, tomatoes, squash

EGGS

1. Hard boiled
2. Deviled (use different flavors)
3. Egg salad spread
4. Eggs any style that can be managed
5. Egg as a part of other recipes
6. Eggnog

FRUITS

1. Use standard fruits, but be adventurous: pomegranates, cranberries, pears, peaches, apricots, plums, berries, pineapples, melons, grapes, grapefruit, tangerines
2. Kabobs and salads
3. Juices and juice blends
4. In muffins, yogurt, milk beverages
5. Fruit "sandwiches"
6. Stuffed dates, prunes, etc.
7. Dried fruits (raisins, currants, prunes, apples, peaches, apricots, dates, figs)

VEGETABLES

1. Variety—sweet and white potatoes, cherry tomatoes, broccoli, cauliflower, radishes, peppers, mushrooms, zucchini, all squashes, rutabaga, avocados, eggplant, okra, pea pods, turnips, pumpkin, sprouts, spinach
2. Almost any vegetable can be served raw with or without dip
3. Salads, kabobs, cutouts
4. Juices and juice blends
5. Soup in a cup (hot or cold)
6. Stuffed—celery, cucumbers, zucchini, spinach, lettuce, cabbage, squash, potatoes, tomatoes
7. Vegetable spreads
8. Sandwiches

DRIED PEAS AND BEANS

1. Peanuts, kidney beans, garbanzos, limas, lentils, yellow and green peas, pintos, black beans
2. Beans and peas mashed as dips or spreads
3. Bean, pea, or lentil soup in a cup
4. Roasted soybean-peanut mix
5. Three-bean salad

PASTAS

1. Different shapes and thicknesses
2. Pasta with butter and poppy seeds

3. Cold pasta salad
4. Lasagne noodles (cut for small sandwiches)
5. Chow mein noodles (wheat or rice)

BREADS

1. Use a variety of grains—whole wheat, cracked wheat, rye, cornmeal, oatmeal, bran, grits, etc.
2. Use a variety of breads—tortillas, pocket breads, crepes, pancakes, muffins, biscuits, bagels, popovers, English muffins
3. Toast—plain, buttered, with spreads, cinnamon
4. Homemade yeast and quick breads
5. Fill and roll up crepes, pancakes
6. Waffle sandwiches

CEREALS, GRAINS, SEEDS

1. Granola
2. Slices of rice loaf or rice cakes
3. Dry cereal mixes (not pre-sweetened)
4. Seed mixes (pumpkin, sunflower, sesame, poppy, caraway, etc.)
5. Roasted wheat berries, wheat germ, bran as roll-ins, toppers, or as finger mix
6. Popcorn with toppers of grated cheese, flavored butters, mixed nuts
7. Stir into muffins or use as a topper

Multimedia:

The following resources can be found in educational catalogs:

1. Rogers, Fred. *A Place of Our Own* [record].

2. "Around the House" on *Sounds Around Us* [record]. Glenview, IL: Scott Foresman.

3. *The Sleepy Family* [record]. New York: Young People's Records.

4. *Small Voice, Big Voice with Dick, Laurie, and Jed* [record]. Folkway Records and Service Corp.

5. *The Playroom* [Apple/IBM/Mac software, PK-2]. Broderbund.

6. *Learning to Tell Time* [video]. Tele-Story.

Books:

The following books can be used to complement the theme:

1. Greenspun, Adele A. (1991). *Daddies*. New York: Putnam Publishing Group.

2. Hallinan, P. K. (1990). *We're Very Good Friends, My Father and I*. Nashville, TN: Ideals Publishing Corp.

3. Hallinan, P. K. (1990). *We're Very Good Friends, My Mother and I*. Nashville, TN: Ideals Publishing Corp.

4. Corey, Dorothy. (1992). *Will There Be a Lap for Me?* Morton Grove, IL: Albert Whitman and Co.

5. Asch, Frank, & Vagin, Vladmir. (1992). *Dear Brother*. New York: Scholastic, Inc.

6. Birdseye, Tom. (1991). *Waiting for Baby*. New York: Holiday House, Inc.

7. Franklin, Jonathan. (1991). *Don't Wake Baby*. New York: Farrar, Straus and Giroux, Inc.

8. Holabird, Katharine. (1991). *Angelina's Baby Sister*. New York: Crown Books for Young Readers.

9. Hutchins, Pat. (1992). *Silly Billy*. New York: Greenwillow Books.

10. Levinson, Riki. (1991). *Me Baby!* New York: Dutton Children's Books.

11. Mcphail, David. (1990). *Sisters*. San Diego: Harcourt Brace Jovanovich.

12. Steptoe, John. (1992). *Baby Says*. New York: William Morrow and Co.

13. Henkes, Kevin. (1990). *Julius, The Baby of the World*. New York: Greenwillow.

14. Crews, Donald. (1991). *Big Mama's*. New York: Greenwillow.

15. Dorros, Arthur. (1992). *This Is My House*. New York: Scholastic.

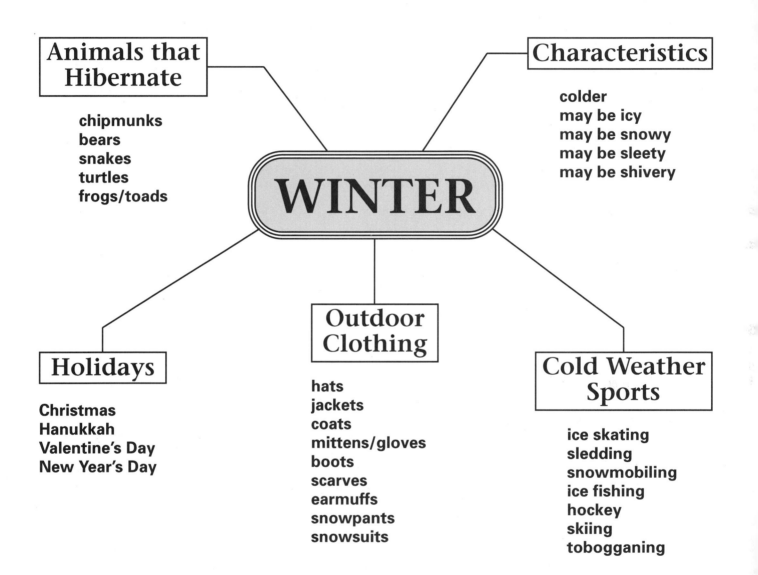

Animals that Hibernate

chipmunks
bears
snakes
turtles
frogs/toads

Characteristics

colder
may be icy
may be snowy
may be sleety
may be shivery

WINTER

Holidays

Christmas
Hanukkah
Valentine's Day
New Year's Day

Outdoor Clothing

hats
jackets
coats
mittens/gloves
boots
scarves
earmuffs
snowpants
snowsuits

Cold Weather Sports

ice skating
sledding
snowmobiling
ice fishing
hockey
skiing
tobogganing

Theme Goals:

Through participating in the experiences provided by this theme, the children may learn:

1. Winter holidays.
2. Characteristics of winter weather.
3. Winter sports.
4. Winter clothing.
5. Hibernating animals.

Concepts for the Children to Learn:

1. Winter is one of the four seasons.
2. Winter is usually the coldest season.
3. It snows in the winter in some areas.
4. People wear warmer clothes in the winter.
5. Some animals hibernate in the winter.
6. Trees may lose their leaves in the winter.
7. Lakes, ponds, and water may freeze in the winter.
8. Sledding, skiing, toboganning, and ice skating are winter sports in colder areas.
9. To remove snow, people shovel and plow.
10. December, January, and February are winter months.

Vocabulary:

1. **ice**—frozen water.
2. **cold**—not warm.
3. **frost**—very small ice pieces.
4. **snow**—frozen particles of water that fall to the ground.
5. **temperature**—how hot or cold something is.
6. **sleet**—mixture of rain and snow.
7. **hibernate**—to sleep during the winter.
8. **snowperson**—snow shaped in the form of a person.
9. **ski**—a runner that moves over snow and ice.
10. **icicle**—a hanging piece of frozen ice.
11. **sled**—transportation for moving over snow and ice.
12. **boots**—clothing worn on feet to keep them dry and warm.
13. **shiver**—to shake from cold or fear.

Bulletin Board

The purpose of this bulletin board is to provide the children with an opportunity to match patterns. Construct several pairs of mittens out of tagboard, each with a different pattern, as illustrated. Laminate them. On the bulletin board, string one of each pair of the mittens through a rope or clothesline (one or two rows). Tie enough clothespins in place by putting the line through the wire spring of the clip clothespins to put up the matching mittens. (Tie the clothespins beside the first mitten.) Children can match the mittens by hanging the second next to the first with a clothespin. This is a good matching exercise for twos, who sometimes need help with the clothespins. It is mainly a small motor exercise for older children, unless you make the mittens fairly similar so that finding the correct pairs is a more difficult task.

Parent Letter

Dear Parents,

We are beginning a unit on winter. The children will be learning about the coldest season by taking a look at winter clothing, changes that occur during this season indoors and outdoors, and winter sports. Throughout the unit, the children will develop an awareness of winter activities.

At School

Some of our learning experiences related to winter include:

- creating cottonball snowpeople.
- sorting mittens by size, shape, and color.
- enjoying stories about winter.
- setting up an ice-skating rink in the dramatic play area.
- experiencing snow and ice in the sensory table.

At Home [Delete this paragraph if snow is unavailable.]

To experience winter at home, try this activity—snow in the bathtub! Bring in some snow from outside and place in your bathtub. Also place some measuring cups, spoons, and scoops in the bathtub and let your child use mittens to play in the snow. In addition, a spray bottle filled with colored water (made with food coloring) will allow your child to make colorful sculptures. This is sure to keep your children busy and will develop an awareness of the senses.

From all of us!

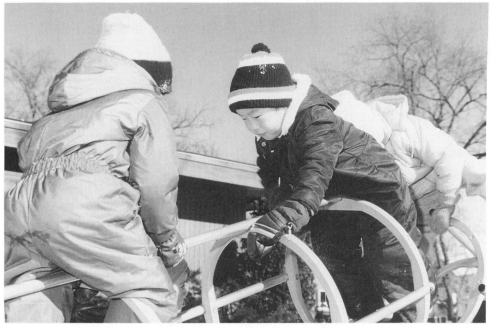

Some children live in areas where there is no snow in the winter.

Music:

1. **"Snowperson"**
   (Sing to the tune of "Twinkle, Twinkle, Little Star")

   Snowperson, snowperson, where did you go?
   I built you yesterday out of snow.
   I built you high and I built you fat.
   I put on eyes and a nose and a hat.
   Now you're gone all melted away
   But it's sunny outside so I'll go and play.

2. **"Winter Clothes"**
   (Sing to the tune of "Did you Ever See a Lassie?")

   Children put your coats on, your coats on, your coats on.
   Children put your coats on, one, two, and three.

   (hats, boots, mittens, etc.)

3. **"Mitten Song"**

   Thumbs in the thumb place, fingers all together.
   This is the song we sing in mitten weather.

Fingerplays:

FIVE LITTLE SNOWPEOPLE

Five little snowpeople standing in the door.
This one melted and then there were four.
   (hold up all five fingers, put down thumb)
Four little snowpeople underneath a tree.
This one melted and then there were three.
   (put down pointer finger)
Three little snowpeople with hats and mittens too.
This one melted and then there were two.
   (put down middle finger)
Two little snowpeople outside in the sun.
This one melted and then there was one.
   (put down ring finger)
One little snowperson trying hard to run.
He melted too, and then there were none.
   (put down pinky)

Variations:
- Make five little snowpeople finger puppets and remove them one by one.
- Make five stick puppets for children to hold and sit down one by one at appropriate times during fingerplay.

MAKING A SNOWPERSON

Roll it, roll it, get a pile of snow.
    (make rolling motions with hands)
Rolling, rolling, rolling, rolling, rolling here we go.
Pat it, pat it, face it to the south.
    (patting motion)
Now my little snowperson's done, eyes and nose and mouth.
    (point to eyes, nose and mouth)

ZIPPERS

Three little zippers on my snowsuit,
    (hold up three fingers)
Fasten up as snug as snug can be
It's a very easy thing as you can see
Just zip, zip, zip!
    (do three zipping motions)
I work the zippers on my snowsuit.
Zippers really do save time for me
I can fasten them myself with one, two, three.
Just zip, zip, zip!
    (do three zipping motions)

THE SNOWPERSON AND THE BUNNY

A chubby little snowperson
    (make a fist)
Had a carrot nose.
    (poke thumb out)
Along came a bunny
And what do you suppose?
    (other hand, make rabbit ears)
That hungry little bunny
Looking for his lunch
    (bunny hops around)
Ate that snowperson's carrot nose.
    (bunny nibbles at thumb)
Crunch, crunch, crunch.

BUILD A SNOWPERSON

First you make a snowball,
    (rolling motion)
Big and fat and round.
    (extend arms in large circle)
Then you roll the snowball,
    (rolling motion)
All along the ground.
Then you build the snowperson

One-two-three!
    (place three pretend balls on top of each other)
Then you have a snowperson,
Don't you see?
    (point to eyes)
Then the sun shines all around and
Melts the snowperson to the ground.
    (drop to the ground in a melting motion)

Science:

1. **Weather Doll**

   Make a felt weather doll. Encourage the children to dress and undress the doll according to the weather.

2. **Make Frost**

   Changes in temperature cause dew. When dew freezes it is called frost. Materials needed are a tin can with no lid, rock salt, and crushed ice. Measure and pour 2 cups of crushed ice and 1/2 cup rock salt in a can. Stir rapidly. Let the mixture sit for 30 minutes. After 30 minutes, the outside of the can will have dew on it. Wait longer and the dew will change to frost. To hasten the process, place in a freezer.

3. **Make Birdfeeders**

   Roll pinecones in peanut butter and then bird-seed. Attach a string to the pinecones and hang them outside. Encourage the children to check the birdfeeders frequently.

   A birdfeeder can also be prepared from suet. To do this, wrap suet in a netting. Gather the edges up and tie together with a long string. Another method is to place suet in a net citrus fruit bag.

4. **Snow**

   Bring a large container of snow into the class-room. After it is melted, add colored water and place the container outdoors. When frozen, bring a colored block of ice back into the class-room and observe it melt.

5. **Examine Snowflakes**

Examine snowflakes with a magnifying glass. Each is unique. For classrooms located in warmer climates, make a snow-like substance by crushing ice.

6. **Catching Snowflakes**

Cover a piece of cardboard with dark felt. Place the cardboard piece in the freezer. Go outside and let snowflakes land on the board. Snowflakes will last longer for examination.

7. **Coloring Snow**

Provide children with spray bottles containing colored water, preferably red, yellow, and blue. Allow them to spray the snow and mix colors.

8. **Thermometers**

Experiment with a thermometer. Begin introducing the concept by observing and discussing what happens when the thermometer is placed in a bowl of warm water and a bowl of cold water. Demonstrate to the children and encourage them to experiment under supervision during the self-selected activity period.

9. **Signs and Sounds of Winter**

On a winter walk in colder climates have the children watch and listen for signs and sounds of winter. The signs of winter are weather: cold, ice, daylight is shorter, darkness is earlier; plants: all but evergreen trees are bare; and people: we wear warmer clothes, we play inside more, we shovel snow, we play in the snow. Some of the sounds of winter are: boots crunching, rain splashing, wind howling, etc. (Adapt this activity to the signs of winter in your climate.)

Dramatic Play:

1. **Ice-skating Palace**

Make a masking tape border on a carpeted floor. Give child 2 pieces of waxed paper. Show children how to fasten waxed paper to their ankles with rubber bands. Play instrumental music and encourage the children to skate around on the carpeted floor.

2. **Dress Up**

If available, put outdoor winter clothing such as coats, boots, hats, mittens, scarves, and earmuffs in the dramatic play area of the classroom with a large mirror. The children may enjoy trying on a variety of clothing items.

Arts and Crafts:

1. **Whipped Soap Painting**

Mix 1 cup Ivory Snow flakes with 1/2 cup warm water in bowl. The children can beat with a hand eggbeater until mixture is fluffy. Apply mixture to dark construction paper with various tools (toothbrushes, rollers, tongue depressors, brushes, etc.). To create variety, food coloring can be added to paint mixture.

2. **Cottonball Snowperson**

Cut a snowperson figure from dark construction paper. Provide the children with cottonballs and glue. They can decorate the snowperson by gluing on cottonballs.

3. **Snowflakes**

Cut different-sized squares out of white construction paper. Fold the squares in half, and then in half again. Demonstrate and encourage the children to cut and open their own designs. The snowflakes can be hung in the entry or classroom for decoration.

4. **Windowpane Frost**

On a piece of construction paper, draw an outline of a window. Spread glue around and on the frame and sprinkle with glitter.

5. **Winter Mobile**

Cut out pictures of winter from magazines or have children create their own winter pictures. Attach several pictures with string or yarn to a branch, hanger (masking taped), or paper plate. Glitter can be added.

6. **Ice Cube Art**

Place a popsicle stick in each ice compartment of a tray and fill with water. Freeze. Sprinkle dry tempera paint on paper. Then to make their own design, the children can move an ice cube on the paper.

7. **Frosted Pictures**

Mix 1 part Epsom salts with 1 part boiling water. Let the mixture cool. Encourage the children to make a crayon design on paper. The mixture can be brushed over the picture. Observe how the crystals form as the mixture dries.

8. **Winter Shape Printing**

Cut sponges into various winter shapes such as boots, snowmen, mittens, snowflakes, fir trees, and stars. The children can use the sponges as a tool to print on different pieces of colored construction paper.

9. **Easel Ideas**

Feature white paint at the easel for snow pictures on colored paper. Or, cut easel paper into winter shapes: snowmen, hats, mittens, scarves, snowflakes, etc.

10. **Snow Drawings**

White chalk and dark construction paper can be placed in the art area.

11. **Snow Painting**

Using old spray bottles filled with colored water, let the children make pictures in the snow outside. This activity is limited to areas where snow is available.

Sensory:

The following items can be placed in the sensory table.

- snow and ice (plain or colored with drops of food coloring)
- cottonballs with measuring/balancing scale
- pinecones
- ice cubes (colored or plain)
- snow and magnifying glasses

Large Muscle:

1. **Freeze**

Play music and have the children walk around in a circle. When the music stops, the children freeze by standing still in a stooped position. Vary the activity by substituting other actions such as hopping, skipping, galloping, sliding, etc.

2. **Snowperson**

During outdoor play make a snowperson. Decorate with radish eyes, carrot nose, scarf, hat, and holding a stick. Other novel accessories can be substituted by using the children's ideas.

3. **Snowpeople**

After a snowfall, have the children lie down in the snow and move their arms and legs to make shapes.

4. **Snowball Target**

Since children love throwing snowballs, set up a target outside for children to throw at.

5. **Shovel**

Provide child-sized shovels for the children to help shovel a walk.

6. **Balance**

Make various tracks in the snow, such as a straight line, a zig-zag line, a circle, square, triangle, and rectangle.

Field Trips/Resource People:

1. Visit an ice-skating rink. Observe the ice and watch how it is cleaned.

2. Visit a sledding hill. Bring sleds along and go sledding.

3. Invite a snowplow operator to school to talk to the children. After a snowfall, the children can observe the plowing.

4. Take the children to a grocery store and view the freezer area. Also, observe a refrigerated delivery truck.

Math:

1. **Shape Sequence**

   Cut three different-sized white circles from construction paper for each child to make a snowperson. Which is the largest? Smallest? How many do you have? What shape? Then have children sequence the circles from largest to smallest and smallest to largest.

2. **Mitten Match**

   From construction paper or tagboard design and cut several pairs of mittens. On one pair of mittens write a numeral and on the other, the corresponding number of dots. The children can match the dots to the numerals locating the pairs of mittens.

3. **Winter Dominoes**

   Trace and cut 30 squares out of white tagboard. Section each square into four spaces diagonally. In each of the four spaces, draw different winter objects or stick winter stickers on. The children can match the pictures by playing dominoes.

4. **Dot to Dot**

   Make a dot-to-dot snowperson. The children connect the dots in numerical order. You can also make dot-to-dot patterns of other winter objects such as hats, snowflakes, mittens, etc. This activity requires numeral recognition and order, so it is restricted to the school-aged child.

5. **Puzzles**

   Mount winter pictures or posters on tagboard sheets. Cut into pieces. The number of pieces cut will be dependent upon the children's developmental age. Place in the small manipulative area of the classroom for use during self-selected activity periods.

Social Studies:

1. **Travel**

   Discuss ways people travel in winter such as sled, toboggan, snowmobile, snowshoes, skis, etc.

2. **Winter Happenings**

   Display pictures of different winter happenings, sports, clothing, snow, etc., around the room at the children's eye level.

3. **Winter Book**

   Encourage the children to make a book about winter. Do one page a day. The following titles could be used:

   - What I wear in winter.
   - What I like to do outside in winter.
   - What I like to do inside in winter.
   - My favorite food during winter.
   - My favorite thing about winter.
   (This activity may be more appropriate for the school-aged child.)

4. **Winter Clothing Match**

   Draw a large paper figure of a boy and of a girl. Design and cut winter clothing to fit each figure. The children can dress the figures for outdoor play.

Group Time (games, language):

1. **Who Has the Mitten?**

   Ask the children to sit in a circle. One child should sit in the middle. Make a very small mitten out of felt or construction paper. Tell the children to pass the mitten around the circle. All the children should imitate the passing actions even if they do not have the mitten in hand. When the verse starts the child in the middle tries to guess who has the mitten. Chant the following verse while passing a mitten.

   I pass the mitten from me to you,
   I pass the mitten and that is what I do.

2. Hat Chart

Prepare a hat chart by listing all the types and colors of hats worn by the children in the classroom.

Cooking:

1. Banana Snowpeople

2 cups raisins
2 bananas
shredded coconut

Chop the bananas and raisins in a blender. Then place them in a mixing bowl. Refrigerate until mixture is cool enough to be handled. Roll the mixture into balls and into shredded coconut. Stack three balls and fasten with toothpicks.

2. Hot Chocolate

Add warm water or milk to instant hot chocolate and mix. Heat as needed.

3. Snow Cones

Crush ice and spoon into small paper cups. Pour a fruit juice over the ice. Serve.

4. Snowballs—China

1/4 cup walnuts, ground
1/4 cup almonds, ground
1/4 cup sesame seeds, toasted
1/2 cup sugar
1 tablespoon shortening
1 pound glutenous rice flour

In a bowl, mix nuts, sesame seeds, sugar, and shortening. Form mixture into 1/2-inch balls. Fill a big mixing bowl with 1/2-inch layer of rice flour. Moisten the nut balls by dipping them into water. Place balls individually in floured bowl and shake bowl back and forth, coating the balls with flour. Redip coated balls in water and coat three times. Slip balls into boiling water and gently boil for about 5 minutes until balls float to the surface. Add a cup of cold water and boil for about 3 to 4 minutes. Serve about 4 to each person along with the hot liquid. This activity requires supervision.

Multimedia:

The following records can be found in educational catalogs:

1. Jenkins, Ella. *Seasons for Singing* [record].

2. "Alpine Blizzard," *Environment* [record]. Syntonic Research, Inc.

Books:

The following books can be used to complement the theme:

1. Neitzel, Shirley. (1993). *The Jacket I Wear in the Snow*. New York: Morrow.

2. London, Jonathan. (1993). *The Owl Who Became the Moon*. New York: Dutton.

3. Cowcher, Helen. (1990). *Antarctica*. New York: Farrar, Straus & Giroux.

4. Martin, Bill, Jr. (1991). *Polar Bear, Polar Bear What Do You Hear?* New York: Henry Holt.

5. Sing, Rachel. (1992). *Chinese New Year's Dragon*. Cleveland, OH: Modern Curriculum Press.

6. Tran, Kim-Lan. (1992). *Têt: The New Year*. Cleveland, OH: Modern Curriculum Press.

7. Hoban, Julia. (1993). *Amy Loves the Snow*. New York: Harper Collins.

8. Keown, Elizabeth. (1992). *Emily's Snowball: The World's Biggest*. New York: Macmillan.

9. Tibo, Gilles. (1991). *Simon and the Snowflakes*. Plattsburgh, NY: Tundra Books.

10. Chlad, Dorothy. (1991). *Playing Outdoors in the Winter*. Chicago: Children's Press.

11. Fowler, Allan. (1991). *How Do You Know It's Winter?* Chicago: Children's Press.

12. Good, Elaine W. (1991). *White Wonderful Winter*. Intercourse, PA: Good Books.

13. Hirschi, Ron. (1990). *Winter*. New York: Dutton Children's Books.

14. Moncure, Jane B. (1990). *Step into Winter: A New Season*. Mankato, MN: Child's World, Inc.

15. Adams, Pam. (1990). *On a Cold and Frosty Morning*. New York: Child's Play—International.

16. Blades, Ann. (1990). *Winter*. New York: Lothrop, Lee, & Shepard Books.

17. Ewart, Claire. (1992). *One Cold Night*. New York: Putnam Publishing Group.

18. Erickson, Gina, & Foster, Kelli C. (1991). *The Sled Surprise*. Hauppauge, NY: Barron's Educational Series, Inc.

19. Lewis, Rob. (1990). *Henrietta's First Winter*. New York: Farrar, Straus and Giroux, Inc.

20. Rice, Eve. (1993). *Oh, Lewis!* New York: William Morrow and Co., Inc.

21. Stevenson, James. (1991). *Brrr!* New York: Greenwillow Books.

22. Velthuijs, Max. (1993). *Frog in Winter*. New York: William Morrow and Co., Inc.

23. Sanchez, Isidro, & Peris, Carme. (1992). *Winter Sports*. Hauppauge, NY: Barron's Educational Series, Inc.

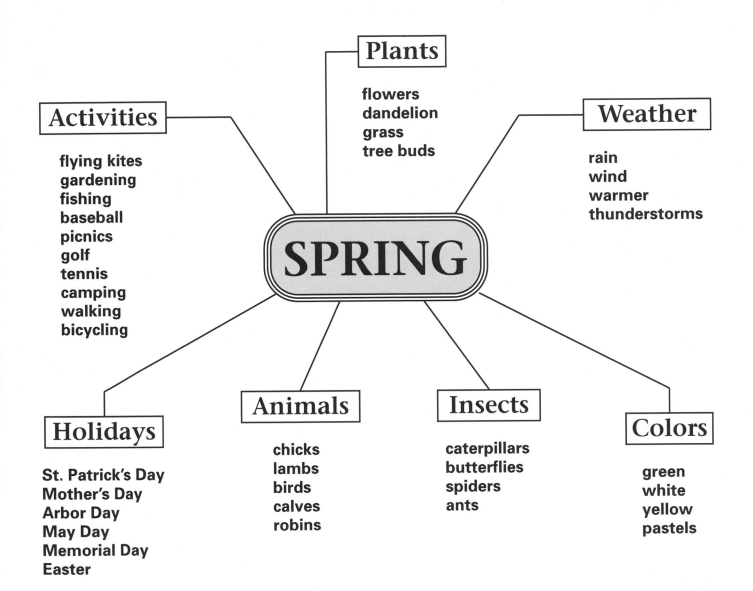

Plants

flowers
dandelion
grass
tree buds

Activities

flying kites
gardening
fishing
baseball
picnics
golf
tennis
camping
walking
bicycling

Weather

rain
wind
warmer
thunderstorms

SPRING

Holidays

St. Patrick's Day
Mother's Day
Arbor Day
May Day
Memorial Day
Easter

Animals

chicks
lambs
birds
calves
robins

Insects

caterpillars
butterflies
spiders
ants

Colors

green
white
yellow
pastels

Theme Goals:

Through participating in the experiences provided by this theme, the children may learn:

1. Spring colors.

2. Spring weather.

3. Plants that grow in the spring.

4. Insects seen during the spring.

5. Springtime holidays.

6. Spring animals.

7. Spring activities.

Concepts for the Children to Learn:

1. Spring is a season.

2. It rains in the spring.

3. Light colors are seen during the spring.

4. Caterpillars and butterflies are insects seen in the spring.

5. Some holidays are celebrated in the spring: Mother's Day, Easter, St. Patrick's Day, May Day, Arbor Day, and Memorial Day.

6. Chicks, lambs, and birds are springtime animals.

7. Some people go on picnics in the spring.

8. Many gardens are planted in the spring.

9. Flowers, dandelions, and grass are spring plants.

Vocabulary:

1. **spring**—the season that comes after winter and before summer.

2. **garden**—a place where plants and flowers are grown.

3. **rain**—water from the clouds.

Bulletin Board

The purpose of this bulletin board is to have the children place the proper number of ribbons on each kite tail. To do this, they need to look at the number of dots on the kite. Construct kites and print the numerals beginning with one and the corresponding number of dots on each. Construct ribbons for the tails of the kites as illustrated. Color the kites and tails and laminate. Staple kites to bulletin board. Affix magnetic strips to each kite as the string. Affix a magnetic piece in the middle of each ribbon.

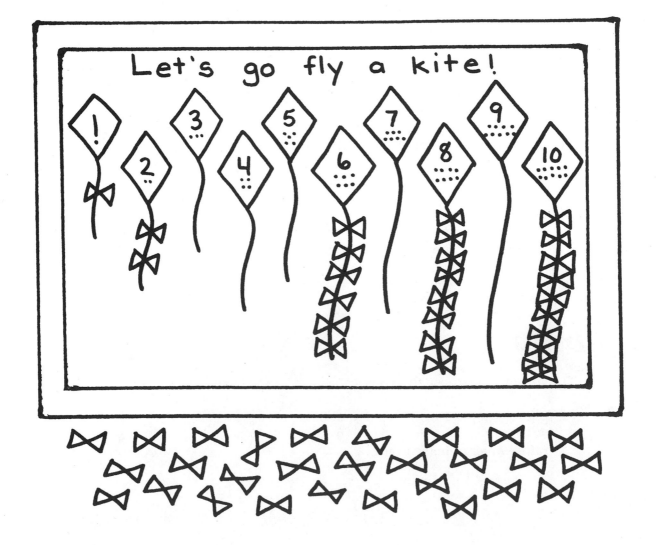

Parent Letter

Dear Parents,

The temperature is slowly rising, and there are patches of green grass on the playground. In other words, spring is here! And spring is the subject we will be exploring at school. Throughout the week, the children will become more aware of the many changes that take place during this season, as well as common spring activities.

At School

Some of the learning experiences for this curriculum unit include:

- finding a suitable place on the playground to plant flowers.
- taking a walk around the neighborhood to observe signs of spring.
- planting grass seed in empty eggshells at the science table.
- creating pictures and designs with pastel watercolor markers in the art area.

At Home

To foster concepts of spring at home, save seeds from fruits such as oranges and apples. Assist your child in planting the seeds. Your child can also sort the seeds by color, size, or type to develop classification skills. The seeds could also be used for counting. Happy seed collecting!

Enjoy your child as you explore concepts related to spring.

Bears wake up from long naps in the spring.

Music:

1. **"Catch One If You Can"**
   (Sing to the tune of "Skip to My Lou")

   Butterflies are flying. Won't you try and catch one?
   Butterflies are flying. Won't you try and catch one?
   Butterflies are flying. Won't you try and catch one?
   Catch one if you can.

   Raindrops are falling. Won't you try and catch one?
   Raindrops are falling. Won't you try and catch one?
   Raindrops are falling. Won't you try and catch one?
   Catch one if you can.

2. **"Signs of Spring"**
   (Sing to the tune of "Muffin Man")

   Do you see a sign of spring,
   A sign of spring, a sign of spring?
   Do you see a sign of spring?
   Tell us what you see.

3. **Let's Be Windmills**
   (Sing to the tune of "If I Were a Lassie")

   Oh I wish I were a windmill, a windmill, a windmill.
   Oh I wish I were a windmill. I know what I'd do.
   I'd swing this way and that way, and this way and that way.

   Oh I wish I were a windmill, when the wind blew.

Fingerplays:

SEE, SEE, SEE

See, see, see
  (shade eyes with hands)
Three birds are in a tree.
  (hold up three fingers)
One can chirp
  (point to thumb)
And one can sing.
  (point to index finger)
One is just a tiny thing.
  (point to middle finger, then rock baby bird in arms)
See, see, see
Three birds are in a tree
  (hold up three fingers)

Look, look, look
  (shade eyes)
Three ducks are in a brook.
  (hold up three fingers)
One is white, and one is brown.
One is swimming upside down.
  (point to a finger each time)
Look, look, look
Three ducks are in a brook.
  (hold up three fingers)

122

THIS LITTLE CALF

(extend fingers, push each down in succession)

This little calf eats grass.
This little calf eats hay.
This little calf drinks water.
This little calf runs away.
This little calf does nothing
But just lies down all day.
    (rest last finger in palm of hand)

RAINDROPS

Rain is falling down.
Rain is falling down.
    (raise arm, flutter fingers to ground, tapping
    the floor)
Pitter-patter
Pitter-patter
Rain is falling down.

CREEPY CRAWLY CATERPILLAR

A creepy crawly caterpillar that I see
    (shade eyes)
Makes a chrysalis in the big oak tree.
    (make body into a ball)
He stays there and I know why
    (slowly stand up)
Because soon he will be a butterfly.
    (flap arms)

MY GARDEN

This is my garden.
    (extend one hand forward, palm up)
I'll rake it with care
    (make raking motion on palm with three
    other fingers)
And then some flower seeds
I'll plant there.
    (planting motion)
The sun will shine
    (make circle with hands)
And the rain will fall.
    (let fingers flutter down to lap)
And my garden will blossom
And grow straight and tall.
    (cup hands together, extend upwards slowly)

CATERPILLAR

The caterpillar crawled from a plant, you see.
    (left hand crawls up and down right arm)

"I think I'll take a nap," said he.
So over the ground he began to creep
    (right hand crawls over left arm)
To spin a chrysalis, and he fell asleep.
    (cover right fist with left hand)
All winter he slept in his bed
Till spring came along and he said,
"Wake up, it's time to get out of bed!"
    (shake fist and pointer finger)
So he opened his eyes that sunny spring day.
    (spread fingers and look into hand)
"Look I'm a butterfly!"…and he flew away.
    (interlock thumbs and fly hands away)

Science:

1. **Alfalfa Sprouts**

   Each child who wishes to participate should be provided with a small paper cup, soil, and a few alfalfa seeds. The seeds and soil can be placed in the cup and watered. Place the cups in the sun and watch the sprouts grow. The sprouts can be eaten for snack. A variation is to plant the sprouts in eggshells as an Easter activity.

2. **Weather Chart**

   A weather chart can be constructed that depicts weather conditions such as sunny, rainy, warm, cold, windy, etc. Attach at least two arrows to the center of the chart so that the children can point the arrow at the appropriate weather conditions.

3. **Thermometers**

   On the science table place a variety of outdoor thermometers. Also, post a thermometer outside of a window, at a low position, so the children can read it.

4. **Sprouting Carrots**

   Cut the large end off a fresh carrot and place it in a small cup of water. In a few days, a green top will begin to sprout.

5. **Nesting Materials**

   Place string, cotton, yarn, and other small items outside on the ground. Birds will collect these items to use in their nest building.

6. **Grass Growing**

Grass seeds can be sprinkled on a wet sponge. Within a few days the seeds will begin to sprout.

7. **Ant Farm**

An ant farm can by made by using a large jar with a cover. Fill the jar 2/3 full with sand and soil, and add ants. Punch a few air holes in the cover of the jar, and secure the cover to the top of the jar. The children can watch the ants build tunnels.

Dramatic Play:

1. **Fishing**

Using short dowels prepare fishing poles with a string taped to one end. Attach a magnet piece to the loose end of the string. Construct fish from tagboard and attach a paper clip to each fish. The magnet will attract the paper clip, allowing the children to catch the fish. Add a tackle box, canteen, hats, and life jackets for interest.

2. **Garden**

A small plastic hoe, rake, and garden shovel can be placed outdoors to encourage gardening. A watering can, flower pots, seed packages, and sun hats will also stimulate interest.

3. **Flower Shop**

Collect plastic flowers, vases, wrapping paper, seed packages, and catalogs and place in the dramatic play area. A cash register and play money can be added.

4. **Spring Cleaning**

Small mops, brooms, feather dusters, and empty pails can be placed in the dramatic play area. A spray bottle filled with blue water, which can be used to wash designated windows, can also be provided.

Arts and Crafts:

1. **Butterfly Wings**

Fold a sheet of light-colored paper in half. Show the children how to paint on only one side of the paper. The paper can be folded again and pressed. The result will be a symmetrical painting. Antennas can be added to make butterflies using crayons and markers.

2. **Pussy Willow Fingerprints**

Trace around a tongue depressor with a colored marker. Then using ink pads or finger-paint, the children can press their finger on the ink pad and transfer their fingerprint to the paper. This will produce pussy willow buds.

3. **Caterpillars**

Horizontally cut egg cartons in half. Place the pieces on the art table with short pieces of pipe cleaners, markers, and crayons. From these materials, the children can make caterpillars.

4. **Kites**

Provide diamond-shaped construction paper, string, hole punch, crepe paper, glue, glitter, and markers. For older children, provide the paper with a diamond already traced. This provides them an opportunity to practice finger motor skills by cutting out the shapes. Using the triangle shapes, the children can create kites, and use them outdoors.

Sensory:

The following items can be added to the sensory table:

- string, hay, sticks, and yarn to make birds' nests
- tadpoles and water
- dirt with worms
- seeds
- water and boats
- ice cubes to watch them melt

124

Large Muscle:

1. Windmills

The children can stand up, swing their arms from side to side, and pretend to be windmills. A fan can be added to the classroom for added interest. Sing the song, "Let's Be Windmills," which is listed under music.

2. Puddles

Construct puddles out of tagboard and cover with aluminum foil. Place the puddles on the floor. The children can jump from puddle to puddle. A variation would be to do this activity outside, using chalk to mark puddles on the ground.

3. Caterpillar Crawl

During a transition time, the children can imitate caterpillar movements.

Field Trips:

1. Nature Walk

Walk around your neighborhood, looking for signs of spring. Robins and other birds are often first signs of spring and can usually be observed in most areas of the country.

2. Farm

Arrange a field trip to a farm. It is an interesting place to visit during the spring. Ask the farmer to show you the farm equipment, buildings, crops, and animals.

Math:

1. Seed Counting

On an index card, mark a numeral. The number of cards prepared will depend upon the developmental appropriateness for the children. The children are to glue the appropriate number of seeds onto the card.

2. Insect Seriation

Construct flannel board pieces representing a ladybug, an ant, a caterpillar, a butterfly, etc. The children can arrange them on the flannel board from smallest to largest.

Social Studies:

1. Animal Babies

Collect pictures of animals and their young. Place the adult animal pictures in one basket and the pictures of the baby animals in another basket. The children can match adult animals to their offspring.

2. Spring Cleanup

Each child should be provided with a paper bag to collect litter on a walk to a park, in your neighborhood, or even on your playground. The litter should be discarded when you return to the center. Also, the children should be instructed to wash their hands.

3. Dressing for Spring

Flannel board figures with clothing items should be provided. The children can dress the figures for different kinds of spring weather.

4. Spring Clothing

Collect several pieces of spring clothing such as a jacket, hat, galoshes, and short-sleeved shirts. Add these to the dramatic play area.

Group Time (games, language):

1. What's Inside?

Inside a large box, place many spring items. Include a kite, an umbrella, a hat, a fishing pole, etc. Select an item without showing the children. Describe the object and give clues about how the item can be used. The children should try to identify the item.

2. Insect Movement

During transition time, ask the children to move like the following insects: worm, grasshopper, spider, caterpillar, butterfly, bumblebee, etc.

Cooking:

1. **Lemonade**

   1 lemon
   2 to 3 tablespoons sugar
   1 1/4 cups water
   2 ice cubes

Squeeze lemon juice out of lemon. Add the sugar and water. Stir to dissolve the sugar. This makes one serving. Adjust the recipe to accommodate your class size.

2. **Watermelon Popsicles**

Remove the seeds and rind from a watermelon. Puree the melon in a blender or food processor. Pour into small paper cups. Insert popsicle sticks and freeze. These fruit popsicles can be served at snack time.

SCIENCE ACTIVITIES

Twenty-five other interesting science activities include:

1. Observe **food forms** such as potatoes in the raw, shredded, or sliced form. Fruits can be juiced, sliced, or sectioned.

2. **Prepare tomatoes** in several ways, such as sliced, juiced, stewed, baked, and pureed.

3. **Show corn** in all forms including on the cob, popcorn, fresh cooked, and canned.

4. **Sort** picture cards into piles, living and non-living.

5. **Tape record voices.** Encourage the children to recognize each others' voices.

6. **Tape record familiar sounds** from their environment. Include a ticking clock, telephone ringing, doorbell, toilet flushing, horn beeping, etc.

7. Take the children on a **sensory walk.** Prepare by filling dishpan-sized containers with different items. Foam, sand, leaves, pebbles, mud, cold and warm water, and grains can be used. Have the children remove their shoes and socks to walk through.

8. **Enjoy a nature walk.** Provide each child with a grocery bag and instructions to collect leaves, rocks, soil, insects, etc.

9. Provide the children with **bubbles**. To make the solution, mix 2 quarts of water, 3/4 cup liquid soap, and 1/4 cup glycerine (available from a local druggist). Dip plastic berry baskets and plastic six-pack holders into the solution. Wave to produce bubbles.

10. Show the children how to feel their **heartbeat** after a vigorous activity.

11. Observe **popcorn** popping.

12. Record **body weights and heights**.

13. Prepare **hair and eye color charts**. This information can be made into bar graphs.

14. If climate permits, **freeze water outdoors**. Return it to the class and observe the effects of heat.

15. **Introduce water absorption** by providing containers with water. Allow the children to experiment with coffee filters, paper towels, newspaper, sponges, dishcloths, waxed paper, aluminum foil, and plastic wrap.

16. Explore **magnets**. Provide magnets of assorted sizes, shapes, and strengths. With magnets, place paper clips, nuts, bolts, aluminum foil, copper pennies, metal spoons, jar lids, feathers, etc.

17. Plan a **seed party**. Provide the children with peanuts, walnuts, pecans, and coconuts. Observe the different sizes, shapes, textures, and flavors.

18. Make a **desk garden**. Cut carrots, turnips, and a pineapple 1 1/2 inches from the stem. Place the stem in a shallow pan of water.

19. Create a **worm farm**. Place gravel and soil in a clear, large-mouth jar. Add worms and keep soil moist. Place lettuce, corn, or cereal on top of the soil. Tape black construction paper around the outside of the jar. Remove the paper temporarily and see the tunnels.

20. Place a **celery stalk** with leaves in a clear container of water. Add blue or red food coloring. Observe the plant's absorption of the colored water. A similar experiment can be introduced with a white carnation.

21. Make a **rainbow** with a garden hose on a sunny day. Spray water across the sun rays. The rays of the sun contain all of the colors, but the water, acting as a prism, separates the colors.

22. Make **shadows**. In a darkened room, use a flashlight. Place a hand or object in front of the light source, making a shadow.

23. Produce **static electricity** by rubbing wool fabric over inflated balloons.

24. Install a **birdfeeder** outside the classroom window.

25. During large group, play the **What's missing game**. Provide children with a variety of small familiar items. Tell them to cover their eyes or put their heads down. Remove one item. Then tell the children to uncover. Ask them what is missing. As children gain skill, remove a second and a third item.

Multimedia:

The following resources can be found in educational catalogs:

1. Jenkins, Ella. *Seasons for Singing* [record].

2. Wood, Lucille. *Springtime Walk* [record].

3. *All About Spring* [record]. Lyons Publishers.

4. Palmer, Hap. "Sunshine," *Modern Tunes for Rhythm and Instruments* [record].

5. *Raindrops* [record]. Melody House Records.

Books:

The following books can be used to complement the theme:

1. Suyenaga, R., et al. (1992). *Korean Children's Day*. Cleveland, OH: Modern Curriculum Press.

2. Good, Elaine W. (1987). *That's What Happens When It's Spring!* Intercourse, PA: Good Books.

3. Updike, David. (1989). *A Spring Story.* Ann Arbor, MI: Pippin.

4. Hautzig, Deborah. (1989). *Happy Mother's Day.* New York: Random House.

5. Brown, Craig. (1993). *In the Spring.* New York: Greenwillow Books.

6. Barker, Cicely M. (1991). *Flower Fairies of the Spring.* New York: Frederick Warne and Co.

7. Fowler, Allan. (1991). *How Do You Know It's Spring?* Chicago: Children's Press.

8. Hirschi, Ron. (1990). *Spring.* New York: Dutton Children's Books.

9. Moncure, Jane B. (1990). *Step into Spring: A New Season.* Mankato, MN: Child's World, Inc.

10. Zimmerman, H. Werner. (1991). *Alphonse Knows…the Colour of Spring.* New York: Oxford University Press, Inc.

11. Chmielarz, Sharon. (1992). *End of Winter.* New York: Crown Books for Young Readers.

12. Tibo, Gilles. (1990). *Simon Welcomes Spring.* Plattsburgh, NY: Tundra Books of Northern New York.

13. Katz, Bobbi (Ed.). (1992). *Puddle Wonderful: Poems to Welcome Spring.* New York: Random House Books for Young Readers.

Holidays

Bastille Day
Memorial Day
Labor Day
Fourth of July
Father's Day
Grandparent's Day

Weather

warm
sunny
rainy
humid

SUMMER

Clothing

shorts
swimsuits
sunglasses
sundress
lightweight fabrics

Activities

vacationing
swimming
biking
water games
sunbathing
boating
water sports
baseball
camping
golfing
picnics

Theme Goals:

Through participating in the experiences provided by this theme, the children may learn:

1. Summer holidays.

2. Types of summer clothing.

3. Summer clothing needs.

4. Summer activities.

Concepts for the Children to Learn:

1. Summer is usually the warmest season.

2. Summer months are usually warm and sunny.

3. Lightweight clothing is worn in the summer.

4. Shade trees protect us from the sun during the summer.

5. Memorial Day, Father's Day, Grandparent's Day, the Fourth of July, Bastille Day, and Labor Day are all summer holidays.

6. Swimming, biking, and camping are all summer activities.

Vocabulary:

1. **shorts**—short pants worn in warm weather.

2. **swimming**—a water sport usually enjoyed by many people during the summer months.

3. **hot**—a warm temperature experienced during summer months.

4. **beach**—a sandy place used for sunbathing and playing.

5. **shade**—being in the shadow of something.

Bulletin Board

The purpose of this bulletin board is to promote the identification of written numerals as well as matching sets of objects to a written numeral. Pairs of pails are constructed out of various scraps of tagboard. Using a black marker print a different numeral on each pail. The number of pairs made and numerals used should depend upon the developmental level of the children. Cut seashells out of tagboard and decorate as desired. Laminate all pieces. Attach pails to the bulletin board by stapling them along the side and bottom edges, leaving the tops of the pails open. The children should place the corresponding sets of shells in each pail.

Parent Letter

Dear Parents,

Summer is the favorite season of most children. As summer approaches, we will be starting a unit on the season. Through this unit, the children will become more aware of summer weather, activities, food, and clothing.

At School

Learning experiences planned to highlight summer concepts include:

- exploring the outside and inside of a watermelon and then eating it!
- trying on shorts, sunglasses, and sandals in the dramatic play area.
- preparing fruit juice popsicles.
- eating a picnic lunch on Wednesday. We will be walking to Wilson Park at 11:45. Please feel free to pack a sack lunch and meet us there!

At Home

To reinforce summer concepts at home, try the following:

- Plan a family picnic and allow your child to help plan what food and items will be needed.
- Take part in or observe any summer activity such as boating, fishing, biking, or camping.

Have a good summer!

Summer means a lot of outdoor activities.

Music:

1. **"Summer Clothing"**
(Sing to the tune of "The Farmer in the Dell.")

Oh, if you are wearing shorts,
If you are wearing shorts,
You may walk right to the door,
If you are wearing shorts.

Also include: stripes, sandals, tennis shoes,
flowers, a sundress, blue jeans, belt, barrettes,
etc.

This song can be used during transition times
to point out children's summer clothing.

2. **"Summer Activities"**
(Sing to the tune of "Skip to My Lou.")

Swim, swim, swim in a circle.
Swim, swim, swim in a circle.
Swim, swim, swim in a circle.
Swim in a circle now.

Also include: jump, hop, skip, run, walk, etc.
Use this song as a transition song to introduce
summer activities.

Fingerplays:

HERE IS THE BEE HIVE

Here is the bee hive. Where are the bees?
   (make a fist)
They're hiding away so nobody sees.
Soon they're coming creeping out of their hive,
1, 2, 3, 4, 5. Buzz-z-z-z-z.
   (draw fingers out of fist on each count)

GREEN LEAF

Here's a green leaf
   (show hand)
And here's a green leaf.
   (show other hand)
That you see, makes two.

Here's a bud.
   (cup hands together)
That makes a flower;
Watch it bloom for you!
   (open cupped hands gradually)

A ROLY-POLY CATERPILLAR

Roly-poly caterpillar
Into a corner crept.
Spun around himself a blanket
   (spin around)

Then for a long time slept.
  (place head on folded hands)

Roly-poly caterpillar
Wakened by and by.
  (stretch)
Found himself with beautiful wings
Changed into a butterfly.
  (flutter arms like wings)

Science:

1. **Science Table**

   Add the following items to the science table:

   - all kinds of sunglasses with different-colored shades
   - plant grass seeds in small cups of dirt, water daily
   - dirt and grass with magnifying glasses
   - sand with scales and magnifying glasses
   - pinwheels (children use their own wind to make them move)
   - blow bubbles outdoors

2. **Water and Air Make Bubbles**

   Bubble Solution Recipe

   3/4 cup liquid soap
   1/4 cup glycerine (obtain at a drugstore)
   2 quarts water

   Place mixed solution in a shallow pan and let children place the bubble makers in the solution. Bubble makers can be successfully made from the following:

   - plastic six-pack holder
   - straws
   - bent wire with no sharp edges
   - funnels

3. **Flying Kites**

   On a windy day, make and fly kites.

4. **Making Rainbows**

   If you have a hose available the children can spray the hose into the sun. The rays of the sun contain all the colors mixed together. The water acts as a prism and separates the water into colors creating a rainbow.

Dramatic Play:

1. **Juice Stand**

   Set up a lemonade or orange juice stand. To prepare use real oranges and lemons and let the children squeeze them and make the juice. The juice can be served at snack time.

2. **Ice Cream Stand**

   Trace and cut ice cream cones from brown construction paper. Cotton balls or small yarn pompoms can be used to represent ice cream. The addition of ice cream buckets and ice cream scoopers can make this activity more inviting during self-selected play periods.

3. **Indoors or Outdoors Picnic**

   A blanket, picnic basket, plastic foods, purses, small cooler, paper plates, plastic silverware, napkins, etc., can be placed in the classroom to stimulate play.

4. **The Beach**

   In the dramatic play area place beach blankets, lawn chairs, buckets, sunglasses, beach balls, magazines, and books. If the activity is used outdoors, a sun umbrella can be added to stimulate interest in play.

5. **Camping Fun**

   A small freestanding tent can be set up indoors, if room permits, or outdoors. Sleeping bags can also be provided. Blocks or logs could represent a campfire.

6. **Traveling by Air**

   Place a telephone, tickets, travel brochures, and suitcases in the dramatic play area.

Arts and Crafts:

1. **Outdoor Painting**

   An easel can be placed outside. The children choose to use the easel during outdoor playtime. If the sun is shining, encourage the children to observe how quickly the paint dries.

2. Chalk Drawings

Large pieces of chalk should be provided for the children to draw on the sidewalks outdoors. Small plastic berry baskets make handy chalk containers.

3. Foot Painting

This may be used as an outdoor activity. The children can dip their feet in a thick tempera paint mixture and make prints by stepping on large sheets of paper. Sponges and pans of soapy water should be available for cleanup.

4. Shake Painting

Tape a large piece of butcher paper on a fence or wall outdoors. Let the children dip their brushes in paint and stand two feet from the paper. Then show them how to shake the brush, allowing the paint to fly onto the paper.

5. Sailboats

Color styrofoam meat trays with markers. Stick a pipe cleaner in the center of the tray and secure by bending the end underneath the carton. Prepare a sail and glue to the pipe cleaner.

Sensory:

Sensory Table

The following items can be added to the sensory table:

- sand with toys
- colored sand
- sand and water
- water with toy boats
- shells
- small rocks and pebbles
- grass and hay

Large Muscle:

1. Barefoot Walk

Check the playground to ensure that it is free of debris. Then sprinkle part of the grass and sandbox with water. Go on a barefoot walk.

2. Balls

In the outdoor play yard place a variety of large balls.

3. Catching Balloons

Balloons can be used indoors and outdoors. Close supervision is required. *If a balloon breaks it should be immediately removed.*

4. Parachute Play

Use a real parachute or a sheet to represent one. The children should hold onto the edges. Say a number and then have the children count and wave the parachute in the air that number of times.

5. Balloon Racket Ball

Bend coat hangers into diamond shapes. Bend the handles closed and tape for safety. Then pull nylon stockings over the diamond shapes to form swatters. The children can use the swatters to keep the balloons up in the air by hitting them.

Field Trips/Resource People:

1. Picnic at the Park

A picnic lunch can be prepared and eaten at a park or in the play yard.

2. Resource People

The following resource people may be invited to the classroom:

- A lifeguard to talk about water safety.
- A camp counselor can talk to the children about camping and sing some camp songs with the children.

Math:

Sand Numbers and Shapes

During outdoor play informally make shapes and numbers in the sand and let children identify the shape or number.

Social Studies:

1. Making Floats

To celebrate the Fourth of July, decorate the trikes, wagons, and scooters with crepe paper, streamers, balloons, etc. Parade around the school or neighborhood.

2. Summer at School

Take pictures or slides of community summer activities. Construction workers, parades, children playing, sports activities, people swimming, library hours, picnics, band concerts, and people driving are examples. Show the slides and discuss them during group time.

3. Summer Fun Book

Magazines should be provided for the children to find pictures of summer activities. The pictures can be pasted on a sheet of paper. Bind the pages by stapling them together to make a book.

Group Time (games, language):

1. Exploring a Watermelon

Serve watermelon for snack. Talk about the color of the outside, which is called the rind. Next cut the watermelon into pieces. Give each child a piece to look at. Examine it carefully. "What color is the inside? Are there seeds? Do we eat the seeds? What can we do with them?" The children can remove all the seeds from their piece of watermelon. Then eat the watermelon. Collect all of the seeds. After circle time, wash the seeds. When dry, they can be used for a collage.

2. Puppet Show

Weather permitting, bring puppets and a puppet stage outdoors and have an outdoor puppet show.

Cooking:

1. Popsicles

pineapple juice
grape juice
cranapple juice
popsicle sticks
small paper cups

If frozen juice is used, mix according to the directions on the can. Fill the paper cups 3/4 full of juice. Place the cups in the freezer. When the juice begins to freeze, insert a popsicle stick in the middle of each cup. When frozen, peel the cup away and serve.

2. Watermelon Popsicles

Remove the seeds and rind from watermelon. Puree the melon in a blender. Follow the recipe for popsicles.

3. Zippy Drink

2 ripe bananas
2 cups orange juice
2 cups orange sherbet
ice cubes
orange slices

Peel the bananas, place in a bowl and mash with a fork. Add orange juice and sherbet and beat with a rotary beater until smooth. Pour into pitcher. Add ice cubes and orange slices.

4. Kulfi (Indian Ice Cream)

1 quart milk
1/2 pint heavy cream
1/4 cup sugar
1/2 cup chopped pistachio nuts
1/2 cup chopped almonds
1 tablespoon vanilla
2 drops red food coloring

Combine milk and heavy cream in a saucepan. Simmer over medium heat for about 20 minutes until thick. Add sugar, pistachio nuts, almonds, vanilla, and food coloring. Mix thoroughly. Let cool. Fill small paper cups halfway with kulfi and place in a freezer for 1 hour until the kulfi has the consistency of soft sherbet. Makes 10 servings.

Source: *Wonderful World Macmillan Early Skills Program*. (1985). New York: Macmillan Educational Company.

Multimedia:

The following resources can be found in educational catalogs:

1. *Action Songs for Indoor Days* [record]. Tom Thumb series.

2. *Children's Games* [record]. Kimbo Records.

3. Palmer, Hap. *Modern Marches* [record].

4. *Pretend to Be Me* [record]. Melody House Records.

5. *Adventures in Sounds* [record]. Melody House Records.

6. *Patriotic Songs of the U.S.* [record]. Melody House Records.

Books:

The following books can be used to complement the theme:

1. Sumiko. (1990). *My Summer Vacation*. New York: David McKay Co., Inc.

2. Barker, Cicely M. (1991). *Flower Fairies of the Summer*. New York: Frederick Warne and Co., Inc.

3. Blades, Ann. (1990). *Summer*. New York: Lothrop, Lee, & Shepard Books.

4. Fowler, Allan. (1992). *How Do You Know It's Summer?* Chicago: Children's Press.

5. Moncure, Jane B. (1990). *Step into Summer: A New Season*. Mankato, MN: Child's World, Inc.

6. Sanchez, Isidro, & Peris, Carme. (1992). *Summer Sports*. Hauppauge, NY: Barron's Educational Series, Inc.

7. Schweninger, Ann. (1992). *Summertime*. New York: Viking Children's Books.

8. Komoda, Beverly. (1991). *The Too Hot Day*. New York: Harper Collins Children's Books.

9. Hayward, Linda. (1989). *Grover's Summer Vacation*. New York: Random House.

10. Ransom, Candace F. (1992). *Shooting Star Summer*. Honesdale, PA: Boyds Mills Press.

11. Brown, Margaret W. (1993). *Summer Noisy Book*. New York: Harper Collins.

T H E M E 15

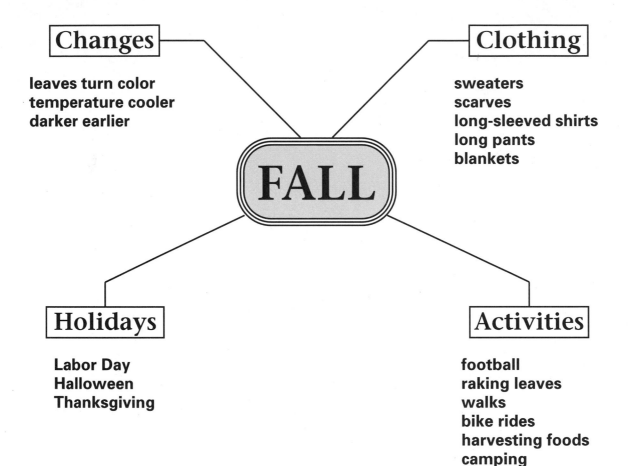

Changes

leaves turn color
temperature cooler
darker earlier

Clothing

sweaters
scarves
long-sleeved shirts
long pants
blankets

FALL

Holidays

Labor Day
Halloween
Thanksgiving

Activities

football
raking leaves
walks
bike rides
harvesting foods
camping
soccer

Theme Goals:

Through participating in the experiences provided by this theme, the children may learn:

1. Characteristics of fall weather.

2. Fall holidays.

3. Fall clothing.

4. Fall activities.

Concepts for the Children to Learn:

1. Fall is one of the four seasons.

2. Fall is the season between summer and winter.

3. Some trees change color in the fall.

4. In some places the weather becomes cooler in the fall.

5. The day becomes shorter in the fall.

6. Leaves fall from some trees in the fall.

7. Labor Day, Halloween, and Thanksgiving are some fall holidays.

8. Scarves and sweaters may need to be worn in the fall in some areas.

9. Pumpkins and apples can be harvested in the fall.

10. Football is a fall sport.

11. Blankets are usually needed on our beds in the fall in some places.

Vocabulary:

1. **fall**—the season between summer and winter.

2. **Halloween**—the holiday when people wear costumes and go trick-or-treating.

3. **Thanksgiving**—a holiday to express thanks.

4. **Labor Day**—a holiday to honor working people.

5. **season**—a time of the year.

Bulletin Board

The purpose of this bulletin board is to foster a positive self-concept as well as develop skills of name recognition. Construct an acorn for each child. Print the children's names on the acorns. See illustration. Laminate and punch holes in the acorns. Children can hang their acorns on a push pin on the bulletin board when they arrive.

Parent Letter

Dear Parents,

Where we live, the days are getting shorter, the temperature is getting colder, and the leaves are changing color. It's the perfect time to introduce our next unit—fall. By participating in the experiences provided throughout this unit, children will become more aware of changes that take place in the fall and common fall activities.

At School

A few of this week's learning experiences include:

- recording the temperature and the changing colors of the leaves.
- making leaf rubbings in the art area.
- raking leaves on our playground during outdoor time.

We will also be taking a fall walk around the neighborhood to observe the trees in their peak changes. We will be leaving Thursday at 10:00 a.m. Please feel free to join us. It will be a scenic tour.

At Home

To develop classification skills help your child sort leaves by their color, type, or size.

Fingerplays promote language and vocabulary skills. This fingerplay is one we will be learning this week. Enjoy it with your child at home!

Autumn

Autumn winds begin to blow.
   (blow)
Colored leaves fall fast and slow.
   (make fast and slow motions with hands)
Twirling, whirling all around,
   (turn around)
`Til at last, they touch the ground.
   (fall to the ground)

Enjoy your child as you explore experiences related to the unit on fall.

Leaves turn different colors during the fall.

Music:

1. **"Little Leaves"**
   (Sing to the tune of "Ten Little Indians")

   One little, two little, three little leaves.
   Four little, five little, six little leaves.
   Seven little, eight little, nine little leaves.
   Ten little leaves fall down.

2. **"Happy Children Tune"**
   (Sing to the tune of "Did You Ever See a Lassie?")

   Happy children in the autumn,
   In the autumn, in the autumn.
   Happy children in the autumn
   Do this way and that.

   While singing the song, children can keep time by pretending to rake leaves, jump in the leaves, etc.

3. **"Pretty Leaves Are Falling Down"**
   (Sing to the tune of "London Bridges")

   Pretty leaves are falling down, falling down, falling down.

   Pretty leaves are falling down, all around the town.
      (wiggle fingers)

   Let's rake them up in a pile, in a pile, in a pile.
   Let's rake them up in a pile, all around the town.
      (make raking motions)

   Let's all jump in and have some fun,
   have some fun, have some fun.
   Let's all jump in and have some fun, all around the town.
      (jump into circle)

Fingerplays:

AUTUMN

   Autumn winds begin to blow.
      (blow)
   Colored leaves fall fast and slow.
      (make fast and slow falling motions with hands)
   Twirling, whirling all around
      (turn around)
   'Til at last, they touch the ground.
      (fall to the ground)

142

LEAVES

Little leaves fall gently down
Red and yellow, orange and brown.
  (flutter hands as leaves falling)
Whirling, whirling around and around.
  (turn around)
Quietly without a sound.
  (put finger to lips)
Falling softly to the ground
  (begin to fall slowly) ·
Down and down and down and down.
  (lie on floor)

LITTLE LEAVES

The little leaves are falling down
  (use hands to make falling motion)
Round and round, round and round.
  (turn around)
The little leaves are falling down,
  (use hands to make falling motion)
Falling to the ground.
  (fall to ground)

TWIRLING LEAVES

The autumn wind blows—Oooo Oooo Oooo.
  (make wind sounds)
The leaves shake and shake then fly into the sky so blue.
  (children shake)
They whirl and whirl around them, twirl and twirl around.
  (turn around in circles)
But when the wind stops, the leaves sink slowly to the ground.
Lower, lower, lower, and land quietly without a sound.
  (sink very slowly and very quietly)

Science:

1. **Leaf Observation**

   Collect leaves from a variety of trees. Place them and a magnifying glass on the science table for the children to explore.

2. **Temperature Watch**

   Place a thermometer outside. A large cardboard thermometer can also be constructed out of tagboard with movable elastic or ribbon for the mercury. The children can match the temperature on the cardboard thermometer with the outdoor one.

3. **Weather Calendar**

   Construct a calendar for the month. Record the changes of weather each day by attaching a symbol to the calendar. Symbols should include clouds, sun, snow, rain, etc.

4. **Color Change Sequence**

   Laminate or cover with contact paper, several leaves of different colors. The children can sort, count, and classify the leaves.

Dramatic Play:

1. **Fall Wear**

   Set out warm clothes such as sweaters, coats, hats, and blankets to indicate cold weather coming on. The children can use the clothes for dressing up.

2. **Football**

   Collect football gear including balls, helmets, and jerseys and play on the outdoor playground.

Arts and Crafts:

1. **Fall Collage**

   After taking a walk to collect objects such as grass, twigs, leaves, nuts, and weeds, collages can be made in the art area.

2. **Leaf Rubbings**

   Collect leaves, paper, and crayons and show the children how to place several leaves under a sheet of paper. Using the flat edge of crayon color rub over paper. The image of the leaves will appear.

3. **Pumpkin Seed Collage**

   Wash and dry pumpkin seeds and place them in the art area with glue and paper. The children can make pumpkin seed collages.

4. Leaf Spatter Painting

Use a lid from a box that is approximately 9 inches x 12 inches x 12 inches. Cut a rectangle from top of lid leaving a 1 1/2-inch border. Invert the lid and place a wire screen over the opening. Tape the screen to the border. Arrange the leaves on a sheet of paper. Place the lid over the arrangement. Dip a toothbrush into thin tempera paint and brush across screen. When the tempera paint dries, remove the leaves.

Sensory:

Leaves

Place a variety of leaves in the sensory table. Try to include moist and dry examples for the children to compare.

Large Muscle:

Raking Leaves

Child-sized rakes can be provided. The children can be encouraged to rake leaves into piles.

Field Trips:

1. **Neighborhood Walk**

Take a walk around the neighborhood when the leaves are at their peak of changing colors. Discuss differences in color and size.

2. **Apple Orchard**

Visit an apple orchard. Observe the apples being picked and processed. If possible let children pick their own apples from a tree.

3. **Pumpkin Patch**

Visit a pumpkin patch. Discuss and observe how pumpkins grow, their size, shape, and color. Let the children pick a pumpkin to bring back to the classroom.

Math:

1. **Weighing Acorns and Pinecones**

A scale, acorns, and pinecones for the children to weigh can be added to the science table.

2. **Leaf Math**

Out of construction paper or tagboard, prepare pairs of various-shaped leaves. The children can match the identical leaves.

Social Studies:

Bulletin Board

Construct a bulletin board using bare branches to represent a tree. Cut out leaves from colored construction paper and print one child's name on each. At the beginning of the day, children can hang their name on the tree when they arrive.

Cooking:

1. **Apple Banana Frosty**

1 golden delicious apple, diced
1 peeled sliced banana
1/4 cup milk
3 ice cubes

Blend all the ingredients in a blender. Serves 4 children.

2. **Apple Salad**

6 medium apples
1/2 cup raisins
1/2 teaspoon cinnamon
1/2 cup chopped nuts
1/4 cup white grape juice

Peel and chop the apples. Mix well and add the remaining ingredients. Serves 10 children.

NATURE RECIPES

Cattails

Use them in their natural color or tint by shaking metallic powder over them. Handle carefully. The cattail is dry and feels crumbly. It will fall apart easily.

Crystal Garden*

Place broken pieces of brick or terra cotta clay in a glass bowl or jar. Pour the following solution over this:

4 teaspoons water
1 teaspoon ammonia
4 teaspoons bluing
1 teaspoon Mercurochrome
4 teaspoons salt

Add more of this solution each day until the crystal garden has grown to the desired size. (Adult supervision required.)

* This activity should be carefully observed if in a classroom with preschool children.

Drying Plants for Winter Bouquets

Strip the leaves from the flowers immediately. Tie the flowers by their stems with string and hang them with the heads down in a cool dry place away from the light. Darkness is essential for preserving their color. Thorough drying takes about 2 weeks.

Preserving Fall Leaves

Place alternate layers of powdered borax and leaves in a box. The leaves must be completely covered. Allow them to stand for four days. Shake off the borax and wipe each with liquid floor wax. Rub a warm iron over a cake of paraffin, then press the iron over front and back of leaves.

Preserving Magnolia Leaves

Mix two parts of water with one part of glycerine. Place stems of the magnolia leaves in the mixture and let them stand for several days. The leaves will turn brown and last several years. Their surface may be painted or sprayed with silver or gold paint.

Pressing Wild Flowers

When gathering specimens, include the roots, leaves, flowers and seed pods. Place between newspapers, laying two layers of blotters underneath the newspaper and two on top to absorb the moisture. Change the newspapers three times during the week. Place between two sheets of corrugated cardboard and press. It usually takes seven to ten days to press specimens. Cardboard covered with cotton batting is the mounting base. Lay the flower on the cotton and cover with cellophane or plastic wrap to preserve the color.

Treating Gourds

Soak gourds for two hours in water. Scrape them clean with a knife. Rub with fine sandpaper. While still damp cut an opening to remove seeds.

Multimedia:

The following resources can be found in educational catalogs:

1. James, Dixie, & Becht, Linda. *The Singing Calendar* [record].

2. McLaughlin, Roberta, & Wood, Lucille. *Sing a Song of Holidays and Seasons* [record]. Bowman Records.

Books:

The following books can be used to complement the theme:

1. Tejima, Keizaburo. (1986). *The Bears' Autumn*. Chicago: Children's Press.

2. Allington, Richard L., & Kroll, Kathleen. (1985). *Autumn*. Milwaukee: Raintree.

3. Maass, Robert. (1990). *When Autumn Comes*. New York: Henry Holt & Co.

4. Updike, David. (1988). *An Autumn Tale*. New York: Pippin Press.

5. Hains, Harriet. (1993). *My New School*. New York: Dorling Kindersley.

6. Baer, Edith. (1990). *This Is the Way We Go to School: A Book about Children around the World*. New York: Scholastic.

7. Arnosky, Jim. (1993). *Every Autumn Comes the Bear*. New York: Putnam.

8. Fowler, Allan. (1992). *How Do You Know It's Fall?* Chicago: Children's Press.

9. Moncure, Jane B. (1990). *Step Into Fall: A New Season*. Mankato, MN: Child's World, Inc.

Purpose

share feelings
show love

Colors

red
pink
white

VALENTINE'S DAY

Symbols

hearts
Cupid
cards
candy
arrows
flowers

Activities

parties
card giving
flowers
gifts

Theme Goals:

Through participating in the experiences provided by this theme, the children may learn:

1. Valentine's Day colors.

2. Valentine's Day activities.

3. Symbols of Valentine's Day.

4. Purpose of Valentine's Day.

Concepts for the Children to Learn:

1. Red, pink, and white are Valentine's Day colors.

2. On Valentine's Day we share our love with others.

3. Hearts, Cupids, and flowers are symbols of Valentine's Day.

4. People send cards on Valentine's Day.

Vocabulary:

1. **heart**—a symbol of love.

2. **Valentine**—a card designed for someone special.

3. **Cupid**—a symbol of Valentine's Day, usually a baby boy with a bow and arrows.

4. **card**—a decorative paper with a written message.

Bulletin Board

The purpose of this bulletin board is to have the children place the correct number of hearts in the corresponding numbered box. Using boxes as illustrated, a Valentine's Day bulletin board can be made. The bottom of each box should be cut, so it can be taped shut while putting hearts in and easily opened to release the hearts. Mark each box with a numeral and a corresponding number of hearts. The number of numerals will depend upon developmental appropriateness. Attach the boxes to the bulletin board using push pins or staples. Next, construct many small hearts.

Parent Letter

Dear Parents,

Valentine's Day is a special day, so this unit celebrates Valentine's Day. It is a day when we share our good feelings about special people. This day also provides an opportunity to talk about the importance of sharing, giving, loving, and friendship.

At School

Some of the activities related to Valentine's Day will include:

- having a post office in dramatic play to mail valentines to friends.
- constructing valentine mobiles to decorate our room.
- constructing a "What a Friend Is…" chart to hang in our room.
- sending and receiving valentines.

At Home

Try to set aside time to have a heart-to-heart chat with your child. To develop self-esteem talk to your child about feelings and why you are proud of him. Also, help your child make a valentine for a grandparent, aunt, uncle, or other person. A special note could be dictated by your child and written by you.

Have a Happy Valentine's Day!

Be my valentine.

Music:

1. **"My Valentine"**
   (Sing to the tune of "The Muffin Man")

   Oh, do you know my valentine,
   My valentine, my valentine?
   Oh, do you know my valentine?
   His name is _____.

   Chosen valentine then picks another child.

2. **"Ten Little Valentines"**
   (Sing to the tune of "Ten Little Indians")

   One little, two little, three little valentines.
   Four little, five little, six little valentines.
   Seven little, eight little, nine little valentines.
   Ten little valentines here!

3. **"Two Little Cupids"**

(Sing to the tune of "Two Little Blackbirds")

Two little cupids sitting on a heart.
   (hold hands behind back)
One named _____. One named _____.
   (bring out one pointer for each name)
Fly away, _____. Fly away, _____.
   (place one pointer behind back for each
   name)
Come back, _____. Come back, _____.
   (bring out pointers one at a time again)
Two little cupids sitting on a heart.
   (hold up two fingers)
One named _____. One named _____.
   (wiggle each pointer separately.)

For each _____ insert a child's name.

Fingerplay:

FIVE LITTLE VALENTINES

Five little valentines were having a race.
The first little valentine was frilly with lace.
   (hold up one finger)
The second little valentine had a funny face.
   (hold up two fingers)
The third little valentine said, "I love you."
   (hold up three fingers)
The fourth little valentine said, "I do too."
   (hold up four fingers)
The fifth little valentine was sly as a fox.
He ran the fastest to the valentine box.
   (make five fingers run behind back.)

Science:

1. **Valentine's Day Flowers**

   In the science area, place various flowers and
   magnifying glasses. The children can observe
   and explore the various parts of the flowers.

2. **Valentine's Day Colors**

   Mixing red and white tempera paint, the
   children can make various shades of red or
   pink.

Dramatic Play:

1. **Mailboxes**

   Construct an individual mailbox for each child using shoeboxes, empty milk cartons, paper bags, or partitioned boxes. Print each child's name on the box or encourage the child to do so. The children can sort mail, letters, and small packages into the boxes.

2. **Florist**

   Plastic flowers, vases, styrofoam pieces, tissue paper, ribbons, candy boxes, a cash register, and play money can be used to make a flower shop.

3. **Card Shop**

   Stencils, paper, markers, scraps, stickers, etc., can be provided to make a card-making shop.

Arts and Crafts:

1. **Easel Painting**

   Mix red, white, and pink paint and place at the easel.

2. **Chalk Drawings**

   White chalk and red and pink construction paper can be used to make chalk drawings.

3. **Classroom Valentine**

   Cut out one large paper heart. Encourage all children to decorate and sign it. The valentine can be hung in the classroom or be given to a classroom friend. The classroom friend may be the cook, janitor, center director, or principal.

4. **Heart Prints**

   On the art table place white paper and various heart-shaped cookie cutters. Mix pink and red tempera paint and pour into shallow pans. The children can print hearts on white construction paper using the cookie cutters as a tool and then paint them.

5. **Heart Materials**

   The children can cut hearts out of construction paper and decorate them with lace scraps, yarn, and glitter to make original Valentine's Day cards. Pre-cut hearts should be available for children who have not mastered the skill. For other children who have cutting skills, a heart shape can be traced on paper for them to cut.

Sensory:

Soap

   Mix dish soap, water, and red food coloring in the sensory table. Provide egg beaters for children to make bubbles.

Large Muscle:

1. **Hug Tag**

   One child is "it" and tries to tag another child. Once tagged, the child is "frozen" until another child gently hugs him to "unfreeze" him.

2. **Balloon Ball**

   Blow up two or three red, pink, or white balloons. Using nylon paddles made by stretching nylon pantyhose over bent coat hangers, the children can hit the balloons to each other. The object is to try to keep the balloon up off the floor or ground. This activity needs to be carefully supervised. If a balloon breaks, it needs to be immediately removed.

Field Trips:

1. **Visit a Post Office**

   Visit the local post office. Valentine's Day cards made in the classroom can be mailed.

2. **Visit a Floral Shop**

Visit a flower store. Observe the different valentine arrangements. Call attention to the beautiful color of the flowers, arrangements, and containers.

Math:

1. **Broken Hearts**

Cut heart shapes out of red and pink tagboard. Print a numeral on one side and a number set of heart stickers or drawings on the other side. Cut the hearts in half as a puzzle. The children can match the puzzle pieces.

2. **Heart Seriation**

Cut various-sized hearts from pink, red, and white construction paper. The children can sequence the heart shapes from small to big or vice versa.

Social Studies:

1. **Sorting Feelings**

Cut pictures of happy and sad people out of magazines. On the outside of two boxes, draw a smiling face on one and a sad face on the other. The children can sort the pictures into the corresponding boxes.

2. **Sign Language**

Show the children how to say, "I love you," in sign language. They can practice with each other. When the parents arrive, the children can share with them.

I	point to self
love	cross arms over chest
you	point outwards

Group Time (games, language):

Valentine March

Place large material hearts with numerals on them on the floor. Include one valentine per child. Play a marching song and encourage children to march from heart to heart. When the music stops, so do the children. Each child then tells the numeral he is standing on. To make the activity developmentally appropriate for young children, use symbols. Examples might include a ball, car, truck, glass, cup, door, etc.

Cooking:

1. **Valentine Cookies**

2/3 cup shortening
1 egg
3/4 cup sugar
1 teaspoon vanilla
1 1/2 cups flour
1 1/2 teaspoons baking powder
4 teaspoons milk
1/4 teaspoon salt

Mix all of the ingredients together. If time permits, refrigerate the dough. Roll out dough. Use heart-shaped cookie cutters. Bake at 375 degrees for 12 minutes. Frost. The children can make two cookies, one for themselves, and one to give to a friend.

2. **Heart-shaped Sandwiches**

1 loaf bread
heart-shaped cookie cutters
strawberry jam or jelly

Give each child 1 or 2 pieces of bread (depending on size of cutter). Cut out 2 heart shapes from bread. Spread on jam or jelly to make a sandwich. Eat at snack time.

MATERIALS TO COLLECT FOR THE ART CENTER

aluminum foil	jars	rug yarn
ball bearings	jugs	safety pins
barrel hoops	lacing	sand
beads	lampshades	sandpaper
belts	leather remnants	seashells
bottles	linoleum	seeds
bracelets	marbles	sheepskin
braiding	masonite	shoelaces
brass	metal foil	shoe polish
buckles	mirrors	snaps
burlap	muslin	soap
buttons	nails	sponges
candles	necklaces	spools
canvas	neckties	stockings
cartons	oilcloth	sweaters
cellophane	ornaments	tacks
chains	pans	tape
chalk	paper bags	thread
chamois	paper boxes	tiles
clay	paper cardboard	tin cans
cloth	paper corrugated	tin foil
colored pictures	paper dishes	tongue depressors
confetti	paper doilies	towels
containers	paper napkins	tubes
copper foil	paper newspaper	twine
cord	paper tissue	wallpaper
cornhusks	paper towels	wax
cornstalks	paper tubes	window shades
costume jewelry	paper wrapping	wire
crayon pieces	phonograph records	wire eyelets
crystals	photographs	wire hairpins
emery cloth	picture frames	wire hooks
eyelets	pinecones	wire mesh
fabrics	pins	wire paper clips
felt	pipe cleaners	wire screen
felt hats	plastic board	wire staples
flannel	plastic paint	wooden beads
floor covering	pocket books	wooden blocks
glass	reeds	wooden clothespins
gourds	ribbon	wooden sticks
hat boxes	rings	wool
hooks	rope	yarn
inner tubes	rubber bands	zippers

Multimedia:

The following resources can be found in educational catalogs:

1. *The Singing Calendar* [record]. Kimbo Records.

2. Palmer, Hap. *Holiday Songs and Rhythms* [record].

Books:

The following books can be used to complement the theme:

1. Modell, Frank. (1987). *One Zillion Valentines*. New York: William Morrow and Company, Inc.

2. St. Pierre, Stephanie. (1990). *Valentine Kittens*. New York: Scholastic, Inc.

3. Watson, Wendy. (1991). *A Valentine for You*. Boston: Houghton Mifflin Co.

4. Blos, Joan W. (1990). *One Very Best Valentine's Day*. New York: Simon and Schuster Trade.

5. Ehrlich, Fred. (1992). *A Valentine for Ms. Vanilla*. New York: Viking Children's Books.

6. Nerlove, Miriam. (1992). *Valentine's Day*. Morton Grove, IL: Albert Whitman and Co.

7. Schweninger, Ann. (1990). *Valentine Friends*. New York: Puffin Books.

8. Stock, Catherine. (1991). *Secret Valentine*. New York: Macmillan Children's Books Group.

9. Bond, Felicia. (1990). *Four Valentines in a Rainstorm*. New York: Harper Collins.

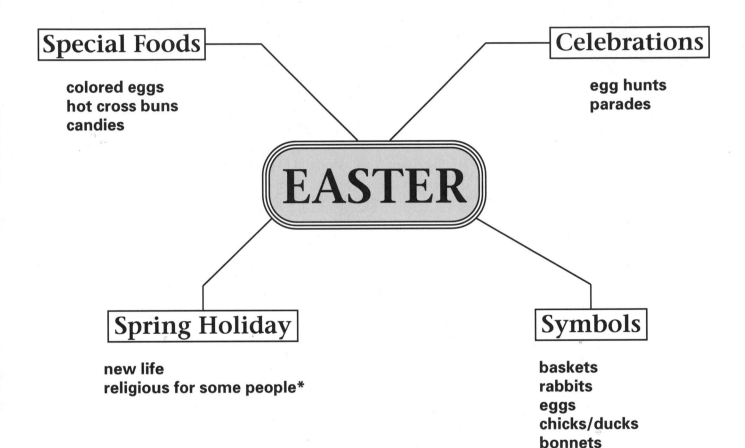

Special Foods

colored eggs
hot cross buns
candies

Celebrations

egg hunts
parades

EASTER

Spring Holiday

new life
religious for some people*

Symbols

baskets
rabbits
eggs
chicks/ducks
bonnets

* Some center personnel may elect to include an Easter
theme with an emphasis on the spring holiday as
opposed to the traditional religious emphasis.

Theme Goals:

Through participating in the experiences provided by this theme, the children may learn:

1. Easter traditions.

2. Easter symbols.

3. Boiled eggs can be dyed and decorated for Easter.

4. Care of rabbits.

Concepts for the Children to Learn:

1. Easter is a holiday.

2. Many families celebrate Easter.

3. At Eastertime eggs are decorated.

4. There are many symbols of Easter, including baby animals, baskets, rabbits, and eggs.

5. Baskets filled with eggs and candy may be hidden.

6. Baby animals born in the spring are a sign of new life.

7. Bonnets (hats) may be worn at Easter time.

Vocabulary:

1. **Easter**—a holiday in spring.

2. **basket**—a woven container.

3. **hatch**—to break out of a shell.

4. **dye**—to change the color.

5. **duckling**—a baby duck.

6. **chick**—a baby chicken.

7. **lamb**—a baby sheep.

8. **bunny**—a baby rabbit.

9. **holiday**—a day of celebration.

10. **spring**—the season of the year when plants begin to grow.

11. **bonnet**—a kind of hat.

Bulletin Board

The purpose of this bulletin board is to promote correspondence of sets to the written numeral. Construct baskets out of stiff tagboard. Write a numeral beginning with the number one on each basket as illustrated. Carefully attach these to the bulletin board stapling all the way around the round bottom of the baskets. Construct many small Easter eggs. Encourage the children to deposit the corresponding number of Easter eggs in the numbered baskets. Care needs to be taken when removing the eggs. The number of baskets should reflect the developmental level of the children. If available, you might want to try using lightweight Easter baskets. They are harder to hang up, but may prove to be more sturdy.

158

Parent Letter

Dear Parents,

"Here comes Peter Cottontail, hopping down the bunny trail…" Easter is on its way, and is the theme we will explore this unit. This is an exciting holiday for children. Through learning experiences planned for the unit, the children will find out about ways that some families celebrate Easter and symbols that represent Easter. Included will be the Easter bunny, Easter baskets, and foods that are associated with Easter.

At School

Learning experiences planned to reinforce concepts of Easter include:

- a special visitor for the week—a rabbit! The children will assist in taking care of the rabbit.
- a hat shop in the dramatic play area with materials to create Easter bonnets.
- Easter grass and plastic eggs in the sensory table.
- an egg hunt! On Friday, we will search our play yard for hidden eggs and place them in our baskets.

At Home

To establish a sense of family history, recall family Easter celebrations that you have had in the past with your child. What special things does your family do together on this holiday? And, of course, dye some Easter eggs!

Be adventurous and try some dyes from natural materials. Natural dying is not new; natural dyes were the original Easter egg colors the world over. To make purple eggs purchase a box of frozen blackberries. Thaw and place in a saucepan. Add eggs and cover with water plus 1 tablespoon of vinegar. Bring the water to a boil and simmer for 20 minutes. Afterward, take the pan off the heat source and let stand for approximately 20 minutes.

To make gold eggs use powdered tumeric. Place eggs in a saucepan and add enough water to cover. Then, add 3 tablespoons of tumeric and bring to a boil. Simmer for 20 minutes. Remove from heat source and cool.

To create pale green eggs, cut spinach and place in the bottom of a pan. Add enough water to cover and add eggs. Bring to a boil and simmer for 20 minutes. Remove from heat and allow to set for more intense color.

From all of us,

Children enjoy being read Easter stories.

Music:

1. **"Did You Ever See a Rabbit?"**
   (Sing to the tune of "Did You Ever See a Lassie?")

   Did you ever see a rabbit, a rabbit, a rabbit?
   Did you ever see a rabbit, a rabbit on Easter morn?
   He hops around so quietly
   And hides all the eggs.
   Did you ever see a rabbit, on Easter morn?

2. **"Easter Bunny"**
   (Sing to the tune of "Ten Little Indians")

   Where, oh, where is the Easter Bunny,
   Where, oh, where is the Easter Bunny,
   Where, oh, where is the Easter Bunny,
   Early Easter morning?

   Find all the eggs and put them in a basket,
   Find all the eggs and put them in a basket,
   Find all the eggs and put them in a basket,
   Early Easter morning.

3. **"Easter Eggs"**
   (Sing to the chorus of "Jingle Bells")

   Easter eggs, Easter eggs,
   Hidden all around.

   Come my children look about
   And see where they are found.

   Easter eggs, Easter eggs
   They're a sight to see.
   One for Tom and one for Ann
   And a special one for me!

   Insert names of children in your classroom.

4. **"Easter Eggs"**
   (Sing to the tune of "Mama's Little Baby Loves Shortnin'")

   Easter eggs here and there,
   Easter eggs everywhere.
   What's the color of the
   Easter egg here?

Fingerplays:

FIVE LITTLE EASTER EGGS

Five little Easter eggs lovely colors wore;
Mother ate the blue one and then there were four.
Four little Easter eggs, two and two, you see;
Daddy ate the red one, and then there were three.
Three little Easter eggs; before I knew
Sister ate the yellow one, then there were two.

Two little Easter eggs; oh what fun.
Brother ate the purple one, then there was one.
One little Easter egg; see me run!
I ate the very last one, and then there were none!

This could be a fingerplay or could be done with colored finger puppet eggs with the children holding a particular color going down when that color is named.

Source: Peck, Don. (1975). *Fingerplays that Motivate.* Minneapolis: T.S. Denison and Company.

KITTY AND BUNNY

Here is a kitty.
  (make a fist with one hand)
Here is a bunny.
  (hold up other hand with pointer and middle fingers up straight)
See his tall ears so pink and funny?
  (wiggle the two extended fingers)
Kitty comes by and licks his face;
  (extend thumb and wiggle near the bunny)
And around and around the garden they race.
  (make circular motions with hands)
And then without a single peep,
They both lie down and go to sleep.
  (fold hands)

Source: Peck, Don. (1975). *Fingerplays that Motivate.* Minneapolis: T.S. Denison and Company.

EASTER BUNNY

Easter Bunny, Easter Bunny
  (make "ears" at head with arms outstretched)
Pink and white
Come fill my basket
  (make filling motion)
Overnight
  (pretend to sleep, lay head on hands)

Source: Overholser, Kathy. (1979). *Let Your Fingers Do the Talking.* Minneapolis: T.S. Denison and Company.

THE DUCK

I waddle when I walk.
  (hold arms elbow high and twist trunk side to side, or squat down)

I quack when I talk.
  (place palms together and open and close)
And I have webbed toes on my feet.
  (spread fingers wide)
Rain coming down
Makes me smile, not frown
  (smile)
And I dive for something to eat.
  (put hands together and make diving motion)

MY RABBIT

My rabbit has two big ears
  (hold up index and middle fingers for ears)
And a funny little nose.
  (join other three fingers for nose)
He likes to nibble carrots
  (move thumb away from other two fingers)
And he hops wherever he goes.
  (move whole hand jerkily)

Science:

1. **Incubate and Hatch Eggs**

   Check the yellow pages of your telephone book to see if any hatcheries are located in your area.

2. **Dying Eggs**

   Use natural products to make egg dye. Beets—deep red, onions—yellow (add soda to make bright yellow), cranberries—light red, spinach leaves—green, and blackberries—blue. To make dyed eggs pick two or three colors from the list. Make the dye by boiling the fruit or vegetable in small amounts of water. Let the children put a cool hard-boiled egg in a nylon stocking and dip it into the dye. Keep the egg in the dye for several minutes. Pull out the nylon and check the color. If it is dark enough, place the egg on a paper towel to dry. If children want to color the eggs with crayons before dying, you can show how the wax keeps liquid from getting on the egg.

3. **Science Table Additions**

   - bird nests
   - empty bird eggs

- different kinds of baskets
- an incubator
- newly planted seeds
- flowers still in bud (children can watch them open)
- pussy willows

4. **Basket Guessing**

Do reach-and-feel using a covered basket. Place an egg, a chick, a rabbit, a doll's hat, some Easter grass, etc., in a large Easter basket. Let the children place their hands into the basket individually and describe the objects they are feeling.

Dramatic Play:

1. **Flower Shop**

Plan a flower shop for the dramatic play area. Include spring plants, baskets, and Easter lilies.

2. **Egg Center**

Create a colored egg center to be used during self-directed play. Some children put stickers on plastic eggs, some sell the eggs, and others buy them.

3. **Costume Shop**

Place costumes for bunny use, Easter baskets, and Easter eggs in the dramatic play area. The children can take turns hiding the eggs and going on hunts.

4. **A Bird Nest**

Place a nest with eggs in the dramatic play area. Also provide bird masks, a perch, and other bird items in the area for use during self-initiated play.

5. **Easter Clothes**

Bring in Easter clothes for the children to dress up in. Suits, dresses, hats, purses, gloves, and dress-up shoes should be included.

6. **Hat Shop**

Make a hat shop. Place hats with ribbons, flowers, netting, and other decorations in the dramatic play area. The children can decorate the hats. If the children are interested, plan an Easter Parade.

Arts and Crafts:

1. **Easter Collages**

Collect eggshells, straw, Easter grass, or plant seeds for making collages. Place on art table with sheets of paper and glue.

2. **Colorful Collages**

Use pastel-colored sand and glue to make collages.

3. **Wet Chalk Eggs**

Use wet chalk to decorate paper cut in the shape of eggs in pastel colors. Show the children the difference between wetting the chalk in vinegar and water. The vinegar color will be brighter.

4. **Easel Ideas**

Cut egg-shaped easel paper or basket-shaped paper. Clip to the easel. Provide pastel paints at the easel. To make the paint more interesting add glitter.

5. **Milk Carton Easter Baskets**

Cut off the bottom four inches of milk cartons. Provide precut construction or wallpaper to cover the baskets, and yarn. Include small bits of paper or bright cloth to glue on. Make a handle using a thin strip of paper that is stapled to the carton. Use the baskets for the children's snack.

6. **Plastic Easter Baskets**

Easter baskets can be made by using the green plastic baskets that strawberries and blueberries come in from the grocery store. Cut thin strips of paper that children can practice weaving through the holes. This activity is most successful with older children.

7. **Color Mixing**

Provide red, yellow, and blue dyed water in shallow pans. Provide the children with medicine droppers and absorbent paper cut in the shape of eggs. Also, the children can use medicine droppers to apply color to the paper. Observe what happens when the colors blend together.

8. **Rabbit Ears**

Construct rabbit ears out of heavy paper. Attach them to a band that can be worn around the head, fitting it for size. These ears may stimulate creative movement as well as dramatic play.

9. **Shape Rabbit**

Provide a large, a medium, and four small circles cut from white paper, as well as two tall thin triangles. Show the children how to put these shapes together to make a rabbit.

Sensory:

1. **Sensory Table Activities**

Add to the sensory table:

- cotton balls with scoops and measuring cups
- birdseed or beans
- straw or hay and plastic eggs
- plastic chicks and ducks with water
- Easter grass, eggs, small straw mats
- dirt with plastic flowers and/or leaves
- dyed, scented water and water toys
- sand, shovels, and scoops

2. **Clay Cutters**

Make scented clay. Place on the art table with rabbit, duck, egg, and flower cookie cutters for the children to use during self-directed or self-initiated play.

Large Muscle:

1. **Bunny Trail**

Set up a bunny trail in the classroom. Place tape on the floor and have children hop over the trail. To make it more challenging, add a balance beam to resemble a bridge.

2. **Eggs in the Basket**

The children can practice throwing egg-shaped or regular bean bags into a large basket or bucket.

3. **Rabbit Tag**

Make the egg-shaped bean bags to play rabbit tag. To play the game, the children stand in a circle, with one child being the rabbit. The rabbit walks around the circle with a bean bag balanced on his head, and drops a second bean bag behind the back of another child. The second child must put the bean bag on his head and follow the rabbit around the circle once. Each child must keep the bean bag balanced—if it drops, it must be picked up and replaced on the head. If the rabbit is tagged, he chooses the next rabbit. If the rabbit returns to the empty spot in the circle, the second child becomes the rabbit. This is an unusual game in that the action is fairly slow, but it's still very exciting.

4. **Egg Rolling**

Place mats on the floor and have children roll across with their arms at their sides. For older children, you can place the mat on a slightly inclined plane and have children roll down, then try to have them roll back up, which is more challenging.

Field Trips:

1. **The Farm**

Take a trip to a farm to see the new baby animals.

2. **The Hatchery**

Visit a hatchery on a day that they are selling baby chicks.

3. **Neighborhood Walk**

Take a walk around the neighborhood and look for signs of new life.

4. **Rabbit Visit**

Bring some rabbits to school for the children to observe.

Math:

1. **Egg Numerals**

Collect five large plastic eggs, such as the kind that nylon stockings can be purchased in. Put numerals from one to five (or ten, for older children) on the eggs. Let the children place the correct number of cotton balls or markers into each egg.

2. **Easter Seriation**

Cut different-sized tagboard eggs, chicks, ducks, and rabbits. The children can place the items in a row from the smallest to the largest.

Social Studies:

1. **Family Easter Traditions**

During large group, ask the children what special activities their families do to celebrate Easter. Their families may go to church, eat together, have egg hunts, or do other things that are special on this day.

2. **Sharing Baskets**

Decorate eggs or baskets to give to a home for the elderly. If possible, take a walk and let the children deliver them.

Group Time (games, language):

1. **The Last Bunny**

This is a game for ten or more players. It is more fun with a large number. An Easter rabbit is chosen by counting out or drawing straws. All the other players stand in a circle.

The Easter rabbit walks around the circle and taps one player on the back saying, "Have you seen my bunny helper?" "What does it look like?" asks the player and the Easter rabbit describes the bunny helper. He may say, "She is wearing a watch and blue shoes." The player tries to guess who it is. When he names the right person, the Easter rabbit says, "That's my helper!" and the other player chases the bunny helper outside and around the circle. If the chaser catches the bunny helper before he can return to his place the chaser becomes the Easter rabbit. If the bunny helper gets there first then the first Easter rabbit must try again. The Easter rabbit takes the place in the circle of whoever is the new Easter rabbit.

Source: Rockwell, Anne. (1973). *Games and How to Play Them.* New York: Thomas Y. Crowell Co.

2. **Outdoor Egg Hunt**

Plan an egg hunt outdoors, if possible. Hide the boiled eggs that the children have decorated, candy eggs in wrappers, or small Easter candies in clear plastic bags. The children can use the baskets they have made to collect their eggs, then, weather permitting, eat the boiled eggs for a snack outdoors.

Cooking:

1. **Decorating Cupcakes**

Let the children use green frosting, dyed coconut shreds, and jelly beans to decorate cupcakes and put them into an Easter basket. As a last touch, add a pipe cleaner handle. Cake mixes can be used to make the cupcakes. Follow the directions on the box. Place paper liners in a muffin pan to ensure easy removability.

2. **Bunny Food**

Carrot sticks, celery, and lettuce can be available for snack.

3. **Egg Sandwiches**

Use the boiled eggs the children have decorated to make egg salad or deviled eggs for snack time.

164

4. Carrot and Raisin Salad

4 cups grated carrots
1 cup raisins
1/2 cup mayonnaise or whipped salad
   dressing

Place ingredients in a bowl and mix
thoroughly.

5. Bunny Salad

For each serving place one lettuce leaf on a plate. Put one canned pear half with the cut side down on top of the lettuce leaf. Add sections of an orange to represent the ears. Decorate the bunny face by adding grated carrots, raisins, nuts, or maraschino cherries to make eyes, a nose, and a mouth.

EASTER EGGS

Where did the custom of coloring Easter eggs come from? No one knows for sure. In any case, the Easter holiday centers around eggs for young children. Here are some projects you might like to try.

To hard cook eggs: Place eggs in a saucepan and add enough cold water to cover at least 1 inch above the eggs. Heat rapidly to boiling and remove from heat. Cover the pan and allow to stand for 22 to 24 minutes. Immediately cool the eggs in cold water.

- Make a vegetable dye solution by adding a teaspoon of vinegar to 1/2 cup of boiling water. Drop in food coloring and stir. The longer the egg is kept in the dye, the deeper the color will be.

- Add a teaspoonful of salad oil to a dye mixture and mix in the oil well. This results in a dye that produces swirls of color. Immerse the egg in the dye for a few minutes.

- Draw a design on an egg with a crayon before dying it. The dye will not take to the areas with the crayon marks and the design will show through.

- Wrap rubber bands, string, yarn, or narrow strips of masking tape around an egg to create stripes and other designs. Dip the egg in a dye and allow to dry before removing the wrapping.

- Drip the wax of a lighted birthday candle over an egg or draw a design on the egg using a piece of wax. Place the egg in dye. Repeat process again, if desired, dipping the egg in another color of dye. (Note: The lighted candle is to be used by an adult only.)

- Felt-tip markers can be used to decorate dyed or undyed eggs.

- Small stickers can be used on eggs.

- Craft items such as sequins, glitter, and ribbons and small pom poms can be used with glue to decorate eggs.

- Apply lengths of yarns, string, or thread to the eggs with glue, creating designs, and allow to dry.

- Egg creatures can be created by using markers, construction paper, feathers, ribbon, lace, cotton balls, fabric, and buttons. To make an egg holder, make small cardboard or construction paper cylinders. A toilet paper or paper towel tube can be cut to make stands as well.

- Save the shells from the eggs to use for eggshell collages. Crumble the shells and sprinkle over a glue design that has been made on paper or cardboard.

Multimedia:

The following resource can be found in educational catalogs:

Palmer, Hap. "Easter Time Is Here Again" on *Holiday Songs and Rhythms* [record]. Freeport, NY: Educational Activities, Inc.

Books:

The following books can be used to complement the theme:

1. Wilhelm, Hans. (1985). *Bunny Trouble*. New York: Scholastic Books.

2. Winthrop, Elizabeth. (1985). *Happy Easter, Mother Duck*. New York: Golden Press.

3. Auch, Mary J. (1992). *The Easter Egg Farm*. New York: Holiday House, Inc.

4. Devlin, Wende, & Devlin, Harry. (1990). *Cranberry Easter*. New York: Macmillan Children's Book Group.

5. Fittro, Charlene C. (1992). *Happy, The Easter Bunny*. Sabina, OH: Children's Books and Music.

6. Gambling, Lois G. (1991). *Elephant and Mouse Get Ready for Easter*. Hauppauge, NY: Barron's Educational Series, Inc.

7. Miller, Edna. (1989). *Mousekin's Easter Basket*. New York: Simon and Schuster Trade.

8. Pienkowski, Jan. (1992). *Easter*. New York: Alfred A. Knopf, Books for Young Readers.

9. Stevenson, James. (1990). *The Great Big Especially Beautiful Easter Egg*. New York: William Morrow and Co.

10. Burgess, Beverly C. (1985). *Is Easter Just for Bunnies?* Tulsa, OK: Harrison House.

11. Gibbons, Gail. (1989). *Easter*. New York: Holiday.

12. Ross, Bill. (1992). *Easter Bunnyheads*. Nashville, TN: Ideals.

13. Ross, Bill. (1992). *Easter Eggheads*. Nashville, TN: Ideals.

14. Stock, Catherine. (1991). *Easter Surprise*. New York: Macmillan Child Group.

15. Tangvald, Christine H. (1993). *The Best Thing About Easter*. Cincinnati, OH: Standard Publishing.

16. Bowman, Pete. (1992). *A Surprise for Easter: A Revolving Picture Book*. New York: Macmillan.

17. Friedrich, Priscilla & Otto. (1993). *The Easter Bunny That Overslept*. New York: Morrow.

18. Moncure, Jane B. (1987). *Word Bird's Easter Words*. Mankato, MN: Child's World.

19. Tudor, Tasha. (1989). *A Tale for Easter*. New York: Random House.

20. Wilhelm, Hans. (1991). *Bunny Trouble*. New York: Scholastic.

21. Adams, Adrienne. (1991). *The Easter Egg Artists*. New York: Macmillan.

THEME 18

Symbols

jack-o-lantern
  (pumpkin)
witch
skeleton
ghosts
black cats

Colors

orange
black

HALLOWEEN

Costumes
and Masks

goblin
witch
ghost
television characters
clowns
animals
gypsy
cartoon characters
funny people

Activities

trick-or-treating
bobbing for apples
parties
costume parades
making costumes
wearing makeup
safety

Theme Goals:

Through participating in the experiences provided by this theme, the children may learn:

1. Halloween colors.

2. Halloween costumes and masks.

3. Halloween activities.

4. Halloween symbols.

Concepts for the Children to Learn:

1. Orange and black are Halloween colors.

2. Costumes and masks are worn on Halloween.

3. Some children make their costumes and wear makeup.

4. A costume is clothes for pretending.

5. A mask is a covering we put over our face.

6. A pumpkin can be cut to look like a face.

7. Ghosts, black cats, and witches are symbols of Halloween.

8. People go trick-or-treating on Halloween.

9. A costume parade is a march with many children who are dressed up.

10. Bobbing for apples is an activity at Halloween parties.

Vocabulary:

1. **Halloween**—a day when children dress up and go trick-or-treating.

2. **jack-o-lantern**—a pumpkin cut to look like a face.

3. **trick-or-treat**—walking from house to house to ask for candy or treats.

4. **witch**—a make-believe person who wears black.

5. **ghost**—a make-believe person who wears all white.

6. **goblin**—a Halloween character.

7. **costume**—clothing worn to pretend.

8. **mask**—face covering worn when pretending.

9. **pretending**—acting like someone else.

Bulletin Board

The purpose of this bulletin board is to have the children practice visual discrimination skills. To prepare the bulletin board, construct pumpkins out of orange-colored tagboard. The number will depend upon the developmental appropriateness for the group of children. An alternative would be to use white tagboard colored orange with paint or markers. Divide the pumpkins into pairs. Draw a different kind of face for each pair of pumpkins. Hang one pumpkin from each pair on the left side of the bulletin board as illustrated. Attach an orange string to each pumpkin. On the right side of the bulletin board, hang the matching pumpkins. See illustration. Attach a push pin to each of these pumpkins. The child can match the faces on the pumpkins by winding the correct string around the correct push pin.

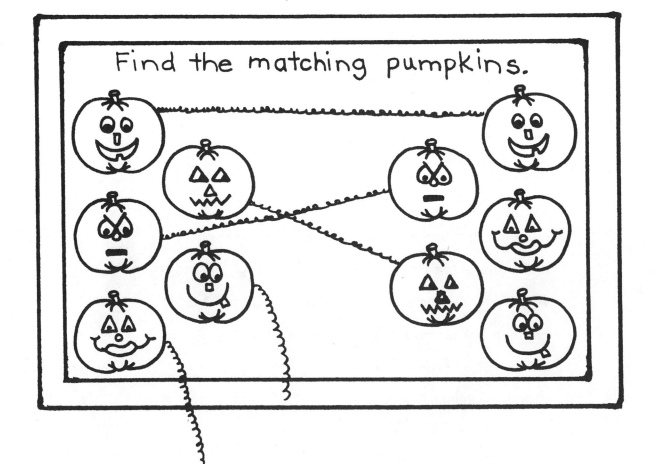

Parent Letter

Dear Parents,

The month of October has a special holiday for children—Halloween! Consequently, our next theme will center on Halloween. Many learning experiences have been planned to promote an awareness of colors that are associated with Halloween, as well as symbols that represent Halloween such as pumpkins, black cats, bats, and witches.

At School

Some of the Halloween activities planned include:

- discussing Halloween safety procedures, especially while trick-or-treating.
- carving a jack-o-lantern for the classroom.
- roasting pumpkin seeds and baking a pumpkin pie.
- trying on a variety of costumes in the dramatic play area.
- creating designs with pumpkin seeds and glue on paper.

Halloween Party!

We will be having a Halloween party on Friday. You are welcome to send a costume to school with your child that day. The costume can be simple. A funny hat, a pair of silly glasses, a wig, or a little makeup would be fine Halloween attire. We would appreciate it if you could send the costume and accessories in a bag that is labeled with your child's name. This will prevent a mix-up of belongings. We will dress in our costumes about 2:00 p.m. Then we will have a small party and parade around in our costumes. It should be a fun day. Join us!

At Home

To get into the spirit of Halloween and to help your child develop language skills, practice the following Halloween rhyme:

"Five Little Pumpkins"

Five little pumpkins sitting on a gate.
The first one said, "Oh my, it's getting late."
The second one said, "There are witches in the air."
The third one said, "But we don't care."
The fourth one said, "Let's run. Let's run."
The fifth one said, "It's Halloween fun!"
"Wooooooooo," went the wind,
And out went the lights.
And the five little pumpkins rolled out of sight.

To ensure a safe Halloween:

- Check to see if your child's costume is flame resistant or at least flame retardant.
- Children can easily trip in long garments. Be sure the hemline is several inches off the ground.
- Masks and hoods can slip and make it difficult for your child to see. If a mask is worn, be sure it is secure and that the holes for the eyes are properly positioned. An alternative to wearing a mask is to use makeup.
- Finally, check the batteries in the flashlight!

Have a safe and happy Halloween.

Masks and pumpkins are symbols of Halloween.

Music:

1. **"Flying Witches"**
   (Sing to the tune of "When the Saints Come Marching In")

   Oh, when the witches
   Come flying by.
   Oh, when the witches come flying by,
   It will be Halloween night,
   When the witches come flying by.

2. **"One Little, Two Little, Three Little Pumpkins"**
   (Sing to the tune of "One Little, Two Little, Three Little Indians")

   One little, two little, three little pumpkins,
   Four little, five little, six little pumpkins,
   Seven little, eight little, nine little pumpkins,
   Ready for Halloween night!

3. **"Have You Made a Jack-O-Lantern?"**
   (Sing to the tune of "Muffin Man")

   Have you made a jack-o-lantern,
   A jack-o-lantern, a jack-o-lantern?
   Have you made a jack-o-lantern
   For Halloween night?

Fingerplays:

JACK-O-LANTERN

I am a pumpkin, big and round.
   (show size with arms)
Once upon a time, I grew on the ground.
   (point to ground)
Now I have a mouth, two eyes, and a nose.
   (point to each)
What are they for do you suppose?
   (point to forehead and "think")
Why—I'll be a jack-o-lantern on Halloween
night.

FIVE LITTLE WITCHES

Five little witches standing by the door.
   (hold up five fingers)
One flew out and then there were four.
   (flying motion with hand)
Four little witches standing by a tree.
   (four fingers)
One went to pick a pumpkin and then there
were three.
   (picking motion, then three fingers)
Three little witches stirring their brew.
   (stir)
One fell in and then there were two.
   (two fingers)
Two little witches went for a run.
   (run with fingers)
One got lost and then there was one.
   (one finger)
One little witch, yes, only one.
   (one finger)
She cast a spell and now there are none.
   (make motions as if to cast spell and then
   put hands in lap)

HALLOWEEN FUN

Goblins and witches in high pointed hats,
   (hands above head to form hat)

172

Riding on broomsticks and chasing black cats.
(ride broomstick)
Children in costumes might well give a fright.
(look frightened)
Get things in order for Halloween night.
We like our treats
(nod head)
And we'll play no mean pranks.
(shake head)
We'll do you no harm and we'll only say,
"Thanks!"

THE JACK-O-LANTERN

Three little pumpkins growing on a vine.
(three fingers)
Sitting in the sunlight, looking just fine.
(arms up like sun)
Along came a ghost who picked just one
(one finger)
To take on home for some Halloween fun.
(smile)
He gave him two eyes to see where he goes.
(paint two eyes)
He gave him a mouth and a big handsome nose.
(point to mouth and nose)
Then he put a candle in.
(pretend to put in candle)
Now see how he glows.
(wiggle fingers from center of body out until arms are extended)

I'VE A JACK-O-LANTERN

I've a jack-o-lantern
(make a ball with open fist, thumb at top)
With a great big grin.
(grin)
I've got a jack-o-lantern
With a candle in.
(insert other index finger up through bottom of fist)

HALLOWEEN WITCHES

One little, two little, three little witches,
(hold up one hand, nod fingers at each count)
Fly over the haystacks
(fly hand in up-and-down motion)
Fly over ditches
Slide down moonbeams without any hitches
(glide hand downward)
Heigh-ho! Halloween's here!

THE FRIENDLY GHOST

I'm a friendly ghost—almost!
(point to self)
And I chase you, too!
(point to child)
I'll just cover me with a sheet
(pretend to cover self ending with hands covering face)
And then call "scat" to you.
(uncover face quickly and call out "scat")

WITCHES' CAT

I am the witches' cat.
(make a fist with two fingers extended for cat)
Meoow. Meoow.
(stroke fist with other hand)
My fur is black as darkest night.
My eyes are glaring green and bright.
(circle eyes with thumb and forefingers)
I am the witches' cat.
(make a fist again with two fingers extended and stroke fist with other hand)

MY PUMPKIN

See my pumpkin round and fat.
(make circle with hands, fingers spread wide, touching)
See my pumpkin yellow.
(make a smaller circle)
Watch him grin on Halloween.
(point to mouth, which is grinning wide)
He is a very funny fellow.

Science:

1. **Carve Pumpkins**

   Purchase several pumpkins. Carve them and save the seeds for roasting. An alternative activity would be to use a black felt-tip marker to draw facial features on the pumpkin. Pumpkins can also have added accessories. For example, a large carrot can be used for a nose, parsley for hair, cut green peppers for ears, radishes for eyes, and a small green onion can be placed in a cut mouth for teeth.

2. Roasting Pumpkin Seeds

Wash and dry pumpkin seeds. Then spread the seeds out on a cookie sheet to dry. Bake the seeds in a preheated oven at 350 degrees until brown. Salt, cool, and eat at snack time.

3. Plant Pumpkin Seeds

Purchase a packet of pumpkin seeds. Plant the pumpkin seeds in small paper cups. Set the paper cups with the pumpkin seeds in a sunny place. Water as needed. Observe to see if there is growth on a daily basis.

Dramatic Play:

Costume

Add Halloween costumes to the dramatic play area. (Some teachers purchase these at thrift stores or sales. From year to year they are stored in a Halloween prop box.)

Arts and Crafts:

1. Spooky Easel

Provide orange and black paint at the paint easels.

2. Pumpkin Seed Pictures

Dye pumpkin seeds many colors. Place the seeds with paste and paper on a table in the art area. The children then can create their own pictures.

3. Crayon Wash

On the art table, place paper, light-colored crayons, tempera paint, and brushes. The children can draw on paper with light-colored crayons. After this, they can paint over the entire picture.

4. Masks

Yarn, paper plates, felt-tip markers, and any other accessories needed to make masks

interesting can be placed on a table in the art area. If desired, yarn can be used as hair on the mask.

Sensory:

1. Measuring Seeds

Pumpkin seeds and measuring cups can be added to the sensory table. The children will enjoy feeling and pouring seeds.

2. Goop

Add dry cornstarch to the sensory table. Slowly add enough water to make it a "goopy" consistency. If desired, add coloring to make it black or orange.

Large Muscle:

Ghost, Ghost, Witch

This game is played like "Duck, Duck, Goose." Form a circle and kneel. Choose one child to walk around the outside of the circle chanting, "Ghost, ghost, ghost." When the child taps another child and says "witch," the child tapped chases the initiator around the circle, attempting to tag the child. If the child who is "it" returns to the tapped child's spot before the other, he can lose his turn. If not, the child continues walking around the circle, repeating the same procedure.

Field Trips/Resource People:

1. Pumpkin Patch

Visit a pumpkin patch. During the tour point out various-sized pumpkins. Discuss how the pumpkins grow, as well as their shapes, sizes, etc.

2. Halloween Safety

A police officer can be invited to talk with the children about Halloween safety.

Math:

1. Counting Pumpkin Seeds

Cut circles from construction paper. The number needed will depend upon the developmental level of the children. Write a numeral on each paper circle and place each into a pie tin. The children may count pumpkin seeds into the tins matching the circles.

2. Weighing Pumpkin Seeds

In the math area, place a scale and pumpkin seeds. The children may elect to experiment by balancing the scale with the pumpkin seeds.

Group Time (games, language):

1. Thank-you Note

Write a thank-you note to any resource person. Encourage all of the children to participate by sharing what they liked or saw.

2. Costume Parade

On Halloween day, the children can dress up in costumes and march around the room and throughout the school to music. If available, a walk to a local nursing home may be enjoyed by the children as well as the elderly.

Cooking:

1. Pumpkin Pie

1 unbaked pie shell
2 cups (16–17 ounces) pumpkin
1 can sweetened condensed milk
1 egg
1/2 teaspoon salt
2 teaspoons pumpkin pie spice

Blend all of the ingredients in a large mixing bowl. Pour the mixture into the pie shell. Bake the pie in an oven preheated to 375 degrees for 50 to 55 minutes or until a sharp knife blade inserted near center of pie is clean when removed. Cool and refrigerate the pie for 1 hour before serving. Top with whipped cream if desired.

2. Pumpkin Patch Muffins

3 cups flour
1 cup sugar
4 teaspoons baking powder
1 teaspoon salt
1 teaspoon pumpkin pie spice
1 cup milk
1 cup canned pumpkin
1/2 cup (1 stick) butter or margarine, melted
2 eggs, beaten

Sift the flour, sugar, baking powder, salt, and pumpkin pie spice into a large mixing bowl. Add the milk, pumpkin, melted butter, and eggs. Mix with a wooden spoon just until flour is moist. (Batter will be lumpy.) Place paper liners in the muffin tins and fill 2/3 full with batter. Bake in a preheated 400-degree oven 20 minutes or until muffins are golden. Cool in muffin tins 10 minutes on a wire rack. Remove muffins from muffin tins and finish cooling on wire racks. Pile into serving baskets and serve warm for snack.

3. Witches' Brew

5 cups cranberry juice, unsweetened
5 cups apple cider, unsweetened
1 or 2 cinnamon sticks
1/4 teaspoon ground nutmeg

Place ingredients in a large saucepan. Cover, heat, and simmer for 10 minutes. Serve warm.

4. Roasted Pumpkin Seeds

Soak pumpkin seeds for 24 hours in saltwater (1/4 cup salt to 1 cup water). Spread on cloth-covered cookie sheet and roast at 100 degrees for 2 hours. Turn oven off and leave seeds overnight.

5. Non-bake Pumpkin Pie

1 can prepared pumpkin pie
1 package vanilla instant pudding
1 cup milk

Mix and pour into baked pie shell or graham cracker pie shell.

DECORATING A PUMPKIN

In carving or decorating a pumpkin with the children you can discuss:

- the physical properties of pumpkins—color, texture, size, shape (both outside and inside).
- food category to which pumpkins belong.
- what other forms pumpkin can be made into after scooped out of the shell.
- where pumpkins grow (plant some of the seeds).

- what size and shape to make the features of the pumpkin, including eyes, nose, mouth, and what kind of expression to make.

Accessories:

1 bunch parsley (hair)
1 carrot (nose)
2 string beans (eyebrows)
2 radishes (eyes)

1 green pepper (ears)
1 stalk celery (teeth)
1 large pumpkin (head)

Prepare the pumpkin in the usual manner; that is, cut off the cap and scoop out the seeds inside. Save the seeds for roasting. If desired, individual vegetable pieces may be attached by carving or inserting toothpicks.

Multimedia:

The following resources can be found in educational catalogs:

1. Palmer, Hap. *Holiday Songs and Rhythms* [record].

2. *Holiday Songs for All Occasions* [record]. Kimbo Records.

3. *Holiday Action Songs* [record]. Kimbo Records.

4. *Why We Celebrate* [30-minute video]. Edu-Vid.

Books:

The following books can be used to complement the theme:

1. Alexander, Sue. (1990). *Who Goes Out on Halloween*. New York: Bantam Books, Inc.

2. Berenstain, Stan & Janice. (1989). *The Berenstain Bears Trick or Treat*. New York: Random House Books for Young Readers.

3. Barkan, Jeanne. (1991). *The Very Scary Jack 'O Lantern*. New York: Scholastic Inc.

4. Cassedy, Sylvia. (1990). *Best Cat Suit of All*. New York: Dial Books for Young Readers.

5. Craig, Janet. (1988). *Joey the Jack-O'-Lantern*. Mahwah, NJ: Troll Associates.

6. Gardner, Beau. (1990). *Whooo's a Fright on Halloween Night*. New York: Putnam Publishing Group.

7. George, Diann. (1992). *The Peanut Butter Witch*. New York: Carlton Press, Inc.

8. Silverman, Erica. (1992). *Big Pumpkin*. New York: Macmillan Children's Book Group.

9. Titherington, Jeanne. (1990). *Pumpkin Pumpkin*. New York: William Morrow and Co., Inc.

10. Wojciechowski, Susan. (1992). *The Best Halloween of All*. New York: Crown Books for Young Readers.

11. Ziefert, Harriet. (1992). *Halloween Parade*. New York: Viking Children's Books.

12. Gantos, Jack. (1988). *Rotten Ralph's Trick or Treat*. Boston: Houghton Mifflin.

13. Himmelman, John. (1987). *Amanda & The Witch Switch*. New York: Puffin.

14. Merriam, Eve. (1987). *Halloween ABC*. New York: Macmillan.

15. Moncure, Jane B. (1987). *Word Bird's Halloween Words*. Mankato, MN: Child's World.

16. Nerlove, Miriam. (1989). *Halloween*. Morton Grove, IL: Albert Whitman.

17. Reeves, Mona R. (1989). *The Spooky Eerie Night*. New York: Macmillan.

18. Stock, Catherine. (1990). *Halloween Monster*. New York: Bradbury Press.

19. Leaf, Margaret. (1987). *Eyes of the Dragon*. New York: Lothrop, Lee & Shepard.

20. Bauer, Caroline F. (Ed.). (1989). *Halloween: Stories & Poems*. New York: Harper Collins.

21. Ziefert, Harriet. (1992). *What Is Halloween?* New York: Harper Collins.

22. Bunting, Eve. (1989). *Ghost's Hour, Spook's Hour*. Boston: Houghton Mifflin.

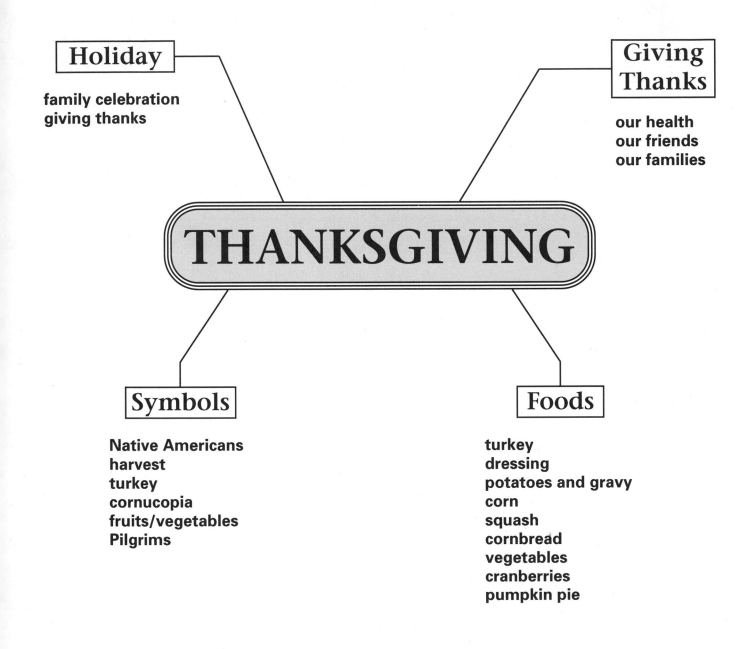

Holiday

family celebration
giving thanks

Giving Thanks

our health
our friends
our families

THANKSGIVING

Symbols

Native Americans
harvest
turkey
cornucopia
fruits/vegetables
Pilgrims

Foods

turkey
dressing
potatoes and gravy
corn
squash
cornbread
vegetables
cranberries
pumpkin pie

Theme Goals:

Through participating in the experiences provided by this theme, the children may learn:

1. Purpose of Thanksgiving.

2. Thanksgiving celebration.

3. Thanksgiving foods.

4. Thanksgiving symbols.

Concepts for the Children to Learn:

1. Thanksgiving is a holiday.

2. Thanksgiving is a time for giving thanks.

3. Families celebrate together on Thanksgiving.

4. Turkey, dressing, potatoes, vegetables, cranberries, and pumpkin pie are eaten on Thanksgiving by many families.

5. A turkey, cornucopia, Pilgrims, and Native Americans are Thanksgiving symbols.

Vocabulary:

1. **Thanksgiving**—a holiday in November.

2. **Pilgrims**—early settlers who sailed to America.

3. **thankful**—expressing thanks.

4. **turkey**—large bird that is cooked for Thanksgiving.

5. **Native Americans**—natives who lived in America when the Pilgrims first arrived.

6. **cornucopia**—a horn-shaped container with fruits, vegetables, and flowers.

Bulletin Board

The purpose of this bulletin board is to have the children hang the color-coded card onto the corresponding colored feather. Construct a large turkey out of tagboard. Color each feather a different color. Hang the turkey on the bulletin board. Hang a push pin in each feather. On small index cards, make a circle of each color and write the color name above it. Use a hole punch to make a hole in each card.

Parent Letter

Dear Parents,

Each year during the month of November we celebrate Thanksgiving. To coincide with this holiday, at school we will be focusing our curriculum on Thanksgiving. Through activities provided, the children will develop an understanding of the foods of Thanksgiving, as well as become more aware of the many people and things for which we are thankful.

At School

Planned learning experiences related to Thanksgiving include:

- popping corn.
- creating hand turkeys.
- visiting a turkey farm.
- exploring various types of corn with scales and magnifying glasses.

At Home

There are many ways for you to incorporate Thanksgiving concepts at home. Talk with your child about the special ways your family celebrates Thanksgiving. Involve your child in the preparation of a traditional Thanksgiving dish. Also, emphasize things and people for which you are thankful.

Reminder

There will be no school on Thursday, November 27th.

For those of you who are traveling during the Thanksgiving weekend, drive safely!

Happy Thanksgiving from the staff!

Families like to celebrate Thanksgiving.

Music:

1. **"Popcorn Song"**
   (Sing to the tune of "I'm a Little Teapot")

   I'm a little popcorn in a pot.
   Heat me up and watch me pop.
   When I get all fat and white, then I'm done.
   Popping corn is lots of fun.

2. **"If You're Thankful"**
   (Sing to the tune of "If You're Happy")

   If you're thankful and you know it clap your
   hands.
   If you're thankful and you know it clap your
   hands.
   If you're thankful and you know it, then your
   face will surely show it,
   If you're thankful and you know it, clap your
   hands.

   Additional verses could include stamp your
   feet, tap your head, turn around, shout hooray,
   etc.

Fingerplays:

THANKSGIVING DINNER

Everyday we eat our dinner.
Our table is very small.
   (palms of hands close together)
There's room for father, mother, sister, brother,
and me—that's all.
   (point to each finger)
But when it's Thanksgiving Day and the
company comes,
You'd scarcely believe your eyes.
   (rub eyes)
For that very same reason, the table stretches
until it is just this size!
   (stretch arms wide)

THE BIG TURKEY

The big turkey on the farm is so very proud.
   (form fist)
He spreads his tail like a fan
   (spread fingers of fist)
And struts through the animal crowd.
   (move two fingers of fist as walking)
If you talk to him as he wobbles along;

He'll answer back with a gobbling song.
"Gobble, gobble, gobble."
(open and close hand)

Science:

1. **Corn**

   Display several types of corn on the science table. Include field corn, popcorn, and popped popcorn.

2. **Wishbone**

   Bring in a wishbone from a turkey and place it in a bottle. Pour some vinegar in the bottle to cover the wishbone. Leave the wishbone in the bottle for 24 hours. Remove it and feel it. It will feel and bend like rubber.

Sensory:

The following items can be placed in the sensory area for the children to discover:

- unpopped or popped popcorn
- pinecones
- cornmeal and measuring cups

Dramatic Play:

Shopping

Set up a grocery store in the dramatic play area. To stimulate play, provide a cash register, shopping bags, as well as empty food containers including boxes, packages, and plastic bottles.

Arts and Crafts:

1. **Thanksgiving Collage**

   Place magazines on the art table for the children to cut out things they are thankful for. After the pictures are cut, they can be pasted on paper to form a collage.

2. **Thanksgiving Feast**

   Place food items cut from magazines and the newspaper on a table along with paste and paper plates. Let the children select the foods they would like to eat for their Thanksgiving feast.

3. **Cornmeal Playdough**

   Make cornmeal playdough. Mix 2 1/2 cups flour with 1 cup cornmeal. Add 1 tablespoon oil and 1 cup water. Additional water can be added to make desired texture. The dough should have a grainy texture. Cooky cutters and rolling pins can extend this activity.

4. **Popcorn Collage**

   Place popped popcorn and dried tempera paint into small sealable bags. Have children shake bags to color the popcorn. Then have them create designs and pictures by gluing the popcorn onto the paper. You can also use unpopped colored popcorn. Make sure the children do not eat any of the popcorn after it has been mixed with paint.

5. **Hand Turkey**

   Paper, crayons, or pencils are needed. Begin by instructing the child to place a hand on a piece of paper. Then tell them to spread their fingers. If possible, have the child trace his own fingers. Otherwise, you need to trace them. The hand can be decorated to create a turkey. Eyes, a beak, and a wattle can be added to the outline of the thumb. The fingers can be colored to represent the turkey's feathers. Then legs can be added below the outline of the palm.

Large Muscle:

Popping Corn

Pretend to be popping corn. Begin by demonstrating how to curl down on the floor, explaining that everyone is a kernel of corn. Then plug in the popcorn popper and listen to the sounds. Upon hearing popping sounds, jump up and down to the sounds.

Field Trip:

Turkey Farm

Visit a turkey farm. The children can observe the behavior of the turkeys as well as the food they eat.

Math:

1. **Turkey Shapes**

   Give children several geometric shapes to create their own turkeys with circles, squares, and triangles. Have children identify the shapes and colors as they create their turkeys.

2. **Colored Popcorn**

   Provide the children with colored popcorn seeds. Place corresponding colored circles in the bottom of muffin tins or egg cartons. Encourage the children to sort the seeds by color.

Group Time (games, language):

1. **Turkey Chase**

   Have the children sit in a circle formation. The game requires two balls of different colors. Vary the size, depending on the age of the children. Generally, the younger the child, the larger the ball size. Begin by explaining that the first ball passed is the "turkey." The second ball is the "turkey farmer." The first ball should be passed from child to child around the circle. Shortly after, pass the second ball in the same direction. The game ends when the turkey farmer, the second ball, catches up to the turkey, the first ball. This game is played like hot potato.

2. **Feast**

   Place several kinds of food on a plate in the middle of the circle. Tell the children to cover their eyes. Choose one child to take something from the plate to eat. The child hides one item, and the others open their eyes and try to guess which food item the child has eaten! The number of items included in this activity should be determined by the children's developmental age. Even to begin the activity, it may be advisable to begin with only two food items.

3. **Turkey Keeper**

   To play this game, a turkey cut from cardboard or even a small plastic replica is needed. Instruct one child to cover his eyes. Then quietly hide the turkey in the classroom. After this, instruct the child to open his eyes and begin to look for the turkey. When the child begins walking in the direction of the turkey, the rest of the children quietly provide a clue by saying, "gobble gobble." As the child approaches the turkey, the children's voices serve as a clue by becoming louder. Once the turkey is located, another child becomes the turkey keeper.

4. **Drop the Wishbone**

   Tell the children to sit in a circle formation. Choose one child to walk around the outside of the circle and drop a wishbone behind another child. (If a real wishbone is unavailable, a wishbone can be cut from cardboard.) The child who had the wishbone dropped behind him must pick it up and chase the first child. If the first child is tagged before he runs around the circle and sits in the second child's place, he is "it" again. If not, the second child is "it." This is a variation of "Drop the Handkerchief."

5. **Turkey Waddle**

   Provide the children with verbal and visual clues to waddle like turkeys. The following terms may be used:

   - fat turkey
   - little turkey
   - fast turkey
   - slow turkey
   - tired turkey
   - happy turkey
   - proud turkey
   - sad turkey
   - hungry turkey
   - full turkey

Cooking:

1. **Fu Fu—West Africa**

   3 or 4 yams
   water
   1/2 teaspoon salt
   1/8 teaspoon pepper
   Optional: 3 tablespoons honey or sugar

   Wash and peel yams and cut into 1/2-inch slices. Place slices in a large saucepan and add water to cover them. Bring to a boil over a hot plate or stove. Reduce heat, cover saucepan, and simmer for 20 to 25 minutes, until yams are soft enough to mash. Remove saucepan from stove and drain off liquid into a small bowl. Let yams cool for 15 minutes. Place yam slices in a medium-sized mixing bowl, mash with a fork, add salt and pepper, and mash again until smooth. Roll mixture into small, walnut-sized balls. If mixture is too dry, moisten it with a tablespoon of the reserved yam liquid. For sweeter Fu Fu, roll yam balls in a dish of honey or sugar. Makes 24 balls.

2. **Muffins**

   1 egg
   3/4 cup milk
   1/2 cup vegetable oil
   2 cups all-purpose flour
   1/3 cup sugar
   3 tablespoons baking powder
   1 teaspoon salt

   Heat oven to 400 degrees. Grease bottoms only of 12 medium muffin cups. Beat egg. Stir in milk and oil. Stir in remaining ingredients all at once, just until flour is moistened. Batter will be lumpy. Fill muffin cups about 3/4 full. Bake until golden brown about 20 minutes. For pumpkin muffins: stir in 1/2 cup pumpkin and 1/2 cup raisins with the milk and 2 teaspoons pumpkin pie spice with the flour.

   For cranberry-orange muffins: stir in 1 cup cranberry halves and 1 tablespoon grated orange peel with milk.

3. **Cranberry Freeze**

   16-ounce can (2 cups) whole cranberry sauce
   8-ounce can (1 cup) crushed pineapple, drained
   1 cup sour cream or yogurt

   In a medium bowl, combine all the ingredients and mix well. Pour the mixture into an 8-inch square pan or an ice cube tray. Freeze 2 hours or until firm. To serve cut into squares or pop out of the ice cube tray.

Multimedia:

The following resources can be found in educational catalogs:

1. Palmer, Hap. "Things I Am Thankful For," *Holiday Songs and Rhymes* [record].

2. *Why We Celebrate…Thanksgiving* [30-minute video]. Edu-vid.

Books:

The following books can be used to complement the theme:

1. Nikola-Lisa, W. (1991). *One, Two, Three Thanksgiving!* Morton Grove, IL: Albert Whitman.

2. George, Jean C. (1993). *First Thanksgiving*. New York: Putnam.

3. Ziefert, Harriet. (1992). *What Is Thanksgiving?* New York: Harper Collins.

4. Fradin, Dennis B. (1990). *Thanksgiving Day*. Hillside, NJ: Enslow Publishers.

5. Hoban, Lillian. (1991). *Silly Tilly's Thanksgiving Dinner*. New York: Harper Collins.

6. Parker, Margot. (1988). *What Is Thanksgiving Day?* Chicago: Children's Press.

7. Berenstain, Stan & Janice. (1990). *The Berenstain Bears and the Prize Pumpkin*. New York: Random House Books for Young Readers.

8. Bunting, Eve. (1991). *A Turkey for Thanksgiving*. Boston: Houghton Mifflin Co.

9. Bunting, Eve. (1990). *Daisy's Crazy Thanksgiving*. New York: Henry Hold and Co.

10. Dragonwagon, Crescent. (1992). *Alligator Arrived with Apples: A Potluck Alphabet Feast*. New York: Macmillan Children's Book Group.

11. Pilkey, Dav. (1990). *'Twas the Night Before Thanksgiving*. New York: Orchard Books.

12. Stock, Catherine. (1990). *Thanksgiving Treat*. New York: Macmillan Children's Book Group.

13. Watson, Wendy. (1991). *Thanksgiving at Our House*. Boston: Houghton Mifflin Co.

Symbols

menorah
Star of David
dreidel
synagogue/temple

Foods

latkes
honey-spice cookies
ka'achei sumsum
matzo

HANUKKAH
(CHANUKAH)

Celebrations

lighting the menorah
gift giving
family togetherness

Theme Goals:

Through participating in the experiences provided by this theme, the children may learn:

1. The story of Hanukkah.

2. Symbols of Hanukkah.

3. Hanukkah celebrations.

Concepts for the Children to Learn:

1. Hanukkah is a Jewish holiday.

2. Hanukkah is a time for giving and sharing with others.

3. The menorah and the dreidel are symbols of Hanukkah.

4. Hanukkah is celebrated for eight days.

5. Some foods eaten during Hanukkah include latkes, honey-spice cookies, ka'achei sumsum, and matzo.

Vocabulary:

1. **latkes**—potato pancakes eaten during Hanukkah.

2. **dreidel**—four-sided toy that spins like a top.

3. **Star of David**—six-sided star-shaped figure, is a Jewish symbol.

4. **menorah**—eight-branched candlestick. The middle or ninth candle is taller than the other eight and is called the shammash.

5. **Hanukkah**—eight-day Jewish festival of lights. A celebration of the Jewish people's fight long ago to retain/keep the right to practice their religion. One candle is lighted on the menorah each day.

Bulletin Board

The purpose of this bulletin board is to develop an awareness of the passage of time as well as the math concept of sets. This bulletin board starts out with the base of the menorah. Each day of Hanukkah the children work together to construct a candle and a flame to add to the menorah. Candles and flames are most interesting when made using a wide variation of mediums: sequins, feathers, cut construction paper, yarn, etc.

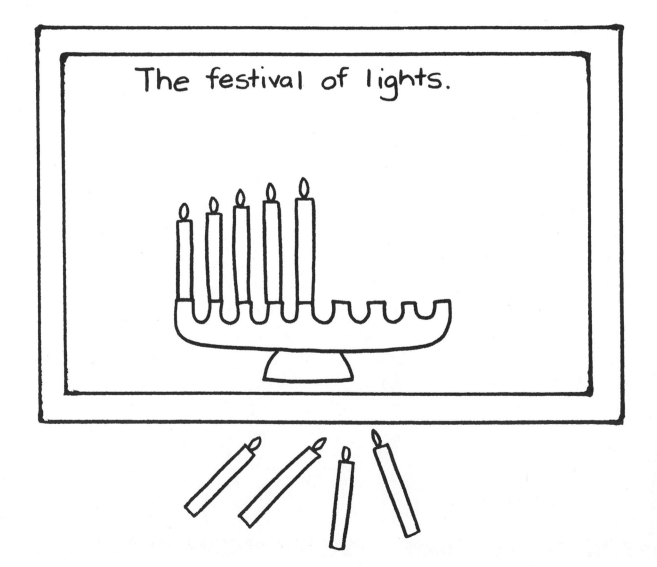

Parent Letter

Dear Parents,

For the next eight days, we will be celebrating Hanukkah. Hanukkah commemorates the victory of the Jews over the Syrians. Hanukkah, also known as the Festival of Lights, is celebrated for eight days in either November or December. In 175 B.C. a Syrian King, Antiochus, ordered the Jewish Temple defiled. After the Syrians desecrated the Temple, Judah Maccabee formed a small but powerful army to defend the Jews. The Maccabees rebuilt the Temple and the legend states that when it was time to light the Temple lamp for rededication, there was only enough sacred oil to burn for one day. Miraculously, it burned for eight days!

Hanukkah is celebrated by the lighting of a special candelabra called a menorah. On the menorah there is one holder for each of the eight nights and one for the shammash. Shammash means helper in Hebrew; this is the candle that is used to light the others. The candles are lit beginning on the right side and moving to the left.

Each night, after the lighting of the menorah, the children are given small gifts. Traditionally this gift was gelt, money to be used while playing the dreidel game.

Unlike most Jewish holidays, work and schooling continues during the eight-day celebration.

At School

Some of the learning experiences the children will participate in include:

- playing a game with a dreidel, which is similar to a toy top.
- preparing latkes (potato pancakes) for snack.
- creating wax-resist drawings at the art table.

Happy Hanukkah!

Learning about Hanukkah and other religious holidays is an important social studies activity.

Music:

"Menorah Candles"
(Sing to the tune of "Twinkle, Twinkle, Little Star")

Twinkle, twinkle candles in the night,
Standing on the menorah bright,
Burning slow we all know,
Burning bright to give us light.
Twinkle, twinkle candles in the night,
Standing on the menorah bright.

Fingerplays:

THE MENORAH CANDLE

I'm a menorah candle
(stand, point at self)
Growing shorter you can see
(bend down slowly)
Melting all my wax
(go down more)
Until there's nothing left to see.
(sit down)

HANUKKAH LIGHTS

One light, two lights, three lights, and four
(hold up four fingers, one at a time)
Five lights, six lights, and three more,
(hold up five fingers on other hand)
Twinkle, twinkle nine pretty lights,
(move fingers)
In a golden menorah bright!
(make cup with palm of hand)

MY DREIDEL

I have a little dreidel.
(cup hands to form a square)
I made it out of clay.
(move fingers in a molding motion)
And when it's dry and ready
(flatten hands as if to hold in hand—palm
up, pinkies together)
Then with it I will play.
(pretend to spin dreidel on the floor)

Science:

1. **Potato Sprouts**

Provide each child with a clear plastic cup. Fill the plastic cup half-full with water. Place a potato part way in the water supported by toothpicks to keep it from dropping into the cup. Put the end with tubers into the water. The other end should stick out of the water. Refill with fresh water as it evaporates and watch the roots begin to grow and leaves start to sprout.

2. **Candle Snuffer**

   Demonstrate how a candle snuffer is used to put out a flame. (Check licensing regulations prior to the activity.)

3. **Light**

   Light a candle. Discuss other sources of light. (Examples: sun, lamp, flashlight, traffic lights, etc.)

4. **Sunlight Power**

   Fill two glasses half-full of warm water. Stir some flour into one glass. In the other, dissolve a little yeast in the water, then add flour. Now set them both in a warm place for an hour and watch the results.

Dramatic Play:

1. **Family Celebration**

   Collect materials for a special family meal. These may include dresses, hats, coats, plates, cups, plastic food, napkins, etc. The children can have a holiday meal.

2. **Gift Wrapping Center**

   Collect various-sized boxes, wrapping paper, tape, and ribbon. The children can wrap presents for Hanukkah.

Sensory:

Sand Temples

Fill the sensory table with sand and moisten until the sand begins to adhere. The children may pack sand into cans to mold into desired shapes and build sand temples from the molded forms.

Arts and Crafts:

1. **Star of David**

   Provide the children with triangles cut from blue construction paper. Demonstrate to the children how to invert one triangle over the other to form a star. The stars may be glued to construction paper.

2. **Potato Art**

   Slice potatoes in half. The children may dip the potato halves in shallow pans containing various colors of tempera paint and then create designs on construction paper.

3. **Hanukkah Handprints**

   Provide the children with construction paper, brushes, and tempera paint in shallow pans. Paint each of the children's hands with a brush that has been dipped in tempera paint. The children then may place their hands on the construction paper, creating handprints.

4. **Dreidel Top**

   Collect and wash out 1/2-pint milk containers. Tape the top down so that the carton forms a square. Provide construction paper squares for the children to paste to the sides of the milk carton. The children may decorate with crayons or felt-tip markers. Upon completion, punch an unsharpened pencil through the milk container so that the children may spin it like a top.

5. **Star of David Mobile**

   Provide each child with two drinking straws. Demonstrate to the children how to bend the straws so that they make triangles. Glue the straw triangles together, inverting one over the other to make a six-pointed star. Tie string to the star and hang from a window or ceiling. This activity is appropriate for 6-, 7-, and 8-year-olds.

Resource People:

Invite a rabbi or parent of the Jewish faith to come and talk about Hanukkah and how it is celebrated.

Large Muscle:

1. Dreidel Dance

The children can dance the dreidel dance by standing in a circle and spinning as they sing this song to the tune of "Row, Row, Row, Your Boat."

Dreidel, dreidel, dreidel,
A-spinning I will go.
Speed it up and slow it down,
And on the ground I'll go!

2. Frying Donuts—Dramatic Play

Children can act out frying donuts as they sing this song to the tune of "I Have a Little Turtle."

I have a little donut,
It is so nice and light,
And when it's all done cooking,
I'm going to take a bite!

Frying donuts usually pop up and out of the frying oil when they are finished cooking. The children can act out these motions. The oil used in frying the donuts is significant in the Hanukkah celebration. It signifies the oil burned in the Temple lamp.

Math:

1. Sort the Stars

Provide children with various-colored stars. The children can match the colors. A variation would be to have stars of various sizes. The children could sequence the stars from largest to smallest.

2. Hanukkah Puzzles

Mount pictures of a menorah and the Star of David on tagboard. Cut into pieces. Laminate. The number of pieces will depend upon the children's developmental age.

3. Candle Holder and Candle Match

Have a variety of candle holders set out with candles. The children will have to match the candles to the correct-sized candle holder.

Group Time (games, language):

1. Hot Potato

Ask the children to sit in a circle. Provide one child with a real, a plastic, or a potato constructed from tagboard. Play music. As the music is playing, the children pass the potato around the circle until the music stops. The one holding the potato is out of the circle. Game continues until one child is left or the children no longer wish to play.

2. Dreidel Game

Each player starts with 10 to 15 pennies, nuts, or raisins. Each player places an object in the center of the circle. The dreidel is spun by one of the players, while the following verse is chanted:

I have a little dreidel.
I made it out of clay.
And when it's dry and ready.
Then with it I will play.

Whether the spinning player wins or loses depends on which side of the dreidel lands upward when it falls. The following may be used as a guide:

Nun (N) means nothing: player receives nothing from the pot.
Gimmel (G) means all: player receives everything from the pot.
Hay (H) means half: player takes 1/2 of the pot.
Shin (S) means put in: player adds two objects to the pot.

When one player has won all of the objects, the game is completed.

3. Gelt Hunt

Make a silver coin by cutting out a 4-inch round piece of cardboard and covering it with aluminum foil. Hide the coin (gelt) in the classroom and play a hide-and-seek game. For younger children hide the gelt in an obvious place.

(Gelt is the Yiddish word for money. Traditionally, small amounts of gelt are given to children each night of Hanukkah.)

Social Studies:

1. Menorah

Glue eight wooden or styrofoam spools of equal size to a piece of wood, leaving a space in the middle. Glue a larger spool in the middle, thus having four smaller spools on each side. Spray with gold or silver paint. The menorah can be lit during the eight days of Hanukkah during group time. Explain the meaning of the menorah to the group as well.

2. Hanukkah Celebration

Display pictures at the child's eye level of the Hanukkah celebration. Examples would include such pictures as lighting the menorah, a family meal, etc.

3. Human Menorah

The children can make a human menorah by positioning themselves to resemble a menorah. A menorah is a lamp with nine flames that is used to celebrate Hanukkah. Two children can lie head-to-toe on the floor to form the base. Have nine children stand behind the base to form the candles. The tallest child can stand in the middle and be the shammash. The shammash is the center candle that lights the other candles. The children can make pretend flames out of construction paper for the candles to hold as if they are lit.

Cooking:

1. Latkes

6 medium-sized potatoes washed, pared, and grated
1 egg
3 tablespoons flour
1/2 teaspoon baking powder

In a large bowl, mix the egg and the grated potatoes. Add the flour and baking powder. Drop by spoonfuls into hot cooking oil in a frying pan. Brown on both sides. Drain on paper towel. Latkes may be served with a spoonful of applesauce or sour cream.

2. Hanukkah Honey and Spice Cookies

1/2 cup (1 stick) margarine, softened
1/2 cup firmly packed dark brown sugar
1/2 cup honey
2 1/2 cups unsifted flour
2 teaspoons ground ginger
1 teaspoon baking soda
1 teaspoon ground cinnamon
1 teaspoon ground nutmeg
1/2 teaspoon salt
1/4 teaspoon ground cloves

In a large mixing bowl cream margarine and sugar. Beat in honey and egg until well combined. In a small bowl combine flour, ginger, baking soda, cinnamon, nutmeg, salt, and cloves. Add to honey mixture. Beat on low speed until well blended. Cover dough and chill at least 1 hour or up to 3 days. Heat oven to 350 degrees. Grease cookie sheets. Set aside. Working quickly with 1/4 of the dough at a time, roll out on floured surface to 1/4-inch thickness. Cut into desired shapes, including a dreidel, menorah, or star. Using a spatula, place cookies on prepared cookie sheets 1 inch apart. Reroll scraps. Bake for 7 minutes. Transfer to wire racks to cool. Makes about 4 dozen cookies.

3. Ka'achei Sumsum—Bagel Cookies

4 cups flour
1 cup margarine
1 teaspoon salt
3 tablespoons cake-form yeast
1 egg
1 cup lukewarm water
1/4 teaspoon sugar

Place yeast and sugar in a bowl. Pour over lukewarm water. Put in a warm place for 10 minutes or until yeast rises. Prepare a dough from the flour, margarine, salt, and dissolved yeast mixture. Cover dough with a towel, put in a warm place for 2 hours. When dough rises, take small pieces and roll into strips about 4 inches long. Join the ends to form a bagel. Brush each one with beaten egg and place on a greased baking sheet. Bake in a 350-degree oven for 20 to 30 minutes.

Source: Nahoum, Aldo (Ed.). (1970). *The Art of Israeli Cooking*. New York: Holt, Rinehart and Winston.

4. K'naidlach Soup

3 eggs
3 1/2 cups matzo meal
1/2 chicken bouillon cube
1 teaspoon celery leaves, chopped
nutmeg
juice of 1/2 lemon
salt
pepper

Beat eggs well. Add bouillon cube, salt, pepper, and a pinch of nutmeg. Add lemon juice and celery leaves. Continue to beat.

Slowly add matzo meal, using a wooden spoon to stir. When matzo meal thickens, knead by hand. After matzo meal has been thoroughly kneaded, form small balls (1 inch). Arrange in a deep dish and leave in refrigerator for at least 3 hours. Prepare a clear chicken soup and when it reaches boiling, drop in matzo balls. Let cook for 10 to 12 minutes. Serve 3 to 4 balls per bowl of soup. Add lemon juice to taste.

Source: Nahoum, Aldo (Ed.). (1970). *The Art of Israeli Cooking*. New York: Holt, Rinehart and Winston.

Multimedia:

The following resources can be found in educational catalogs:

1. Palmer, Hap. "Hanukkah" in *Holiday Songs and Rhythms* [record].

2. "Hanukkah" in *Holiday Songs for All Occasions* [record]. Kimbo Records.

3. "My Dreidel" in *Kindergarten Songs, Record 1* [record]. Bowmar.

4. "O Hannukah" in *Folk Songs of Israel* [record]. Bowmar.

5. Ben Ezra. *Israeli Children's Songs* [record]. Folkways.

6. *Songs to Share* [record]. United Synagogue Book Service.

Books:

The following books can be used to complement the theme:

1. Fisher, Aileen. (1985). *My First Hanukkah Book*. Chicago: Children's Press.

2. Shostak, Myra. (1986). *Rainbow Candles*. Rockville, MD: Kar Ben.

3. Gellman, Ellie. (1985). *It's Chanukah*. Rockville, MD: Kar Ben.

4. Chaikin, Miriam. (1990). *Hanukkah*. New York: Holiday House, Inc.

5. dePaola, Tomie. (1989). *My First Chanukah*. New York: Putnam Publishing Group.

6. Ehrlich, Amy. (1989). *Story of Hanukkah*. New York: Dial Books for Young Readers.

7. Gertz, Susan E. (1992). *Hanukkah and Christmas at My House*. Middleton, OH: Willow and Laurel Press.

8. Groner, Judye, & Wikler, Madeline. (1992). *Hanukkah Fun: For Little Hands*. Rockville, MD: Kar-Ben Copies, Inc.

9. Katz, Bobbi. (1992). *A Family Hanukkah*. New York: Random House Books for Young Readers.

10. Kimmelman, Leslie, & Kimmelman, John. (1992). *Hanukkah Lights, Hanukkah Nights*. New York: Harper Collins Children's Books.

11. Schotter, Roni. (1990). *Hanukkah*. New York: Little, Brown and Co.

12. Sidi, Smadar S. (1988). *Chanukah A–Z*. Bellmore, NY: Modan/Adama Books.

13. Adler, David A. (1989). *Happy Hanukkah Rebus*. New York: Viking Children's Books.

14. Kimmel, Eric A. (1990). *The Chanukah Guest*. New York: Holiday House, Inc.

15. Manushkin, Fran. (1990). *Latkes and Applesauce: A Hanukkah Story*. New York: Scholastic, Inc.

16. Wolfberg, Carrie. (1991). *The Happy Dreidels: Hanukkah Adventure*. Clearwater, FL: Peartree.

17. Levine, Abby (Ed.). (1989). *Hanukkah*. Morton Grove, IL: Whitman.

18. Zalben, Jane B. (1988). *Beni's First Chanukah*. New York: Holt.

19. Sholem, Aleichem. (1991). *Hanukkah Money*. New York: Morrow.

20. Backman, Aidel. (1990). *One Night, One Hanukkah Night*. Philadelphia: JPS.

21. Rosenberg, Amy. (1991). *Melly's Menorah*. New York: Simon & Schuster.

22. Zwebner, Janet. (1989). *Animated Menorah*. New York: Shapolsky Publications.

CHRISTMAS

Symbols

ornaments
lights
sleigh
gifts
stockings
Christmas cards
candles
Santa Claus
star
garland
snow
elves
wreaths
religious

Sounds

songs (carols)
bells

Plants

trees
poinsettias
mistletoe
holly

Colors

red
green
white

Foods

cookies
eggnog
candy canes
candy

Theme Goals:

Through participating in the experiences provided by this theme, the children may learn:

1. Christmas colors.
2. Christmas foods.
3. Christmas plants.
4. Symbols of Christmas.
5. Sounds heard at Christmas.

Concepts for the Children to Learn:

1. Red, green, and white are Christmas colors.
2. Christmas cookies and candy are special treats for Christmas.
3. Santa Claus, reindeer, stockings, and Christmas trees are symbols of Christmas.
4. Decorating Christmas trees is a Christmas activity.
5. Christmas ornaments and garland are hung on Christmas trees.
6. There are special Christmas songs.
7. Bells and Christmas carols are sounds heard at Christmas.
8. Pointsettias, pine trees, and mistletoe are Christmas plants.
9. Many people spend Christmas with their families and friends.
10. Some people hang special stockings that are filled with candy and small gifts.
11. Christmas for some people is a time for giving and receiving gifts.
12. Christians believe that Jesus was born on Christmas day.

Vocabulary:

1. **Santa Claus**—a jolly man who wears a red suit and symbolizes Christmas.
2. **pine tree**—a tree decorated for the Christmas holidays.
3. **wreath**—a decoration made from evergreen branches.
4. **elf**—Santa's helper.
5. **star**—a treetop decoration.
6. **stocking**—a large Christmas sock.
7. **reindeer**—an animal used to pull Santa's sleigh.
8. **present**—a gift.
9. **ornament**—decoration for the home or tree.
10. **carol**—a Christmas song.
11. **piñata**—brightly colored paper mache figure that is filled with candy and gifts.

Bulletin Board

The purpose of this bulletin board is to foster positive self-concept, as well as name recognition. Construct a stocking out of tagboard for each child in your class. Print the name across the top and punch a hole in the top with a paper punch. Hang a Christmas poster or teacher-made poster in the center of the bulletin board. Next, attach push pins to the bulletin board, allowing enough room for each stocking to hang on a pin. The children can hang their own stocking on the bulletin board as they arrive each day.

Parent Letter

Dear Parents,

The Christmas season is approaching. All we need to do is drive through our neighborhoods to see decorations and busy shoppers everywhere. Songs of Christmas are heard, and Santa is in the thoughts and sentences of many children. At school we will be participating in many Christmas activities. The children will learn the colors, plants, and symbols that are associated with the Christmas season.

At School

A few of the Christmas learning experiences planned include:

- creating ornaments to decorate the classroom Christmas tree.
- painting with pine boughs at the easel.
- making Christmas cookies.
- designing Christmas cards in the art area.
- practicing songs for our holiday program. Keep your eyes open for a special invitation! The program will be held on December 19th at 3:30. Mark your calendar.

At Home

Music and singing are wonderful ways to communicate our feelings, and we often have many feelings this time of year! When singing Christmas carols, encourage traditional songs as well as this new song:

"I'm a Little Pine Tree"
(Sing to the tune of "I'm a Little Teapot")

I'm a little pine tree tall and straight
Here are my branches for you to decorate.
   (extend arms)
First we'll put the shiny star on top.
   (touch head)
Just be careful the balls don't drop.
   (clap hands)
Now be sure to plug in all the lights
So I will look very cheerful and bright.
Then put all the presents under me.
I'm all set for Christmas, as you can see!

Reminder

Our last day of school will be December 23. We will begin school again on January 3 of the new year.

Happy holidays to you and yours!

Santa Claus and Christmas make winter fun.

Music:

1. **"Rudolph the Red-Nosed Reindeer"** (traditional)

2. **"Jingle Bells"** (traditional)

3. **"The Twelve Days of Christmas"** (traditional)

4. **"We Wish You a Merry Christmas"** (traditional)

5. **"Peppermint Stick Song"**

   Oh I took a lick of my
   peppermint stick
   And I thought it tasted yummy.
   Oh it used to hang on my
   Christmas tree,
   But I like it better in my tummy.

6. **"S-A-N-T-A"**
   (Sing to the tune of "B-I-N-G-O")

   There was a man on Christmas Day
   And Santa was his name-o.
   S-A-N-T-A
   S-A-N-T-A
   S-A-N-T-A
   And Santa was his name-o.

7. **"Up on the House Top"** (traditional)

8. **"Santa Claus is Coming to Town"** (traditional)

9. **"Circle Christmas Verse"**

   Two, four, six, eight.
   Santa Claus don't be late;
   Here's my stocking, I can't wait!
   Two, four, six, eight.

10. **"Christmas Chant"**

    With a "hey" and a "Hi" and a "ho-ho-ho,"
    Somebody tickled old Santa Claus' toe.
    Get up ol' Santa, there's work to be done,
    The children must have their holiday fun.
    With a "hey" and a "hi" and a "ho-ho-ho,"
    Santa Claus, Santa Claus,
    GO-GO-GO!

11. **"Santa's in His Shop"**
    (Sing to the tune of "The Farmer in the Dell")

    Santa's in his shop
    Santa's in his shop
    What a scene for Christmas
    Santa's in his shop.

Other verses:

Santa takes a drum
The drum takes a doll
The doll takes a train
The train takes a ball
The ball takes a top
They're all in the shop
The top stays in the shop

Pictures could be constructed for use during the singing of each toy.

Fingerplays:

SANTA'S WORKSHOP

Here is Santa's workshop.
  (form peak with both hands)
Here is Santa Claus.
  (hold up thumb)
Here are Santa's little elves
  (wiggle fingers)
Putting toys upon the shelves.

HERE IS THE CHIMNEY

Here is the chimney.
  (make fist and tuck in thumb)
Here is the top.
  (cover with hand)
Open it up quick
  (lift hand up)
And out Santa will pop.
  (pop out thumb)

FIVE LITTLE CHRISTMAS COOKIES

(hold up five fingers, take one away as directed by poem)

Five little Christmas cookies on a plate by the door,
One was eaten and then there were four.

Four little Christmas cookies, gazing up at me,
One was eaten and then there were three.

Three little Christmas cookies, enough for me and you,
One was eaten and then there were two.

Two little Christmas cookies sitting in the sun,
One was eaten and then there was one.

One little Christmas cookie, better grab it fast,
As you can see the others surely didn't last.

PRESENTS

See all the presents by the Christmas tree?
  (hand shades eyes)
Some for you,
  (point)
And some for me—
  (point)

Long ones,
  (extend arms)
Tall ones,
  (measure hand up from floor)
Short ones, too.
  (hand to floor—low)
And here is a round one
  (circle with arms)
Wrapped in blue.

Isn't it fun to look and see
  (hand shade eyes)
All of the presents by the Christmas tree?
  (arms open wide)

Science:

1. **Making Candles**

Candles can be made for Christmas gifts. This experience provides an opportunity for the children to see how a substance can change from solid to liquid and back to a solid form. The children can place pieces of paraffin in a tin can that is bent at the top, forming a spout. A red or green crayon piece can be used to add color.

The bottom of the tin cans should be placed in a pan of water and heated on the stove until the paraffin is melted. Meanwhile, the children can prepare small paper cups.

In the bottom of each paper cup mold place a wick. Wicks can be made by tying a piece of string to a paper clip and a pencil. Then lay the pencil horizontally across the cup allowing the string to hang vertically into the cup. When the wax is melted, the teacher should carefully pour the wax into the cup. After the wax hardens, the candles can be used as decorations or presents. This activity should be restricted to four- and five-year-old children. Constant supervision of this activity is required for safety.

2. **Add to the Science Area:**

   - pine needles and branches with magnifying glasses
   - pinecones with a balance scale
   - red, green, and white materials representing different textures

3. **Bells**

   Collect bells of various shapes and sizes. Listen for differences in sounds in relation to the sizes of the bells.

4. **Feely Box**

   A feely box containing Christmas items such as bows, cookie cutters, wrapping paper, non-breakable ornaments, stockings, bells, candles, etc., can be placed on the science table.

Dramatic Play:

Gift Wrapping

Collect and place in the dramatic play area empty boxes, scraps of wrapping paper, comic paper, wallpaper books, and scraps. Scissors, tape, bows, and ribbon should also be provided.

Arts and Crafts:

1. **Christmas Chains**

   Cut sheets of red, green, and white construction paper into strips. Demonstrate how to form the links. The links can be pasted, taped, or stapled, depending upon the developmental level of the children.

2. **Cookie Cutter Painting**

   Provide Christmas cookie cutters, paper, and shallow pans containing red and green paint. The children can apply the paint to the paper using the cookie cutters as printing tools.

3. **Rudolph**

   Begin the activity by encouraging the children to trace their shoe. This will be used for Rudolph's face. Then the children should trace both of their hands which will be used as the reindeer's antlers. Finally, cut out a red circle to be used as the reindeer's nose. Have the children paste all the pieces together on a sheet of paper and add facial features.

4. **Designing Wrapping Paper**

   The children can design their own wrapping paper using newsprint, ink stampers, felt-tip colored markers, tempera paint, etc. Glitter can also be glued onto the paper.

5. **Creating Christmas Cards**

   Paper, felt-tip colored markers, and crayons should be available at the art table. Christmas stencils can also be provided.

6. **Pine Branch Painting**

   Collect short pine boughs to use as painting tools. The tools can be placed at the easel or used with a shallow pan of tempera paint at tables.

7. **Candy Cane Marble Painting**

   Cut red construction paper into candy cane shapes. Marble paint with white tempera paint.

8. **Seasonal Stencils**

   Spread glue inside a seasonal stencil. Apply glitter over the glued area.

9. **Glittery Pinecones**

   Paint pinecones with tempera paint, sprinkle with glitter, and allow the paint to dry. The glittery pinecones can be used for classroom decoration, presents, or taken home.

10. **Paper Wreaths**

Purchase green muffin tin liners. To make the paper wreaths, cut out a large ring from light tagboard or construction paper for each child in the class. The children can glue the green muffin tin liners to the ring, adding small pieces of red yarn, crayons, or felt-tip marker symbols to represent berries if desired.

11. **Playdough Cookies**

Using red, green, and white playdough and Christmas cookie cutters, the children can make playdough cookies.

Favorite Playdough

Combine and boil until dissolved:
2 cups water
1/2 cup salt
food coloring or tempera

Mix while very hot:
2 tablespoons salad oil
2 tablespoons alum
2 cups flour

Knead approximately five minutes until smooth. Store in an airtight covered container.

Sensory:

1. **Add to the Sensory Table:**

   - pine branches, needles, and cones
   - scented red and green playdough
   - icicles or snow (if possible) with thermometers
   - water for a sink and float activity; add different Christmas objects such as bells, plastic stars, and cookie cutters
   - Add scents such as peppermint and ginger to water

2. **Holiday Cubes**

   Prepare ice cube trays using water colored with red and green food coloring. Freeze. Place in the sensory table.

Field Trip:

1. **Christmas Tree Farm**

   Plan a trip to a Christmas tree farm so the children can cut down a Christmas tree. Check your state's licensing requirements regarding the use of fresh Christmas trees and decorations in the center or classroom.

2. **Caroling**

   Plan to go Christmas caroling at a local nursing home or even for another group of children. After caroling, Christmas cookies could be shared.

Math:

1. **Christmas Card Sort**

   Place a variety of Christmas cards on a table in the math area. During self-selected or self-initiated periods, the children can sort by color, pictures, size, etc.

2. **Christmas Card Puzzles**

   Collect two sets of identical Christmas cards. Cut the covers off the cards. Cut one of each of the identical sets of cards into puzzle pieces. The matching card can be used as a form for the children to match the pieces on.

Group Time (games, language):

1. **Find the Christmas Bell**

   For this activity the children should be standing in a circle. One child is given a bell. Then the child should hide, while the remainder of the children cover their eyes. After the child has hidden, he begins to ring the bell, signaling the remainder of the children to listen for the sound and identify where the bell is hidden. Turns should be taken, allowing each child an opportunity to hide and ring the bell.

204

2. **"Guess What's Inside"**

Wrap a familiar object inside of a box. Let the children shake, feel, and try to identify the object. After this, open the box and show the children the object. This activity works well in small groups as well as large groups.

Cooking:

1. **Candy Canes**

Prepare the basic sugar dough recipe for cookie cutters. Divide the recipe in half. Add red food coloring to one half of the dough. Show the children how to roll a piece of red dough in a strip about 3 inches long by 1/2 inch wide. Repeat this process using the white dough. Then twist the two strips together, shaping into a candy cane. Bake the cookies in a 350-degree oven for 7 to 10 minutes.

2. **Basic Sugar Dough for Cookie Cutters**

1/2 cup butter
1 cup sugar

1 egg
1/2 teaspoon salt
2 teaspoons baking powder
2 cups flour
1/2 teaspoon vanilla

Cut into desired shapes. Place on lightly greased baking sheets. Bake 8 minutes at 400 degrees. This recipe makes approximately 3 to 4 dozen cookies.

3. **Eggnog**

4 eggs
2 teaspoons vanilla
4 tablespoons honey
4 cups milk

Beat all of the ingredients together until light and foamy. Pour into glasses or cups and shake a little nutmeg on the top of the eggnog. This adds color and flavor. The recipe makes one quart. Eggnog should always be served immediately or refrigerated until snack or lunch. It should not be served to children who are allergic to eggs.

GIFTS FOR PARENTS

Wax Paper Placemats
wax paper that is heavily
    waxed
crayon shavings
paper designs
dish towel
scissors

Use at least one of the
    following:
yarn
fabric
lace
dried leaves

Cut the wax paper into 12-
    inch by 20-inch sheets (2
    per mat). Place crayon
    shavings between the

wax paper. Then decorate with other items. Place towel on wax paper and press with warm iron until crayon melts. Fringe the edges.

**Popsicle Stick Picture
Frames**
popsicle sticks (10 per
    frame)
glue
picture

Make a background of sticks and glue picture in place. Add additional sticks around the edges,

front, and back for the frame and for support. For a freestanding frame add more popsicle sticks to both the front and the back at the bottom.

Refrigerator Magnets
small magnets
glue
any type of decoration
    (paper cut-outs, plaster
    of paris molds, yarn,
    styrofoam pieces,
    buttons, etc.)

Glue the decorations to the
    magnet.

Service Certificate
paper
crayons
pencils
lace
ribbon

Have the children write and decorate a certificate that states some service they will do for their parents. (Example: This certificate is good for washing the dishes; sweeping the floor; picking up my toys; etc.)

Ornaments
plaster of paris
any mold
glitter
yarn
straw

Pour the plaster of paris into the mold. Decorate with glitter and let dry. If so desired, place a straw into the mold and string with yarn or thread.

Refrigerator Clothespin
clothespins
glue
sequins/glitter/beads
small magnet

Let the children put glue on one side of the clothespin. Sprinkle this area with glitter, sequins, or beads. Then assist the child in gluing the magnet to the other side.

Patchwork Flowerpot
precut fabric squares
glue
tins (for glue)
flower pots

Let the children soak the fabric squares one at a time in the glue. Press onto the pot in a patchwork design. Let dry overnight.

Snapshot Magnet
snapshot
plastic lid
scissors (preferably pinking shears)
glue
magnet

Using the lid, trace around the back of the picture. Cut the picture out and glue into the lid. Glue the magnet to the underside of the lid.

Holiday Pin
outline of a heart, wreath etc., cut out of tagboard
glue
sequins, beads, buttons, yarn
purchased backing for a pin

Let the children decorate the cardboard figure with glue and other decorating items. Glue onto purchased backing for a pin.

Flowers with Vase
styrofoam egg carton
pipe cleaner
scissors
glass jar or bottle
liquid starch
colored tissue paper (cut into squares)
glue yarn
paintbrush

Cut individual sections from egg carton and punch a hole in the bottom of each. Insert a pipe cleaner through the hole as a stem. Use the scissors to cut the petals.

For the vase: Using the paintbrush, cover a portion of the jar with liquid starch. Apply the tissue paper squares until the jar is covered. Add another coat of liquid starch. Dip the yarn into the glue and wrap it around the jar. Insert the flower for a decoration.

Pinecone Ornament
pinecones
paint
paintbrush
glue
glitter
yarn

Paint the pinecones. Then roll the pinecones in the glue and then into a dish filled with glitter. Tie a loop of yarn for hanging.

Paper Weights
glass furniture glides
crepe paper
crayons
glue
plaster of paris
felt piece
scissors

Children decorate a picture and then cut it to fit the glide. Place the picture face down into the recessed part of the glide. Pour plaster of paris over the top of the picture and let it dry. Glue a felt piece over the plaster.

Rock Paperweight
large rocks
paint

Let the children paint a design on a rock they have chosen and give to their parents as a present.

Soap Balls

1 cup Ivory Snow detergent
1/8 cup of water
food coloring
colored nylon netting
ribbon

Add the food coloring to the water and then add the Ivory Snow detergent. Shape the mixture into balls or any shape. Wrap in colored netting and tie with ribbon.

Closet Clove Scenter

orange
cloves
netting
ribbon

Have the children push the pointed ends of the cloves into an orange. Cover the orange completely. Wrap netting around the orange and tie it with the ribbon. These make good closet or dresser drawer scenters.

Handprint Wreath

colored construction paper
scissors
glue
pencil
cardboard/tagboard circle

Let the children trace their hand and cut it out. Glue the palm of the hand to the cardboard circle. Using a pencil roll the fingertips of the hand until curly.

Bird's Nest

1 can sweetened condensed milk
2 teaspoons vanilla
3 to 4 cups powdered milk
1 cup confectioners' sugar
yellow food coloring

Mix all the ingredients together and add food coloring to tint the mixture to a yellow-brown color. Give each child a portion and let him mold a bird's nest. Chill for 2 hours. If so desired, green tinted coconut may be added for grass and put in the nest. Add small jelly beans for bird's eggs.

Flower Pots

plaster of paris
1/2-pint milk containers
straws (3 to 4 for each container)
scissors
construction paper
paint
paintbrush
stapler

Cut the cartons in half and use the bottom half. Pour 1 to 3 inches of plaster into the containers. Stick 3 or 4 straws into the plaster and let harden. After plaster has hardened, remove the plaster very carefully from the milk carton. Let the children paint the plaster pot and make flowers from construction paper and staple the flowers to the straws.

Cookie Jar

coffee can with lid or oatmeal box
construction paper
crayons or felt-tip markers
glue
scissors

Cover the can with construction paper and glue to seal. Let the children decorate their cans with crayons or felt-tip markers. For an added gift, make cookies in the classroom to send home in the jars.

Felt Printing

felt
glue
wood block
tempera paint
scissors

Let the children cut the felt pieces into any shape. Glue the shape onto the wood block. Dip into a shallow pan of tempera paint. Print on newspaper to test.

Napkin Holder

paper plates
scissors
yarn
paper punch
crayons
clear shellac

Cut one paper plate in half. Place the inside together and punch holes through the lower half only. Use yarn to lace the plates together. Punch a small hole at the top for hanging. Decorate with crayons or felt-tip markers. Coat with shellac. May be used as a potholder, napkin, or card holder.

Clay Figures

4 cups flour
1 1/2 cup water
1 cup salt paint
paintbrush

Combine flour, water, and salt. Knead for 5 to 10 minutes. Roll and cut dough into figures. (Cookie cutters work well.) Make a hole at the top of the figure. Bake in a 250-degree oven for 2 hours or until hard. When cool, paint to decorate.

Key Holder

8 popsicle sticks
construction paper or a
    cutout from a greeting
    card
self-adhesive picture
    hanger
yarn

Glue five sticks together
edge to edge. Cut a 1
3/4-inch piece of stick
and glue it across the 5
sticks. Glue 2 sticks
across the top parallel to
the 5 sticks. Turn the
sticks over. Cut paper or
a greeting card to fit
between the crossed
sticks. Place on the self-
adhesive hanger and tie
yarn to the top for hang-
ing.

Planter Trivets

7 popsicle sticks
glue

Glue four popsicle sticks
into a square, the top
two overlapping the bot-
tom ones. Fill in the
open space with the
remaining three and
glue into place.

Pencil Holder

empty soup cans
construction paper or
    contact paper
crayons or felt-tip markers
glue
scissors

Cover the can with
construction or contact
paper. Decorate with
crayons or markers and
use as a pencil holder.

Plaster Hand Prints

plaster of paris
1-inch-deep square
    container
paint
paintbrush

Pour plaster of paris into
the container. Have the
child place his hand in
the plaster to make a
mold. Let the mold dry
and remove it from the
container. Let the child
paint the mold and give
as a gift with the following poem:

My Hands

Sometimes you get
    discouraged
Because I am so small
And always have my
    fingerprints
on furniture and walls.
But everyday I'm growing
    up
and soon I'll be so tall
that all those little
    handprints
will be hard for you to
    recall.
So here's a little handprint
just for you to see
Exactly how my fingers
    looked
When I was little me.

Books:

The following books can be used to complement the theme:

1. Schumacher, Claire. (1987). *Santa's Hat*. New York: Prentice Hall Books.

2. Shuttleworth, Cathie (Illus.). (1987). *The Twelve Days of Christmas*. New York: Derrydale Books.

3. Poulet, Virginia. (1987). *Blue Bug's Christmas*. Chicago: Children's Press.

4. Bokich, Obren. (1987). *A Christmas Card for Mr. McFizz*. Chicago: Children's Press.

5. Dubanevich, Arlene. (1989). *Pigs at Christmas*. New York: Macmillan.

6. Gerver, Jane E. (1990). *Happy Bear, Christmas Star*. New York: Random House.

7. Goffin, Jesse. (1991). *Silent Christmas*. Honesdale, PA: Boyds Mills Press.

8. Hayes, Sarah. (1992). *Happy Christmas, Gemma*. New York: Morrow.

9. McCully, Emily A. (1992). *A Christmas Gift*. New York: Harper Collins.

10. Naylor, Phyllis R. (1989). *Keeping a Christmas Secret*. New York: Macmillan.

11. Radzinski, Kandy. (1992). *The Twelve Cats of Christmas*. San Francisco: Chronicle Books.

12. Clifton, Lucille. (1993). *Everett Anderson's Christmas Coming*. New York: Holt.

13. Bishop, Adela. (1991). *The Christmas Polar Bear*. Union City, CA: DOT Garnet.

14. dePaola, Tomie. (1992). *Jingle the Christmas Clown*. New York: Putnam Publishing Group.

15. Garcia-Bengochea, Debbie. (1992). *Gumdrop the Christmas Bear*. Hazelwood, MO: Masterson Publishing Corp.

16. Haung, Benrei. (1992). *Pop-up Merry Christmas*. New York: Putnam Publishing Group.

17. Jerris, Tony. (1991). *The Littlest Spruce*. Caldeonia, NY: Little Spruce Productions.

18. Shpakow, Tanya. (1991). *On the Way to Christmas*. New York: Alfred A. Knopf Books for Young Readers.

19. Jordan, Sandra. (1993). *Christmas Tree Farm*. New York: Orchard Books.

20. Hague, Michael. (1990). *We Wish You a Merry Christmas*. New York: Henry Holt & Co.

21. Kelley, Emily. (1986). *Christmas Around the World*. Minneapolis: Lerner.

22. Angel, Marie. (1991). *Woodland Christmas*. New York: Dial Books.

23. Aloia, Gregory F. (1989). *The Legend of the Golden Straw: A Christmas Story*. Chicago: Loyola.

24. Palangi, Paula. (1992). *Last Straw*. Elgin, IL: Cook.

25. Hague, Michael. (1991). *We Wish You a Merry Christmas*. New York: Henry Holt & Co.

INTERNATIONAL HOLIDAYS

When planning the curriculum, it is important to note international holidays. The exact date of the holiday may vary from year to year; consequently, it is important to check with parents or a reference librarian at a local library. These international holidays for Christians, Buddhists, Eastern Orthodox, Hindus, Jews, and Muslims are as follows:

Christian

Ash Wednesday
Palm Sunday—the Sunday before Easter, which commemorates the triumphant entry of Jesus in Jerusalem.
Holy Thursday—also known as Maundy Thursday; it is the Thursday of Holy Week.
Good Friday—commemorates the crucifixion of Jesus.
Easter—celebrates the resurrection of Jesus.
Christmas Eve
Christmas Day—commemorates the birth of Jesus.

Buddhist

Nirvana Day (Mahayana Sect)—observes the passing of Sakyamuni into Nirvana. He obtained enlightenment and became a Buddha.
Magna Puja (Theravada Sect)—one of the holiest Buddhist holidays; it marks the occasion when 1,250 of Buddha's disciples gathered spontaneously to hear him speak.
Buddha Day (Mahayana Sect)—this service commemorates the birth of Gautama in Lumbini Garden. Amida, the Buddha of Infinite Wisdom and Compassion, manifested himself among men in the person Gautama.
Versakha Piya (Theravada Sect)—the most sacred of the Buddhist days. It celebrates the birth, death, and enlightenment of Buddha.
Maharram—marks the beginning of Buddhist Lent, it is the anniversary of Buddha's sermon to the first five disciples.
Vassana (Theravada Sect)—the beginning of the three-month period when monks stay in their temple to study and meditate.
Bon (Mahayana Sect)—an occasion for rejoicing in the enlightenment offered by the Buddha; often referred to as a "Gathering of Joy." Buddha had saved the life of the mother Moggallana. The day is in remembrance of all those who have passed away.
Pavarana (Theravada Sect)—celebrates Buddha's return to earth after spending one Lent season preaching in heaven.
Bodhi Day (Mahayana Sect)—celebrates the enlightenment of Buddha.

Eastern Orthodox

Christmas
First Day of Lent—begins a period of fasting and penitence in preparation for Easter.
Easter Sunday—celebrates the resurrection of Jesus.
Ascension Day—the 40th day after Easter, commemorates the ascension of Jesus to heaven.
Pentecost—commemorates the descent of the Holy Spirit upon the Apostles, 50 days after Easter Sunday. Marks the beginning of the Christian Church.

Hindu

Pongal Sankrandi—a three-day harvest festival.

Vasanta Pachami—celebrated in honor of Saraswati, the charming and sophisticated goddess of scholars.

Shivarari—a solemn festival devoted to the worship of Shiva, the most powerful of deities of the Hindu pantheon.

Holi—celebrates the advent of spring.

Ganguar—celebrated in honor of Parvari, the consort of Lord Shiva.

Ram Navami—birthday of the God Rama.

Hanuman Jayanti—birthday of Monkey God Humumanji.

Meenakshi Kalyanam—the annual commemoration of the marriage of Meenakshi to Lord Shiva.

Teej—celebrates the arrival of the monsoon; Parvari is the presiding deity.

Jewish

Yom Kippur—the most holy day of the Jewish year, it is marked by fasting and prayer as Jews seek forgiveness from God and man.

Sukkot—commemorates the 40-year wandering of Israelites in the desert on the way to the Promised Land; expresses thanksgiving for the fall harvest.

Simchat Torah—celebrates the conclusion of the public reading of the Pentateuch and its beginning anew, thus affirming that the study of God's word is an unending process. Concludes the Sukkot Festival.

Hanukkah—the eight-day festival that celebrates the rededication of the Temple to the service of God. Commemorates the Maccabean victory over Antiochus, who sought to suppress freedom of worship.

Purim—marks the salvation of the Jews of ancient Persia through the intervention of Queen Esther, from Haman's plot to exterminate them.

Passover—an eight-day festival marking ancient Israel's deliverance from Egyptian bondage.

Yom Hashoah—day of remembrance for victims of Nazi Holocaust.

Sahvout—celebrates the covenant established at Sinai between God and Israel and the revelation of the Ten Commandments.

Rosh Hashanah—the first of the High Holy Days marking the beginning of a ten-day period of penitence and spiritual renewal.

Muslim

Isra and Miraj—commemorates the anniversary of the night journey of the Prophet and his ascension to heaven.

Ramadan—the beginning of the month of fasting from sunrise to sunset.

Id al-Fitr—end of the month of fasting from sunrise to sunset; first day of pilgrimage to Mecca.

Hajj—the first day of pilgrimage to Mecca.

Day of Amfat—gathering of the pilgrims.

Id al-adha—commemorates the Feast of the Sacrifice.

Muharram—the Muslim New Year; marks the beginning of the Hedjra Year 1412.

Id al-Mawlid—commemorates the nativity and death of Prophet Muhammad and his flight from Mecca to Medina.

APPENDIX B

EARLY CHILDHOOD COMMERCIAL SUPPLIERS

ABC School Supply, Inc.
3312 N. Berkeley Lake Road
Delouth, Georgia 30136
(770) 497-0001

American Guidance Service
Publisher's Building
Circle Pines, Minnesota 55014
(612) 786-4343

Beckley Cardy
One East First Street
Duluth, Minnesota 55802
1-800-227-1178

Childcraft Educational Corporation
P.O. Box 3239
Lancaster, Pennsylvania 17604

Children's Press
5440 North Cumberland Avenue
Chicago, Illinois 60656
1-800-621-1115

Classic School Products
174 Semoran Commerce Place, Suite A106
Apopka, Florida 32703
1-800-394-9661

Community Playthings
Route 213
Rifton, New York 12471
(914) 658-8351

Constructive Playthings
1227 East 119th Street
Grandview, Missouri 64030-1117
1-800-832-0224

Cuisenaire Company of America, Inc.
12 Church Street, Box D
New Rochelle, New York 10802
1-800-237-3142

Delmar Publishers
3 Columbia Circle
Box 15-015
Albany, New York 12212-5015
1-800-998-7498

Didax Educational Resources
395 Main Street
Rowley, Massachusetts 01969
(508) 948-2340

Environments, Inc.
P.O. Box 1348
Beaufort, South Carolina 29901-1348
(803) 846-8155

Gryphon House, Inc.
3706 Otis Street
Mt. Rainier, Maryland 20712

The Highsmith Co., Inc.
W5527 Highway 106
P.O. Box 800
Fort Atkinson, Wisconsin 53538-0800
1-800-558-2110

J. L. Hammett
P.O. Box 9057
Braintree, Massachusetts 02184-9704
1-800-333-4600

Judy/Instructo
4325 Hiawatha Avenue
Minneapolis, Minnesota 55406

Kaplan School Supply Corporation
P.O. Box 609
Lewisville, North Carolina 27023-0609
1-800-334-2014

Kentucky School Supply
Dept. 21
P.O. Box 886
Elizabethtown, Kentucky 42702
1-800-626-4405

Kimbo Educational
10 North Third Avenue
Long Branch, New Jersey 07740
1-800-631-2187

Lakeshore Learning Materials
2695 E. Dominguez Street
Carson, California 90749
1-800-421-5354

Latta's School and Office Supplies
P.O. Box 128
2218 Main Street
Cedar Falls, Iowa 50613
(319) 266-3501

Nasco
901 Janesville Avenue
Fort Atkinson, Wisconsin 53538
1-800-558-9595

Primary Educator
1200 Keystone Avenue
P.O. Box 24155
Lansing, Michigan 48909-4155
1-800-444-1773

Redleaf Press
450 North Syndicate
Suite 5
St. Paul, Minnesota 55104-4125
(612) 641-6629

St. Paul Book and Stationery
1233 West County Road E
St. Paul, Minnesota 55112
1-800-338-SPBS (7727)

Valley School Supply
1000 North Bluemound Drive
P.O. Box 1579
Appleton, Wisconsin 54913
1-800-242-3433

Warren's Educational Supplies
980 West San Bernardino Road
Covina, California 91722-4196
(818) 966-1731

RAINY DAY ACTIVITIES*

1. Get Acquainted Game

The children sit in a circle formation. The teacher begins the game by saying, "My name is —— and I'm going to roll the ball to ——." Continue playing the game until every child has a turn. A variation of the game is have the children stand in a circle and bounce the ball to each other. This game is a fun way for the children to learn each other's names.

2. Hide the Ball

Choose several children and ask them to cover their eyes. Then hide a small ball, or other object, in an observable place. Ask the children to uncover their eyes and try to find the ball. The first child to find the ball hides it again.

3. Which Ball is Gone?"

In the center of the circle, place six colored balls, cubes, beads, shapes, etc., in a row. Ask a child to close his eyes. Then ask another child to remove one of the objects and hide it behind him. The first child uncovers his eyes and tells which colored object is missing from the row. The game continues until all the selections have been made. When using with older children, two objects may be removed at a time to further challenge their abilities.

4. "What Sound is That?"

The purpose of this game is to promote the development of listening skills. Begin by asking the children to close their eyes. Make a familiar sound. Then ask a child to identify it. Sources of sound may include:

tearing paper	blowing a pitch pipe	raising or lowering
sharpening a pencil	dropping an object	window shades
walking, running,	moving a desk or	leafing through
shuffling feet	chair	book pages
clapping hands	snapping fingers	cutting with
sneezing, coughing	blowing nose	scissors
tapping on glass,	opening or closing	snapping rubber
wood, or metal	drawer	bands
jingling money	stirring paint in	ringing a bell
opening a window	a jar	clicking the tongue
pouring water	clearing the throat	crumpling paper
shuffling cards	splashing water	opening a box
blowing a whistle	rubbing sandpaper	sighing
banging blocks	together	stamping feet
bouncing ball	chattering teeth	rubbing palms
shaking a rattle	sweeping sound,	together
turning the lights on	such as a brush or	rattling keys
knocking on a door	broom	

A variation of this game could be played by having a child make a sound. Then the other children and the teacher close their eyes and attempt to identify the sound. For older children this game can be varied with the production of two sounds. Begin by asking the children if the sounds are the same or different. Then have them identify the sounds.

5. "Near or Far?"

The purpose of this game is to locate sound. First, tell the children to close their eyes. Then play a sound recorded on a cassette tape. Ask the children to identify the sound as being near or far away.

6. Descriptions

The purpose of this game is to encourage expressive language skills. Begin by asking each child to describe himself. Included with the description can be the color of his eyes, hair, and clothing. The teacher might prefer to use an imaginative introduction such as: "One by one, you may take turns sitting up here in Alfred's magic chair and describe yourself to Alfred." Another approach may be to say, "Pretend that you must meet somebody at a very crowded airport who has never seen you before. How would you describe yourself so that the person would be sure to know who you are?"

A variation for older children would be to have one of the children describe another child without revealing the name of the person he is describing. To illustrate, the teacher might say, "I'm thinking of someone with shiny red hair, blue eyes, many freckles, etc...." The child being described should stand up.

7. Mirrored Movements

The purpose of this game is to encourage awareness of body parts through mirrored movements. Begin the activity by making movements. Encourage the children to mirror your movements. After the children understand the game, they may individually take the leader role.

8. Little Red Wagon Painted Red

As a prop for the game, cut a red wagon with wheels out of construction paper. Then cut rectangles the same size as the box of the red wagon. Include purple, blue, yellow, green, orange, brown, black, and pink colors.

Sing the song to the tune of **"Skip to My Lou."**

*Little red wagon painted **red.***
*Little red wagon painted **red.***
*Little red wagon painted **red.***
What color would it be?

Give each child a turn to pick and name a color. As the song is sung, let the child change the wagon color.

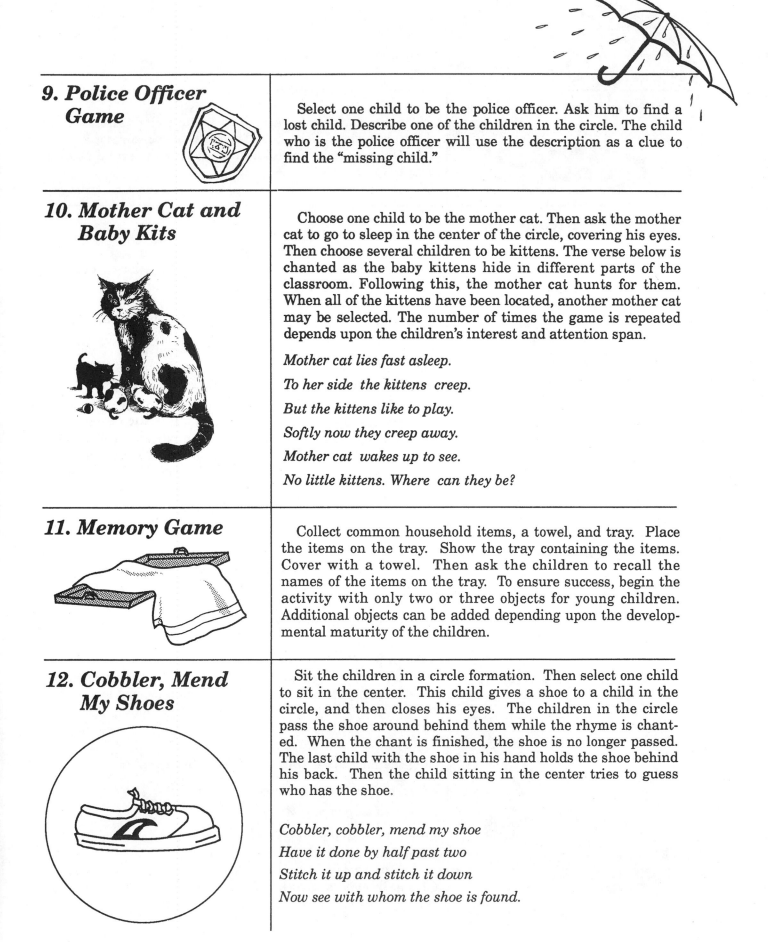

9. Police Officer Game

Select one child to be the police officer. Ask him to find a lost child. Describe one of the children in the circle. The child who is the police officer will use the description as a clue to find the "missing child."

10. Mother Cat and Baby Kits

Choose one child to be the mother cat. Then ask the mother cat to go to sleep in the center of the circle, covering his eyes. Then choose several children to be kittens. The verse below is chanted as the baby kittens hide in different parts of the classroom. Following this, the mother cat hunts for them. When all of the kittens have been located, another mother cat may be selected. The number of times the game is repeated depends upon the children's interest and attention span.

Mother cat lies fast asleep.

To her side the kittens creep.

But the kittens like to play.

Softly now they creep away.

Mother cat wakes up to see.

No little kittens. Where can they be?

11. Memory Game

Collect common household items, a towel, and tray. Place the items on the tray. Show the tray containing the items. Cover with a towel. Then ask the children to recall the names of the items on the tray. To ensure success, begin the activity with only two or three objects for young children. Additional objects can be added depending upon the developmental maturity of the children.

12. Cobbler, Mend My Shoes

Sit the children in a circle formation. Then select one child to sit in the center. This child gives a shoe to a child in the circle, and then closes his eyes. The children in the circle pass the shoe around behind them while the rhyme is chanted. When the chant is finished, the shoe is no longer passed. The last child with the shoe in his hand holds the shoe behind his back. Then the child sitting in the center tries to guess who has the shoe.

Cobbler, cobbler, mend my shoe

Have it done by half past two

Stitch it up and stitch it down

Now see with whom the shoe is found.

216

13. Huckle Buckle Beanstalk

Ask the children to sit in a circle. Once seated, tell them to close their eyes. Then hide a small ball in an obvious place. Say, "Ready." Encourage all of the children to hunt for the object. Each child who spots it returns to a place in the circle and says, "Huckle buckle beanstalk." No one must tell where he has seen the ball until all the children have seen it.

14. What's Different?

Sit all of the children in a circle formation. Ask one child to sit in the center. The rest of the children are told to look closely at the child sitting in the center. Then the children are told to cover their eyes while you change some detail on the child in the center. For example, you may place a hat on the child, untie his shoe, remove a shoe, roll up one sleeve, etc. The children sitting in the circle act as detective to determine "what's different?"

15. Cookie Jar

Sit the children in a circle formation on the floor with their legs crossed. Together they repeat a rhythmic chant while using alternating leg-hand clap to emphasize the rhythm. The chant is as follows.

Someone took the cookies from the cookie jar.

Who took the cookies from the cookie jar?

Mary took the cookies from the cookie jar.

Mary took the cookies from the cookie jar?

Who, me? (Mary)

Yes, you. (all children)

Couldn't be. (Mary)

Then who? (all children)

————— *took the cookies from the cookie jar.* (Mary names another child.)

Use each child's name.

16. Hide and Seek Tonal Matching

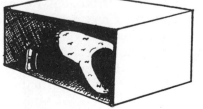

Sit the children in a circle formation. Ask one child to hide in the room while the other children cover their eyes. The children in the circle sing, "Where is ————— hiding?" The child who is hiding responds by singing back, "Here I am." With their eyes remaining closed, the children point in the direction of the hiding child. All open eyes and the child emerges from his hiding place.

17. Listening and Naming

This game is most successful with a small group of children. The children should take turns shutting their eyes and identifying sounds as you tap with a wooden dowel on an object such as glass, triangle, drum, wooden block, cardboard box, rubber ball, etc.

18. Funny Shapes

Ask each child to choose a partner. One partner must make a large shape with his body. The other partner must follow the directions of movement. Roles reverse for the second set of directions. Provide directions such as:

1. Make a big shape.

go *over*

go *under*

go *through*

go *around*

2. Make a small shape.

go *over*

go *under*

go *through*

go *around*

19. Drop the Handkerchief

Direct the children to stand in a circle formation. Ask one child to run around the outside of the circle, dropping a handkerchief behind another child. The child who has the handkerchief dropped behind him must pick it up and chase the child who dropped it. The first child tries to return to the vacated space by running before he is tagged.

20. "If You Please"

This game is a simple variation of "Simon Says." Ask the children to form a circle around a leader who gives directions, some of which are prefaced with "if you please." The children are to follow only the "if you please" directions, ignoring any that do not begin with "if you please." Directions to be used may include walking forward, hopping on one foot, bending forward, standing tall, etc. This game can be varied by having the children follow the directions when the leader says, "do this," and not when he says, "do that." Play only one version of this game on a single day. Too much variety will confuse the children.

218

21. Duck Duck Goose

Ask the children to squat in a circle formation. Then ask one child to walk around the outside of circle, lightly touching each child's head and saying "Duck, Duck." When he touches another child and says "Goose," that child chases him around the circle. If the child who was "it" returns to the "goose's" place without being tagged, he remains. When this happens, the tapped child is "it." This game is appropriate for older four-, five-, six-, and seven-year-old children.

22. Fruit Basket Upset

Ask the children to sit in a circle formation on chairs or on carpet squares. Then ask one child to sit in the middle of the circle as the chef. Hand pictures of various fruits to the rest of the children. Then to continue the game, ask the chef to call out the name of a fruit. The children holding that particular fruit exchange places. If the chef calls out, "fruit basket upset," all of the children must exchange places, including the chef. The child who doesn't find a place is the new chef. A variation of this game would be bread basket upset. For this game use pictures of breads, rolls, bagels, muffins, breadsticks, etc. This game is appropriate for older children.

23. Bear Hunt

This is a rhythmic chant which may easily be varied. Start by chanting each line, encouraging the children to repeat the line.

Teacher: *Let's go on a bear hunt.*

Children: *(Repeat. Imitate walk by slapping knees alternately.)*

Teacher:
I see a wheat field.
Can't go over it;
Can't go under it.
Let's go through it.
(arms straight ahead like you're parting wheat)

I see a bridge.
Can't go over it;
Can't go under it.
Let's swim.
(arms in swimming motion)

I see a tree.
Can't go over it;
Can't go under it.
Let's go up it.
(climb and look)

I see a swamp.
Can't go over it;
Can't go under it.
Let's go through it.
(pull hands up and down slowly)

I see a cave.
Can't go over it;
Can't go under it.
Let's go in.
(walking motion)

I see two eyes. I see two ears.
I see a nose. I see a mouth.
It's a BEAR!!!
(Do all in reverse very fast)

24. "Guess Who?"

Individually tape the children's voices. Play the tape during group time, and let the children identify their classmates' voices.

25. Shadow Fun

Hang a bed sheet up in the classroom for use as a projection screen. Then place a light source such as a slide, filmstrip, or overhead projector a few feet behind the screen. Ask two of the children to stand behind the sheet. Then encourage one of the two children to walk in front of the projector light. When this happens, the children are to give the name of the person who is moving.

26. If This Is Red— Nod Your Head

Point to an object in the room and say, "If this is green, shake your hand. If this is yellow, touch your nose." If the object is not the color stated, children should not imitate the requested action.

27. Freeze

Encourage the children to imitate activities such as washing dishes, cleaning house, dancing, etc. Approximately every 10 to 20 seconds, call out "Freeze!" When this occurs, the children are to stop whatever they are doing and remain frozen until you say, "Thaw" or "Move." A variation of this activity would be to use music. When the music stops, the children freeze their movements.

28. Spy the Object

Designate a large area on the floor as home base. Then select an object and show it to the children. Ask the children to cover their eyes while you place the object in an observable place in the room. Then encourage the children to open their eyes and search for the object. As each child spies the object he quietly returns to the home base area without telling. The other children continue searching until all have found the object. After all the children are seated, they may share where the object is placed.

220

29. Who Is Gone?

This game is played in a circle format. Begin by asking a child to close his eyes. Then point to a child to leave the circle and go to a spot where he can't be seen. The child with his eyes closed opens them at your word, then looks around the circle and identifies the friend who is missing.

30. It's Me

Seat the children in a circle formation, and place a chair in the center. Choose one child to sit on a chair in the circle, closing his eyes. After this, ask another child to walk up softly behind the chair and tap the child on the shoulder. The seated child asks, "Who is tapping?" The other child replies, "It's me." By listening to the response, the seated child identifies the other child.

31. Feeling and Naming

Ask a child to stand with his back to you, placing his hands behind him. Then place an object in the child's hands for identification by feeling it. Nature materials can be used such as leaves, shells, fruit, etc. A ball, doll, block, Lego piece, puzzle piece, crayon, etc., may also be used.

32. Doggy, Doggy, Where's Your Bone?

Sit the children in a circle formation. Then place a chair in the center of the circle. Place a block under the chair. Select one child, the dog, to sit on the chair and close his eyes. Then point to another child. This child must try to get the dog's bone from under the chair without making a noise. After the child returns to his place in the circle, all the children place their hands behind them. Then in unison the children say, "Doggy, Doggy, where's your bone?" During the game, each dog has three guesses as to who has the bone.

Index by Subject